FIGHTERS AND BOMBERS
OF WORLD WAR II

FIGHTERS AND BOMBERS OF WORLD WAR II
1939–45
by
Kenneth Munson

Illustrated by
JOHN W. WOOD

Norman Dinnage
Frank Friend
Brian Hiley
William Hobson
Tony Mitchell
Jack Pelling

PEERAGE BOOKS

First published in Great Britain by Blandford Press Ltd
as two volumes: *Bombers 1939–45* and *Fighters 1939–45*.

This edition published by Peerage Books
59 Grosvenor Street
London W1

© 1969 Blandford Press Ltd

ISBN 0 907408 37 0

Printed in Hong Kong

CONTENTS

Book I
FIGHTERS
Attack and Training Aircraft
1939–45

Introduction to Book I

The middle and late 1930s were years of considerable activity among the world's major aeronautical powers. Apart from the natural process of evolution of the military aeroplane, the advent of Adolf Hitler's National Socialist party to power in Germany, and the increasing strength of the new *Luftwaffe* that followed, led many nations to realise – some less quickly than others – that policies of 'making do' with their air forces' existing equipment for another year or two were extremely unwise. Thus, most of the leading nations in Europe embarked at this time upon schemes for the expansion and re-equipment of their air forces with more modern combat types. Even so, at the time of the outbreak of World War 2 none could yet match the *Luftwaffe* either in numerical strength or in the modernity of its equipment.

The restrictions imposed upon Germany in 1919 by the Treaty of Versailles had included a categorical ban on the manufacture of all but a modest output of light civil aircraft. But with the signing of the Paris Air Agreement seven years later most of the former restrictions were removed, and from this point there began, even before Hitler, the gradual re-establishment of a healthy aviation industry, with factories set up in such countries as Switzerland and the USSR as well as in Germany itself. New military aircraft began to appear, in the early 1930s, ostensibly as 'fast mailplanes', 'sporting single-seaters' and the like for the national airline, Deutsche Lufthansa, or for the re-created *Luftsportverband*, a supposed private flying organisation which was actually turning out military pilots for the new *Luftwaffe*. The practice of allocating civilian registration letters to new prototypes was but the thinnest of disguises for aircraft whose military purpose was all too readily apparent. Little further attempt was made to preserve the fiction after Hitler's accession to power in 1933, and the existence of the *Luftwaffe* was confirmed officially by the German government in 1935. Indicative of the rate at which this air force expanded thereafter is the fact that, at the end of 1935, the industry's output of aircraft was some three hundred a month; by September 1939 it was in excess of a thousand a month.

Germany's eventual ally of the European war, Italy, also embarked upon a re-equipment programme – though by comparison a much more modest one – after the conclusion of its campaigns in Abyssinia during the mid-1930s. But whereas Germany, for its new generations of both fighters and bombers, was clearly pinning its faith on the monoplane, Italy, so far as fighters at least were concerned, was reluctant to eschew the biplanes that had served the *Regia Aeronautica* so well for so long. This reflects the somewhat different conception of the ideal fighting machine held by Italian pilots since the days of World War 1: twenty years later, these airmen still preferred the open cockpit and the lightly armed machine in which outright speed took second place to the ability to out-manoeuvre its opponents.

The Spanish Civil War of 1936–39 afforded several of the major air powers, Germany and Italy among them, an apparently ideal opportunity to try out their new range of military aeroplanes under genuine battle conditions. The ensuing campaigns undoubtedly provided useful experience not only in the evaluation of existing combat types but in drawing attention to future tactical requirements. (For example, it was the Spanish campaigns that led German officials to realise the need for specialised ground-attack aircraft, a realisation that led to the appearance of the Henschel Hs 129 in this role during World War 2.) On the other hand, the aircrews of Germany's *Legion Condor* and Italy's *Aviazione Legionaria* in Spain were so often pitted against markedly inferior opposition that the efficacy of their own aircraft was somewhat over-estimated by world standards.

The peacetime expansion of the RAF during the immediate pre-war years was, by comparison, modest and slow, despite the augmented output resulting from the 'shadow factory' programme, in which the British motor-car industry turned out components or complete aeroplanes to supplement those produced by the recognised aircraft manufacturers. Like Italy, Britain was reluctant to sound the death-knell of the biplane fighter before the monoplane had proved itself, and had ordered the 240 mph (400 km/hr) Gladiator in 1935. Two monoplane fighters, the

Hurricane and the Spitfire, were the subjects of really substantial pre-war orders, but in September 1939 the RAF had in first-line service little more than three hundred Hurricanes and about half as many Spitfires – less than one-tenth of the totals then ordered. With a belated realisation of the RAF's weakness in the event of a war in Europe, a British Purchasing Mission went to the USA in 1938 to order substantial quantities of US combat aircraft to bridge the gap. However, these did not begin to become available in quantity until 1940; when war broke out in Europe Britain's fighter strength of Gladiators, Hurricanes and Spitfires was hugely outnumbered by that of the *Luftwaffe*.

In the initial advances through Poland, France and the Low Countries, the Nazi war machine met opposition which, although intrinsically valiant, was tactically and technically little better than that encountered by the German forces in Spain a year or two earlier. Dive-bombers and ground-attack aircraft, working in support of the ground troops, decimated much of the aerial opposition before it could get into the air, and such fighter opposition as did succeed in taking off was fairly easy prey for the *Luftwaffe*'s Bf 109 fighters.

After the rapid and successful advance to the Channel coast in 1939–40, the *Luftwaffe* began in the late spring of 1940 to step up its bombing campaign against the United Kingdom in preparation for the intended invasion of Britain. In Spain its medium bombers had been able to fly virtually unescorted and with only a light defensive armament, their performance being sufficient in itself to evade most of the fighters ranged against them. Such tactics were soon shown to be inadequate against the faster, well-armed Hurricanes and Spitfires, and twin-engined Messerschmitt Bf 110 long-range fighters were sent to escort the bombers. This revealed the first chink in the *Luftwaffe*'s armour, for the Bf 110 had never before been fully extended in the fighter role, and now proved unequal to its allotted task – so much so that single-engined Bf 109's had to be sent with the formations to escort the escorts.

On 18 June 1940 Winston Churchill told the House of Commons: 'What General Weygand called the Battle of France is over. I expect that the Battle of Britain is about to begin.' Britain's victory in that battle is rightly credited to 'the few', the men and machines that, greatly outnumbered, withstood the

Luftwaffe onslaught during September and October 1940. But 'the few' might have been a great deal fewer without the foresight of Air Chief Marshal Dowding, the C-in-C of RAF Fighter Command, who in May 1940 urged the government to resist the very natural temptation further to deplete its home defence squadrons by sending more and more fighters to support the hard-pressed Allied forces on the Continent.

The defeats inflicted upon its fighters in the Battle of Britain represented the first serious reversal the *Luftwaffe* had suffered during four militant years, and though the bomber *blitz* continued, with a measure of Italian support during the winter of 1940–41, some two thousand German aircraft were lost before the daylight attacks gave way to night bombing. During this phase of the war the Defiant turret-armed fighter, an unfortunate failure in daylight combat, salvaged something of its reputation by serving with some measure of success as a night fighter. The first truly effective night fighters of the war, however, were the twin-engined Beaufighter and Mosquito, both equipped with AI (airborne interception) radar and more effectively armed than the Defiant.

The *Luftwaffe*, attempting to recoup after its losses in 1940, had its efforts largely negated by Hitler's decision to invade the USSR in June 1941, thus creating an additional front along which its resources had to be dispersed. On the credit side, the Bf 109 now began to be joined in service by the superlative Focke-Wulf Fw 190; but when the invasion of Russia was followed less than six months later by the Japanese attack on Pearl Harbor, thus bringing the USA officially into the war, the Axis powers virtually sealed their own fate. The Soviet Union, whose aircraft had also figured in the fighting in Spain (and against the Japanese across the Siberian borders), was, like Britain, France, Poland and other European nations, still in the early stages of its latest modernisation programme at the time of the Nazi invasion. The Soviet Air Force was numerically strong, but its front-line aircraft were not modern by contemporary standards and, like the RAF, it was obliged to rely heavily at first upon large quantities of US warplanes supplied after the passing of the Lend-Lease Act in March 1941. Once it did begin, from 1942, to re-equip with domestically built aircraft it produced a number of combat types which, though of less refined design than the best Western types, were highly efficient weapons and were manufactured in prodigious quantities seldom matched before or since among military aircraft. These were mostly fighters or ground-attack designs, and among them was the archetype of nearly all subsequent ground-attack aircraft, the Ilyushin Il-2.

Pilots of the Japanese air forces shared with those of Italy a predilection for the open cockpit and the lightly armed but highly manoeuvrable fighter. The Japanese, however, had discarded the biplane formula somewhat earlier, all the principal first-line Army and Navy fighters being monoplanes. In the minds of most people, the Japanese fighters of the period are epitomised by the Mitsubishi Zero-Sen single-seater of the Japanese Naval Air Force, which outranked numerically and in renown any other Japanese type produced before 1945. The Zero was without doubt an excellent aeroplane, especially in the early stages of the war, although better fighters produced in smaller numbers included the Navy's Shiden-*Kai* and the Army's Ki-84 and Ki-100. Nor should Nakajima's elegant Hayabusa be omitted from the reckoning, for numerically it was the JAAF's most important fighter, and but for the lack of a more lethal armament would surely have made a greater impact. Japan's conduct of the war can be divided broadly into that on the mainland of south-east Asia, carried out chiefly by the Army Air Force, and that among the numerous island groups in the south-west Pacific, which was essentially the responsibility of the Naval Air Force. So long as it retained its aircraft carriers, the Japanese Fleet was a formidable adversary; but, as the war progressed and its carrier fleet was diminished and demolished, its power in the Pacific was reduced to negligible proportions. The Japanese Army overran the southern mainland of Asia so quickly at the outset of its offensive that its air force became very thinly spread over the vast area that it now had to cover, and eventually home production failed to keep pace with even the normal combat wastage of aircraft by each service.

When the USA entered the war on 7 December 1941, its aviation industry was already committed to the large orders placed in pre-war years by Britain, France and other countries, and to even greater output to meet the 1941 demands of Lend-Lease allocations to the Allies. Once the USA became committed as a combatant, this already huge work load on the domestic aircraft industry was increased still further by large production orders on behalf of its own forces and the acceptance for service of several newly developed combat types. At the outset, nearly one-third of the entire US productive effort was devoted to the manufacture of transport aircraft, and a high percentage of the remaining effort was concerned with the production of medium and heavy bombers and long-range patrol aircraft. It is a measure of the overall US output that, during the ensuing four years, more than 13,000 Warhawk, 20,000 Wildcat and Hellcat, 12,000 Corsair, 15,000 Thunderbolt and 12,000 Mustang fighters were turned out, in addition to lesser quantities of other fighters and miscellaneous other types.

In June 1942 Japan suffered a really serious defeat at US hands in the Battle of Midway Island, in the course of which Japan lost four aircraft carriers and over two hundred and fifty front-line aircraft. The Battle of Midway was a turning-point in the conduct of the Pacific war equal in importance to that of the Battle of Britain to the war in Europe. Within a year of Pearl Harbor, the number of aircraft in service with the US forces had trebled, and most of this strength was serving abroad. One of the first steps taken by the USAAF was the establishment of the US Eighth Air Force at bases in the United Kingdom, and in the autumn of 1942 part of the Eighth was detached to form the basis of the US Twelfth Air Force in North Africa.

In 1943, after the successful conclusion of the North African campaign, first Sicily and then Italy were invaded. By this time Britain's Fleet Air Arm was at last beginning to receive more modern monoplane fighters of British design, to replace its antiquated Sea Gladiator biplanes and augment the American monoplane types received earlier under Lend-Lease. One effect of the mounting bombing campaign against Germany was the wholesale recall of *Luftwaffe* fighter squadrons from other fronts, from which they could ill be spared, to defend the German homeland; moreover, defensive fighters were now outnumbering bombers in the overall *Luftwaffe* establishment, and it was Germany's turn to introduce specialist night fighters into service. Nevertheless, by cutting its reserves to negligible proportions, the *Luftwaffe* was still able to claim a first-line strength in mid-1943 of around four thousand aircraft.

On 8 September 1943 the Italian forces under the command

of Marshal Badoglio surrendered to the Allies, and the aircraft based in Italy became divided into two opposing camps. Those in that half of Italy which had still not been reached by the Allied advance were formed into the *Aviazione della Repubblica Sociale Italiana* and continued to fight alongside the *Luftwaffe*, while those in southern Italy became known as the Italian Co-Belligerent Air Force, which continued to operate with a mixture of Italian, American and British aircraft in support of the Allied cause. Toward the end of 1943 the forthcoming invasion of the Continent was foreshadowed by the setting up in November of the Allied Second Tactical Air Force, and by the increase in ground-attack raids against enemy targets in Europe.

On 6 June 1944 the long-awaited invasion of Normandy began, and was supported strongly by hard-won air superiority and by continual low-level harassing of enemy ground forces by fighter-type aircraft armed with bombs, cannon and rocket projectiles, as well as by sustained heavy bombing attacks on German-held industrial targets. Evidence of desperation in the face of impending defeat manifested itself in both hemispheres during the second half of 1944. In Europe it took the form of Hitler's *Vergeltungs-waffen* (Reprisal Weapons), the V1 and the V2. The V1 flying bombs constituted a slight setback for a time in the autumn of 1944, but their measure was soon taken by the piston-engined Mustangs and Thunderbolts of the USAAF and the Tempests of the RAF, and the latter service's jet-engined Meteor fighters. Repeated attacks on their factories and launching sites finally disposed of the menace both from the V1 and from the V2 rocket missiles which were used against Britain for a time during 1944–45. The hard-hit German aviation industry achieved a partial respite by an extensive dispersal of its factories and by setting up new plants underground, almost exclusively by this time for the production of defensive fighters; but even these new aircraft were prevented from entering service in the numbers needed, due to the continued attentions of Allied bombers to their factories and airfields.

The methods adopted by the Japanese air forces in the latter part of 1944 took an even more extreme form: that of the suicide attack. These attacks, carried out by both Army and Navy pilots, were made for the most part in standard service aircraft of all kinds, carrying bombs or internally stowed explosive; their pilots simply flew them straight into their target and perished in the resulting explosion. Such tactics inevitably had at least an initial effect upon the morale of Allied troops, and so far as results were concerned were quite effective for a time. Incomprehensible as this form of warfare may have been to non-Oriental minds, it was responsible in ten months for more than forty-eight per cent of all American warships damaged, and over twenty-one per cent of those sunk, during the entire course of the war: small wonder that an official survey later rated it 'the single most effective weapon developed by the Japanese in World War 2'. The literally suicidal resistance of the Japanese reached a fantastic peak in the battles for Iwo Jima and Okinawa. In the twelve weeks' battle for Okinawa even the heavy casualties in US troops and weapons paled into insignificance beside the Japanese losses of one hundred and seventeen thousand personnel and three thousand eight hundred aircraft. By this time, however, the USAAF had begun, from bases in the Marianas Islands regained for it by the US Navy, to carry out a sustained bombing of targets within Japan with its long-range, high-flying B-29 Superfortresses; and although Japanese suicide attacks were by no means discontinued, their ferocity and their effect diminished steadily after Okinawa.

In Europe in 1945, neither the advent of the Me 262 and Me 163 jet- and rocket-powered fighters nor the launching of V2 rockets against Britain seriously affected the final outcome of the war, and the *Luftwaffe*, already deprived by Allied bombing of the new fighters it desperately needed, was driven to the final indignity of having its surviving aircraft virtually all grounded for lack of fuel; while the Japanese air forces, driven back to defend their homeland against the American bombers, had all their efforts negated when the atomic *coups de grâce* were delivered upon Hiroshima and Nagasaki in August 1945.

TIGER MOTH (U.K.)

1

De Havilland Tiger Moth II of the R.A.F. (unit unidentified), *ca.* autumn 1940.
Engine: One 130 h.p. de Havilland Gipsy Major 1 inverted-Vee type. *Span:*
29 ft. 4 in. (8·94 m.). *Length:* 23 ft. 11 in. (7·34 m.). *Height:* 8 ft. 9½ in. (2·68 m.).
Normal take-off weight: 1,825 lb. (828 kg.). *Maximum speed:* 109 m.p.h.
(175 km./hr.) at 1,000 ft. (305 m.). *Operational ceiling:* 13,600 ft. (4,145 m.).
Range: 302 miles (486 km.). *Armament:* None.

KAYDET (U.S.A.)

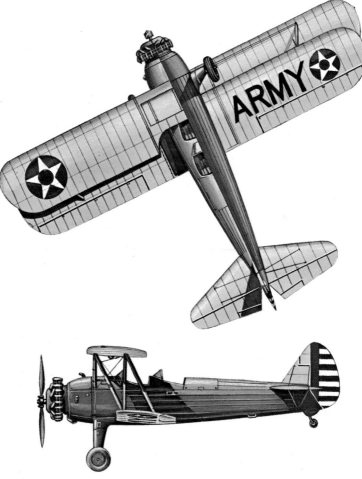

2

Boeing- Stearman PT-13D Kaydet of the U.S.A.A.F., 1942. *Engine:* One 220 h.p. Lycoming R-680-17 radial. *Span:* 32 ft. 2 in. (9·80 m.). *Length:* 25 ft. 0¼ in. (7·63 m.). *Height:* 9 ft 2 in. (2·79 m.). *Normal take-off weight:* 2,717 lb. (1,232 kg.). *Maximum speed:* 124 m.p.h. (200 km./hr.) at sea level. *Operational ceiling:* 11,400 ft. (3,475 m.). *Normal range:* 505 miles (813 km.). *Armament:* None.

HENSCHEL Hs 123 (Germany)

3

Henschel Hs 123A-1 of 8/SG.1, Eastern Front, spring 1942. *Engine:* One 880 h.p. BMW 132Dc radial. *Span:* 34 ft. 5⅜ in. (10·50 m.). *Length:* 27 ft. 4 in. (8·33 m.). *Height:* 10 ft. 6⅜ in. (3·21 m.). *Normal take-off weight:* 4,894 lb. (2,220 kg.). *Maximum speed:* 211 m.p.h. (340 km./hr.) at 3,940 ft. (1,200 m.). *Operational ceiling:* 29,530 ft. (9,000 m.). *Maximum range:* 534 miles (860 km.). *Armament:* Two 7·9 mm. MG 17 machine-guns in upper engine cowling; provision for two 20 mm. MG FF cannon four 110 lb. (50 kg.) bombs or canisters of smaller bombs beneath lower wings.

FIAT C.R.42 (Italy)

4

Fiat C.R.42 (J 11) of the 2nd Air Division, F 9 Wing Royal Swedish Air Force, *ca.* 1941. *Engine:* One 840 h.p. Fiat A.74R.1C 38 radial. *Span:* 31 ft. $9\frac{7}{8}$ in. (9·70 m.). *Length:* 27 ft. $1\frac{1}{8}$ in. (8·26 m.). *Height:* 11 ft. $9\frac{1}{8}$ in. (3·585 m.). *Normal take-off weight:* 5,033 lb. (2,283 kg.). *Maximum speed:* 267 m.p.h. (430 km./hr.) at 17,490 ft. (5,330 m.). *Operational ceiling:* 33,465 ft. (10,200 m.). *Normal range:* 482 miles (775 km.). *Armament:* Two 12·7 mm. Breda-SAFAT machine-guns in upper front fuselage; provision for two similar guns or two 220 lb. (100 kg.) bombs beneath lower wings.

GLADIATOR (U.K.)

5

Gloster Gladiator II of No. 239 Squadron R.A.F., autumn 1940. *Engine:* One 725 h p. Bristol Mercury VIIIA radial. *Span:* 32 ft. 3 in. (9·83 m.). *Length:* 27 ft. 5 in. (8·36 m.). *Height:* 10 ft. 7 in. (3·23 m.). *Normal take-off weight:* 4,864 lb. (2,206 kg.). *Maximum speed:* 257 m.p.h. (414 km./hr.) at 14,600 ft. (4,450 m.). *Operational ceiling:* 33,500 ft. (10,211 m.). *Normal range:* 444 miles (715 km.). *Armament:* Two 0·303 in. Browning machine-guns on sides of front fuselage, and one beneath each lower wing.

PZL P.11c (Poland)

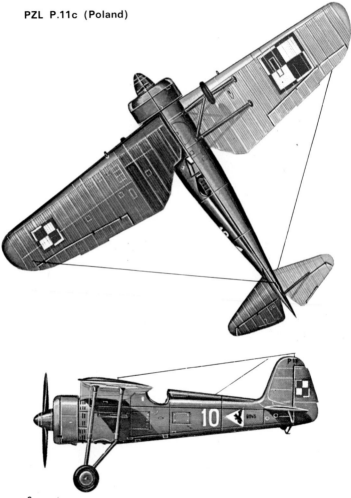

6

PZL P.11c of No. 113 (Owl) Squadron, 1st Air Regiment Polish Air Force, Warsaw, September 1939. *Engine:* One 560 h.p. PZL Skoda-built Bristol Mercury V S2 radial. *Span:* 35 ft. 2 in. (10·72 m.). *Length:* 24 ft. 9¼ in. (7·55 m.). *Height:* 9 ft. 4¼ in. (2·85 m.). *Maximum take-off weight:* 3,505 lb. (1,590 kg.). *Maximum speed:* 230 m.p.h. (370 km./hr.) at 14,760 ft. (4,500 m.). *Operational ceiling:* 31,170 ft. (9,500 m.). *Normal range:* 503 miles (810 km.). *Armament:* Two 0·303 in. Vickers or 7·7 mm. Wzor 37 machine-guns in fuselage sides and (on some aircraft) one in each wing; provision for two 27·5 lb. (12·5 kg.) bombs beneath each wing.

CORSAIR (U.S.A.)

7

Chance Vought F4U-1A Corsair of Squadron VF-17 U.S. Navy, summer 1943.
Engine: One 2,000 h.p. Pratt & Whitney R-2800-8 Double Wasp radial. *Span:*
40 ft. 11¾ in. (12·49 m.). *Length:* 33 ft. 4½ in. (10·17 m.). *Height:* 14 ft. 9¼ in.
(4·50 m.). *Normal take-off weight:* 11,093 lb. (5,032 kg.). *Maximum speed:*
417 m.p.h. (671 km./hr.) at 19,900 ft. (6,065 m.). *Operational ceiling:* 36,900 ft.
(11,247 m.). *Normal range:* 1,015 miles (1,633 km.). *Armament:* Three 0·50 in.
Browning machine-guns in each wing.

WILDCAT (U.S.A.)

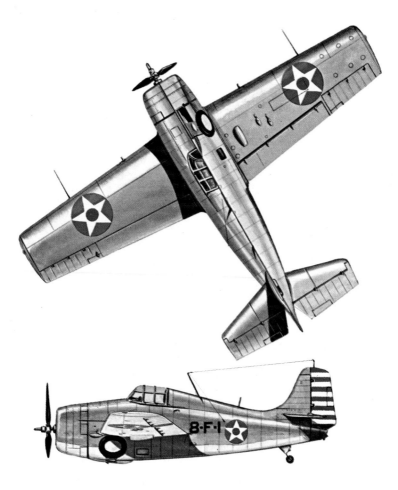

8

Grumman F4F-3 Wildcat of Squadron VF-8, U.S.S. *Hornet*, late 1941. *Engine:* One 1,200 h.p. Pratt & Whitney R-1830-76 Twin Wasp radial. *Span:* 38 ft. 0 in. (11·58 m.). *Length:* 28 ft. 9 in. (8·76 m.). *Height:* 9 ft. 2½ in. (2·81 m.). *Normal take-off weight:* 7,002 lb. (3,176 kg.). *Maximum speed:* 330 m.p.h. (531 km./hr.) at 21,100 ft. (6,431 m.). *Operational ceiling:* 37,500 ft. (11,430 m.). *Normal range:* 845 miles (1,360 km.). *Armament:* Two 0·50 in. M-2 Browning machine-guns in each wing; provision for one 100 lb. (45·4 kg.) bomb beneath each wing.

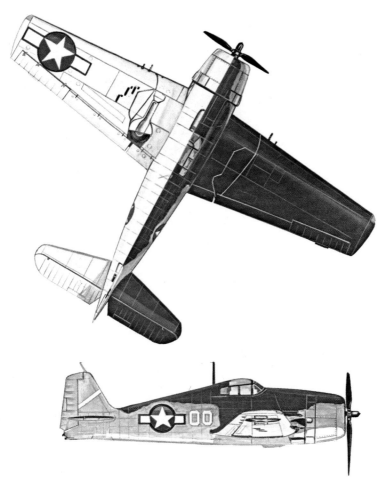

9

Grumman F6F-3 Hellcat of Squadron VF-9, U.S.S. *Yorktown*, September 1943.
Engine: One 2,000 h.p. Pratt & Whitney R-2800-10 Double Wasp radial. *Span:*
42 ft. 10 in. (13·06 m.). *Length:* 33 ft. 7 in. (10·24 m.). *Height:* 14 ft. 5 in.
(4·39 m.). *Normal take-off weight:* 12,441 lb. (5,643 kg.). *Maximum speed:*
375 m.p.h. (604 km./hr.) at 17,300 ft. (5,273 m.). *Operational ceiling:* 37,300 ft.
(11,369 m.). *Normal range:* 1,090 miles (1,754 km.). *Armament:* Three 0·50 in.
Browning M-2 machine-guns in each wing.

THUNDERBOLT (U.S.A.)

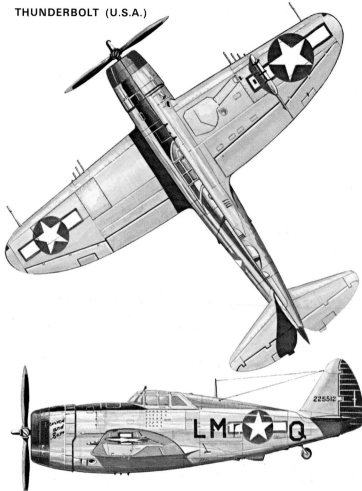

10

Republic P-47D-21-RE of the 61st Fighter Squadron, 56th Fighter Group U.S.A.A.F., U.K. May 1944. *Engine:* One 2,300 h.p. Pratt & Whitney R-2800-21 Double Wasp radial. *Span:* 40 ft. 9¾ in. (12·43 m.). *Length:* 36 ft. 1¾ in. (11·02 m.). *Height:* 14 ft. 7 in. (4·45 m.). *Normal take-off weight:* 13,500 lb. (5,920 kg.). *Maximum speed:* 433 m.p.h. (697 km./hr.) at 30,000 ft. (9,144 m.). *Operational ceiling:* 40,000 ft. (12,192 m.). *Normal range:* 640 miles (1,030 km.). *Armament:* Four 0·50 in. Browning M-2 machine-guns in each wing; provision for one 500 lb. (227 kg.) bomb beneath fuselage and one similar bomb or an auxiliary fuel tank beneath each wing.

BUFFALO (U.S.A.)

11

Brewster B-239 (F2A-1) of Squadron HLeLv 24, Air Regiment LeR 2 Finnish Air Force, 1941–42. *Engine:* One 940 h.p. Wright R-1820-34 Cyclone radial. *Span:* 35 ft. 0 in. (10·67 m.). *Length:* 26 ft. 4 in. (8·03 m.). *Height:* 12 ft. 1 in. (3·68 m.). *Normal take-off weight:* 5,055 lb. (2,293 kg.). *Maximum speed:* 301 m.p.h. (484 km./hr.) at 17,000 ft. (5,182 m.). *Operational ceiling:* 32,500 ft. (9,906 m.). *Normal range:* 1,095 miles (1,762 km.). *Armament:* Two 0·50 in. Colt-Browning machine-guns in upper engine cowling and one in each wing.

NAKAJIMA Ki-27 (Japan)

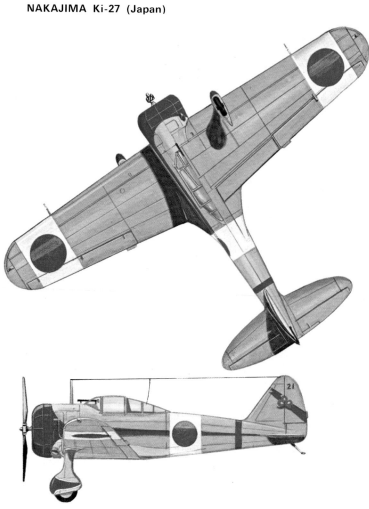

12

Nakajima Ki-27b of the 2nd Squadron, 246th Group J.A.A.F., home defence of Japan, 1942–43. *Engine:* One 710 h.p. Nakajima Ha.1b radial. *Span:* 37 ft. $0\frac{7}{8}$ in. (11·30 m.). *Length:* 24 ft. $8\frac{1}{2}$ in. (7·53 m.). *Height:* 10 ft. 8 in. (3·25 m.). *Normal take-off weight:* 3,638 lb. (1,650 kg.). *Maximum speed:* 286 m.p.h. (460 km./hr.) at 11,485 ft. (3,500 m.). *Normal range:* 388 miles (625 km.). *Armament:* Two 7·7 mm. Type 89 machine-guns in front fuselage; provision for two 55 lb. (25 kg.) bombs beneath each wing.

MITSUBISHI A5M (Japan)

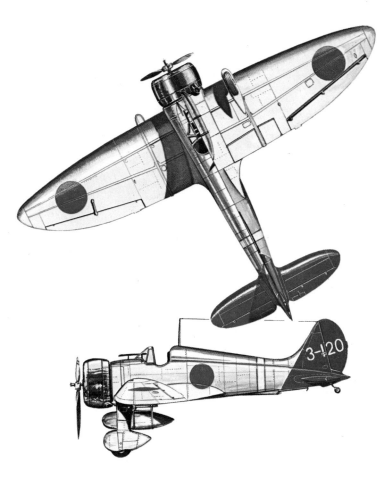

13

Mitsubishi A5M4 Model 24, believed to be an aircraft of No. 12 Air Corps J.N.A.F., late 1939. *Engine:* One 710 h.p. Nakajima Kotobuki 41 radial. *Span:* 36 ft. 1⅛ in. (11·00 m.). *Length:* 24 ft. 9⅞ in. (7·565 m.). *Height:* 10 ft. 6 in. (3·20 m.). *Normal take-off weight:* 3,684 lb. (1,671 kg.). *Maximum speed:* 270 m.p.h. (435 km./hr.) at 9,845 ft. (3,000 m.). *Operational ceiling:* 32,150 ft. (9,800 m.). *Range with auxiliary fuel tank:* 746 miles (1,200 km.). *Armament:* Two 7·7 mm. Type 89 machine-guns in upper front fuselage; provision for two 66 lb. (30 kg.) bombs.

VALIANT (U.S.A.)

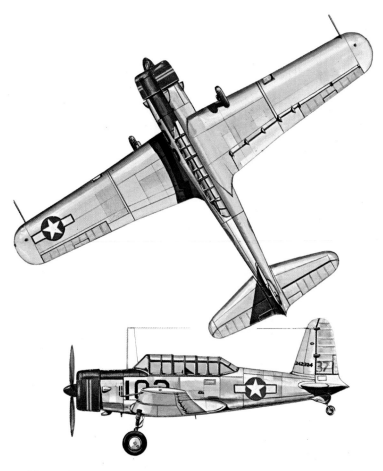

14

Vultee BT-13A Valiant of the U.S.A.A.F., summer 1943. *Engine:* One 450 h.p. Pratt & Whitney R-985-AN-1 Wasp Junior radial. *Span:* 42 ft. 0 in. (12·80 m.). *Length:* 29 ft. 2 in. (8·89 m.). *Height:* 11 ft. 6 in. (3·51 m.). *Normal take-off weight:* 3,991 lb. (1,810 kg.). *Maximum speed:* 182 m.p.h. (293 km./hr.) at sea level. *Operational ceiling:* 21,000 ft. (6,401 m.). *Normal range:* 725 miles (1,167 km.). *Armament:* None.

15

Blackburn Roc of No. 801 Squadron Fleet Air Arm, *ca.* June 1940. *Engine:* One 905 h.p. Bristol Perseus XII radial. *Span:* 46 ft. 0 in. (14·02 m.). *Length:* 35 ft. 7 in. (10·85 m.). *Height:* 12 ft. 1 in. (3·68 m.). *Normal take-off weight:* 8,800 lb. (3,992 kg.). *Maximum speed:* 196 m.p.h. (315 km./hr.) at 6,500 ft. (1,981 m.). *Operational ceiling:* 15,200 ft. (4,633 m.). *Normal range:* 610 miles (982 km.). *Armament:* Four 0·303 in. Browning machine-guns in dorsal turret; provision for four 30 lb. (13·6 kg.) bombs beneath each wing.

BOOMERANG (Australia)

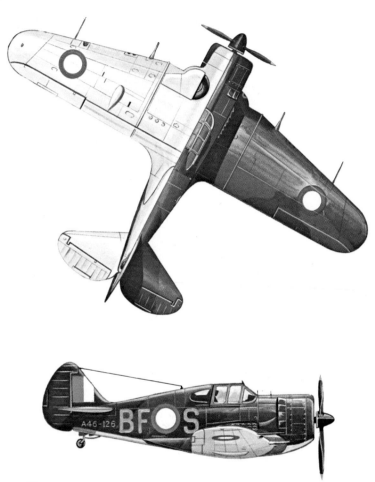

16

Commonwealth CA-13 Boomerang of No. 5 Squadron R.A.A.F., Mareeba (Queensland) March 1944. *Engine:* One 1,200 h.p. CAC-built Pratt & Whitney R-1830-S3C4-G Twin Wasp radial. *Span:* 36 ft. 0 in. (10·97 m.). *Length:* 26 ft. 9 in. (8·15 m.). *Height:* 13 ft. 0 in. (3·96 m.). *Normal take-off weight:* 7,699 lb. (3,492 kg.). *Maximum speed:* 305 m.p.h. (491 km./hr.) at 15,500 ft. (4,724 m.). *Operational ceiling:* 34,000 ft. (10,363 m.). *Normal range:* 930 miles (1,497 km.). *Armament:* One 20 mm Hispano cannon and two 0·303 in. Browning machine-guns in each wing.

POLIKARPOV I-16 (U.S.S.R.)

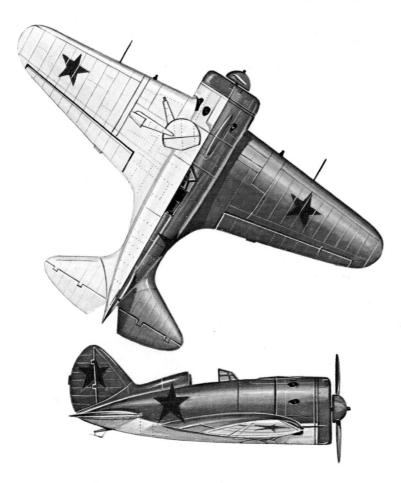

17

Polikarpov I-16 Type 24 of the VVS (Soviet Air Force), 1941. *Engine:* One 1,000 h.p. Shvetsov M-62 radial. *Span:* 29 ft. 6$\frac{3}{8}$ in. (9·00 m.). *Length:* 20 ft. 1$\frac{1}{8}$ in. (6·125 m.). *Height:* 8 ft. 5 in. (2·565 m.). *Maximum take-off weight:* 4,519 lb. (2,050 kg.). *Maximum speed:* 326 m.p.h. (525 km./hr.) at 14,765 ft. (4,500 m.). *Operational ceiling:* 29,530 ft. (9,000 m.). *Normal range:* 249 miles (400 km.). *Armament:* Two 7·62 mm. ShKAS machine-guns in upper front fuselage and one 20 mm. ShVAK cannon in each wing; provision for up to three 82 mm. RS-82 rocket projectiles beneath each wing.

MACCHI C.200 (Italy)

18

Macchi C.200 *Saetta* of the 372° *Squadriglia*, 152° *Gruppo*, 54° *Stormo*,
Cyrenaica autumn 1941. *Engine:* One 870 h.p. Fiat A.74 RC 38 radial. *Span:*
34 ft. 8½ in. (10·58 m.). *Length:* 26 ft. 10⅝ in. (8·196 m.). *Height:* 11 ft. 6¼ in.
(3·51 m.). *Normal take-off weight:* 5,132 lb. (2,328 kg.). *Maximum speed:*
313 m.p.h. (503 km./hr.) at 14,765 ft. (4,500 m.). *Operational ceiling:* 29,200 ft.
(8,900 m.). *Range:* 354 miles (570 km.). *Armament:* Two 12·7 mm. Breda-
SAFAT machine-guns in upper front fuselage; provision for one 110, 220 or
353 lb. (50, 100 or 160 kg.) bomb beneath each wing.

FIAT G.50 (Italy)

19

Fiat G.50*bis* of the 151° *Squadriglia*, 20° *Gruppo*, 51° *Stormo*, Libya *ca.*
November 1941. *Engine:* One 870 h.p. Fiat A.74 RC 38 radial. *Span:* 36 ft. 1⅛ in.
(11·00 m.). *Length:* 27 ft. 2⅜ in. (8·29 m.). *Height:* approx. 11 ft. 9¾ in. (3·60 m.).
Normal take-off weight: 5,512 lb. (2,500 kg.). *Maximum speed:* 302 m.p.h.
(486 km./hr.) at 19,685 ft. (6,000 m.). *Operational ceiling:* 35,270 ft.
(10,750 m.). *Normal range:* 294 miles (473 km.). *Armament:* Two 12·7 mm.
Breda-SAFAT machine-guns in upper front fuselage.

FFVS J 22 (Sweden)

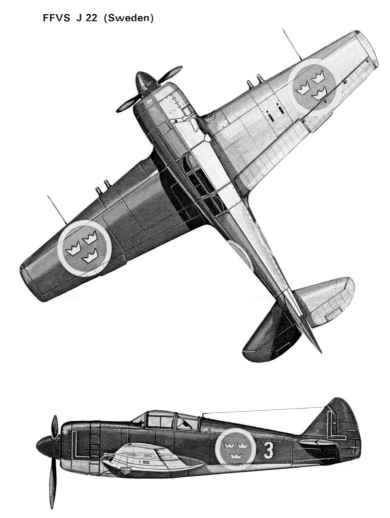

20

FFVS J 22B of the 1st Air Division, F 3 Wing Royal Swedish Air Force, 1945.
Engine: One 1,200 h.p. SFA-built Pratt & Whitney R-1830-S1C3-G Twin Wasp
radial. *Span:* 32 ft. 9¾ in. (10·00 m.). *Length:* 25 ft. 7⅛ in. (7·80 m.). *Height:*
9 ft. 2¼ in. (2·80 m.). *Normal take-off weight:* 6,250 lb. (2,835 kg.). *Maximum
speed:* 357 m.p.h. (575 km./hr.) at 11,485 ft. (3,500 m.). *Operational ceiling:*
30,510 ft. (9,300 m.). *Maximum range:* 789 miles (1,270 km.). *Armament:* Two
13·2 mm. M/39A machine-guns in each wing.

FOCKE-WULF Fw 190 (Germany)

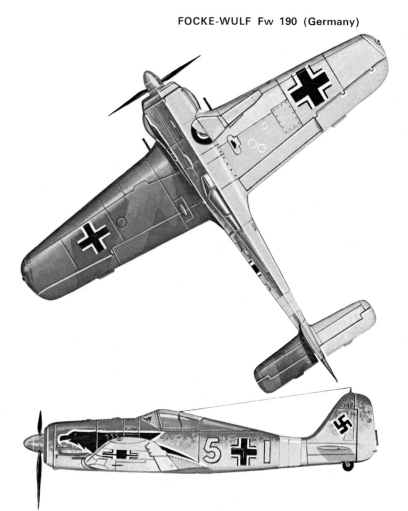

21

Focke-Wulf Fw 190A-4 of 9/JG.2 *Richthofen*, Vannes (France) February 1943.
Engine: One 1,700 h.p. BMW 801D-2 radial (2,100 h.p. at altitude with MW 50
boost). *Span:* 34 ft. 5⅜ in. (10·50 m.). *Length:* 28 ft. 10½ in. (8·80 m.). *Height:*
13 ft. 0 in. (3·96 m.). *Normal take-off weight:* 8,378 lb. (3,800 kg.). *Maximum
speed:* 416 m.p.h. (670 km./hr.) at 20,590 ft. (6,275 m.). *Operational ceiling:*
37,400 ft. (11,400 m.). *Normal range:* 497 miles (800 km.). *Armament:* Two
7·9 mm. MG 17 machine-guns in upper front fuselage, and one 20 mm. MG 151
and one 20 mm. MG FF cannon in each wing.

MYRSKY (Finland)

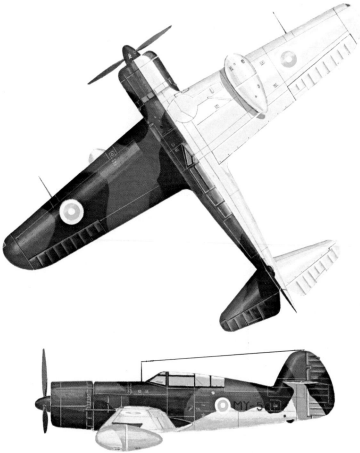

22

IVL Myrsky II of the Finnish Air Force, winter 1944–45. *Engine:* One 1,065 h.p. SFA-built Pratt & Whitney R-1830-S1C3-G Twin Wasp radial. *Span:* 36 ft. 1$\frac{1}{8}$ in. (11·00 m.). *Length:* 27 ft. 4$\frac{3}{4}$ in. (8·35 m.). *Height:* 9 ft. 10$\frac{1}{8}$ in. (3·00 m.). *Normal take-off weight:* 6,504 lb. (2,950 kg.). *Maximum speed:* 329 m.p.h. (530 km./hr.) at 10,665 ft. (3,250 m.). *Operational ceiling:* 29,530 ft. (9,000 m.). *Normal range:* 311 miles (500 km.). *Armament:* Four 12·7 mm. Browning machine-guns in upper front fuselage.

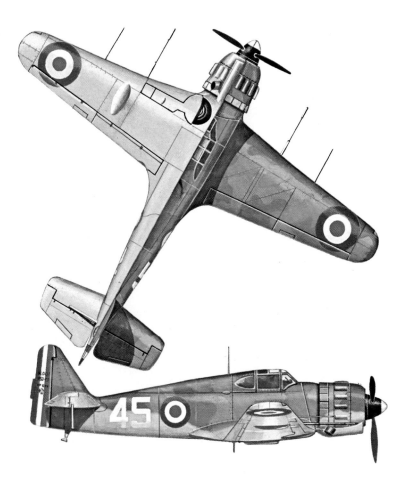

23

Bloch 152-C1 of GC.II/9, *Armée de l'Air*, Clermont Ferrand, June 1940. *Engine:* One 1,060 h.p. Gnome-Rhône 14N-49 radial. *Span:* 34 ft. 7 in. (10·542 m.). *Length:* 29 ft. 10$\frac{3}{8}$ in. (9·104 m.). *Height:* 9 ft. 11$\frac{1}{4}$ in. (3·03 m.). *Normal take-off weight:* 6,058 lb. (2,748 kg.). *Maximum speed:* 316 m.p.h. (509 km./hr.) at 13,125 ft. (4,000 m.). *Operational ceiling:* 32,810 ft. (10,000 m.). *Normal range:* 336 miles (540 km.). *Armament:* One 20 mm. Hispano HS 404 cannon and one 7·5 mm. MAC 1934-M39 machine-gun in each wing.

FOKKER D XXI (Netherlands)

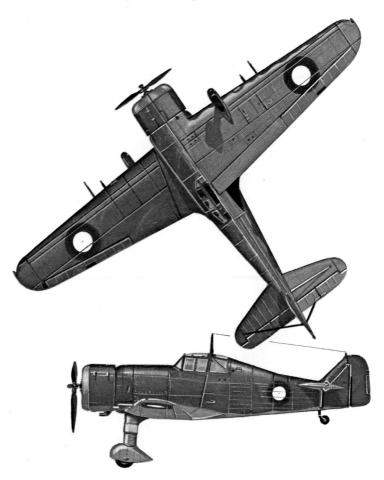

24

Danish-built Fokker D.XXI of No. 2 *Eskadrille*, Royal Danish Aviation Troops, Værløse, early 1940. *Engine:* One 760 h.p. Bristol Mercury VIII radial. *Span:* 36 ft. $1\frac{1}{8}$ in. (11·00 m.). *Length:* 26 ft. $11\frac{1}{4}$ in. (8·21 m.). *Height:* 9 ft. $8\frac{1}{8}$ in. (2·95 m.). *Normal take-off weight:* 4,519 lb. (2,050 kg.). *Maximum speed:* 286 m.p.h. (460 km./hr.) at 16,730 ft. (5,100 m.). *Operational ceiling:* 36,090 ft. (11,000 m.). *Normal range:* 528 miles (850 km.). *Armament:* One 8 mm. DISA machine-gun in each wing; provision for four 27·5 lb. (12·5 kg.) bombs beneath each wing.

MITSUBISHI A6M (Japan)

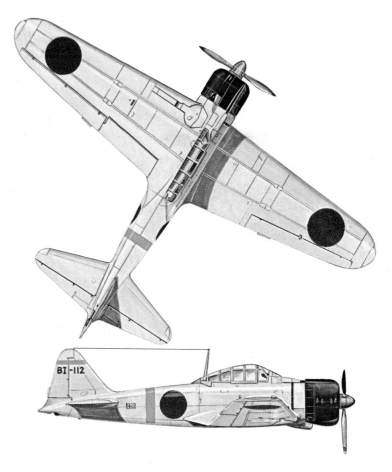

25

Mitsubishi A6M2 Model 21 *Zero-Sen* from the carrier *Soryu*, engaged in the attack on Port Darwin, February 1942. *Engine:* One 940 h.p. Nakajima Sakae 12 radial. *Span:* 39 ft. 4½ in. (12·00 m.). *Length:* 29 ft. 8¾ in. (9·06 m.). *Height:* 10 ft. 0⅛ in. (3·05 m.). *Normal take-off weight:* 5,313 lb. (2,410 kg.). *Maximum speed:* 332 m.p.h. (535 km./hr.) at 14,930 ft. (4,550 m.). *Operational ceiling:* 32,810 ft. (10,000 m.). *Normal range:* 1,162 miles (1,870 km.). *Armament:* Two 7·7 mm. Type 97 machine-guns in upper front fuselage and one 20 mm. Type 99 cannon in each wing; provision for one 132 lb. (60 kg.) bomb beneath each wing.

REGGIANE Re 2000 (Italy)

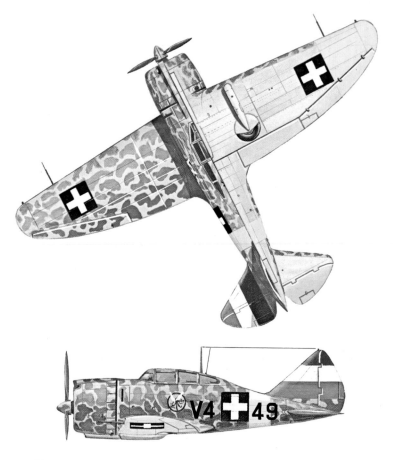

26

Reggiane Re 2000 *Serie* I of No. 1/1 Fighter Squadron Hungarian Independent Fighter Group, Eastern Front summer 1942. *Engine:* One 986 h.p. Piaggio P.XI RC 40 radial. *Span:* 36 ft. $1\frac{1}{8}$ in. (11·00 m.). *Length:* 26 ft. $2\frac{1}{2}$ in. (7·99 m.). *Height:* 10 ft. 6 in. (3·20 m.). *Normal take-off weight:* 6,349 lb. (2,880 kg.). *Maximum speed:* 329 m.p.h. (530 km./hr.) at 16,405 ft. (5,000 m.). *Operational ceiling:* 31,170 ft. (9,500 m.). *Normal range:* 715 miles (1,150 km.). *Armament:* Two 12·7 mm. Breda-SAFAT machine-guns in upper engine cowling.

LAVOCHKIN La-5 (U.S.S.R.)

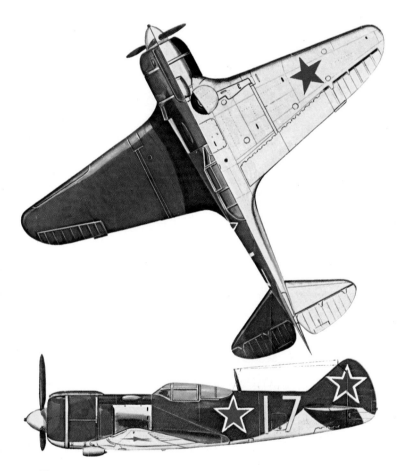

27

Lavochkin La-5FN of the VVS (Soviet Air Force), Eastern Front 1944. *Engine:*
One 1,650 h.p. Shvetsov M-82FN radial. *Span:* 32 ft. $1\frac{7}{8}$ in. (9·80 m.). *Length:*
27 ft. $10\frac{5}{8}$ in. (8·50 m.). *Height:* 8 ft. 4 in. (2·54 m.). *Normal take-off weight:*
7,408 lb. (3,360 kg.). *Maximum speed:* 402 m.p.h. (647 km./hr.) at 16,405 ft.
(5,000 m.). *Operational ceiling:* 32,810 ft. (10,000 m.). *Range:* 435 miles
(700 km.). *Armament:* Two 20 mm. ShVAK or 23 mm. NS cannon in upper engine cowling; provision for two 82 mm. RS-82 rocket projectiles or 331 lb.
(150 kg.) bombs beneath each wing.

NAKAJIMA Ki-43 (Japan)

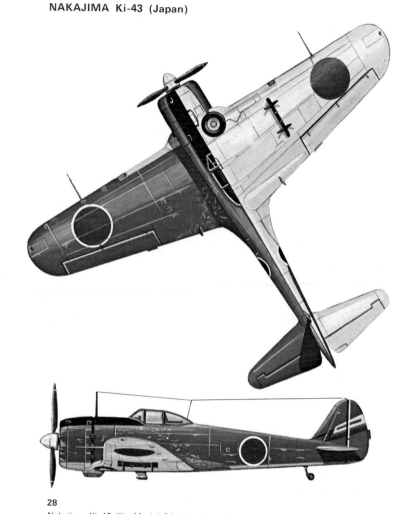

28

Nakajima Ki-43-IIIa Model 3A *Hayabusa* of the 20th Group J.A.A.F., home defence of Japan 1944–45. *Engine:* One 1,190 h.p. Mitsubishi Ha-112 radial. *Span:* 35 ft. 6¾ in. (10·84 m.). *Length:* 29 ft. 3⅛ in. (8·92 m.). *Height:* 10 ft. 8¾ in. (3·27 m.). *Maximum take-off weight:* 6,746 lb. (3,060 kg.). *Maximum speed:* 342 m.p.h. (550 km./hr.) at 19,195 ft. (5,850 m.). *Operational ceiling:* 37,400 ft. (11,400 m.). *Maximum range:* 1,988 miles (3,200 km.). *Armament:* Two 12·7 mm. Type 1 machine-guns in upper engine cowling; provision for one 110 lb. (50 kg.) or 220 lb. (100 kg.) bomb beneath each wing.

NAKAJIMA Ki-44 (Japan)

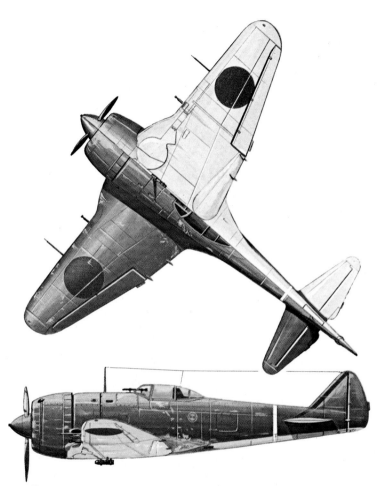

29

Eighth prototype Nakajima Ki-44-I *Shoki*, of the 3rd Flight, 47th Direct Command Squadron J.A.A.F., French Indochina January 1942. *Engine:* One 1,200 h.p. Nakajima Ha-41 radial. *Span:* 31 ft. 0 in. (9·45 m.). *Length:* 28 ft. 8½ in. (8·75 m.). *Height:* 10 ft. 8 in. (3·25 m.). *Normal take-off weight:* 5,512 lb. (2,500 kg.). *Maximum speed:* 360 m.p.h. (580 km./hr.) at 12,140 ft. (3,700 m.). *Operational ceiling:* 35,500 ft. (10,820 m.). *Normal range:* 575 miles (926 km.). *Armament:* Two 7·7 mm. Type 89 machine-guns in upper engine cowling and one 12·7 mm. Type 1 machine-gun in each wing.

NAKAJIMA Ki-84 (Japan)

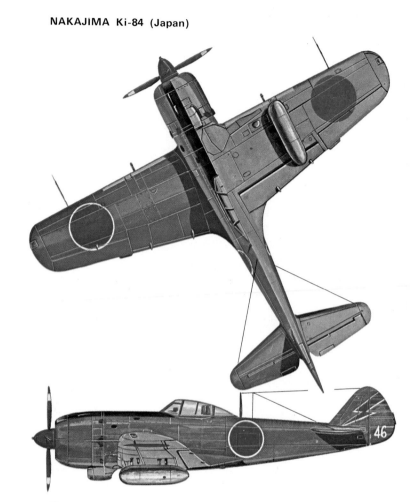

30

Nakajima Ki-84-Ia Model 1A *Hayate* of the 2nd Squadron, 11th Group J.A.A.F., Leyte Island (Philippines) late autumn 1944. *Engine:* One 1,990 h.p. Nakajima Ha-45-21 radial. *Span:* 36 ft. 10⅛ in. (11·238 m.). *Length:* 32 ft. 6½ in. (9·92 m.). *Height:* 11 ft. 1¼ in. (3·385 m.). *Normal take-off weight:* 7,940 lb. (3,602 kg.). *Maximum speed:* 427 m.p.h. (687 km./hr.) at 20,000 ft. (6,096 m.). *Operational ceiling:* 38,000 ft. (11,582 m.). *Normal range:* 780 miles (1,255 km.). *Armament:* Two 12·7 mm. Type 103 machine-guns in upper front fuselage and one 20 mm. Type 5 cannon in each wing; provision for one bomb of up to 551 lb. (250 kg.) size beneath each wing.

MITSUBISHI J2M (Japan)

31

Mitsubishi J2M3 Model 21 *Raiden* of the Tainan Air Corps, J.N.A.F., 1943–44.
Engine: One 1,820 h.p. Mitsubishi Kasei 23a radial. *Span:* 35 ft. $5\frac{1}{4}$ in. (10·80 m.).
Length: 31 ft. $9\frac{3}{4}$ in. (9·695 m.). *Height:* 12 ft. 6 in. (3·81 m.). *Normal take-off weight:* 7,573 lb. (3,435 kg.). *Maximum speed:* 380 m.p.h. (612 km./hr.) at
19,685 ft. (6,000 m.). *Operational ceiling:* 37,795 ft. (11,520 m.). *Normal range:*
656 miles (1,055 km.). *Armament:* One 20 mm. Type 99-I and one Type 99-II
cannon in each wing; provision for one 66 lb. (30 kg.) or 132 lb. (60 kg.) bomb
beneath each wing.

KAWANISHI N1K (Japan)

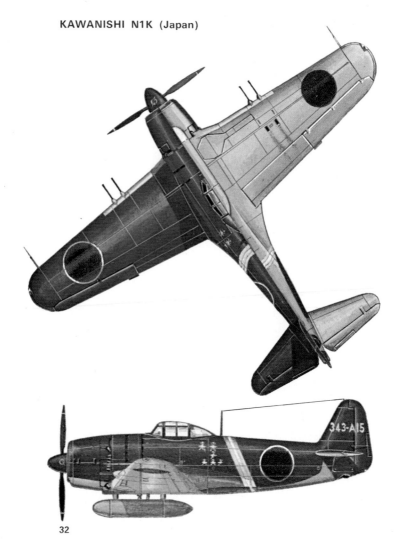

32

Kawanishi N1K2-J Model 21 *Shiden-Kai* of the 343rd Air Corps, J.N.A.F., 1944–45. *Engine:* One 1,990 h.p. Nakajima Homare 21 radial. *Span:* 39 ft. 3¼ in. (11·97 m.). *Length:* 30 ft. 8⅛ in. (9·35 m.). *Height:* 13 ft. 0 in. (3·96 m.). *Normal take-off weight:* 8,818 lb. (4,000 kg.). *Maximum speed:* 369 m.p.h. (594 km./hr.) at 18,375 ft. (5,600 m.). *Operational ceiling:* 35,300 ft. (10,760 m.). *Normal range:* 1,069 miles (1,720 km.). *Armament:* Two 20 mm. Type 99-II cannon in each wing; provision for one 551 lb. (250 kg.) bomb beneath each wing.

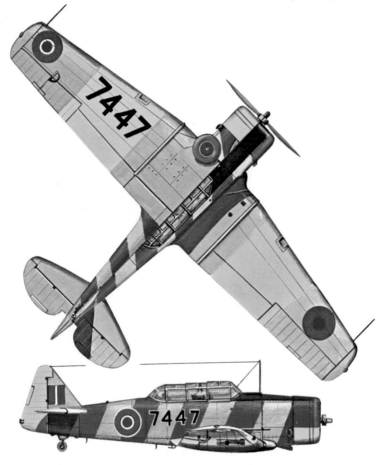

33

North American Harvard III (AT-6D) of No. 22 Air School, Southern Rhodesia Air Force, Vereeniging (Southern Rhodesia), 1944. *Engine:* One 600 h.p. Pratt & Whitney R-1340-AN-1 Wasp radial. *Span:* 42 ft. $0\frac{1}{4}$ in. (12·81 m.). *Length:* 28 ft. $11\frac{7}{8}$ in. (8·84 m.). *Height:* 11 ft. $8\frac{1}{2}$ in. (3·57 m.). *Normal take-off weight:* 5,300 lb. (2,404 kg.). *Maximum speed:* 208 m.p.h. (335 km./hr.) at 5,000 ft. (1,524 m.). *Operational ceiling:* 24,200 ft. (7,376 m.). *Normal range:* 730 miles (1,175 km.). *Armament:* Provision for one 0·30 in. machine-gun in upper front fuselage and one in rear cockpit.

MARTINET (U.K.)

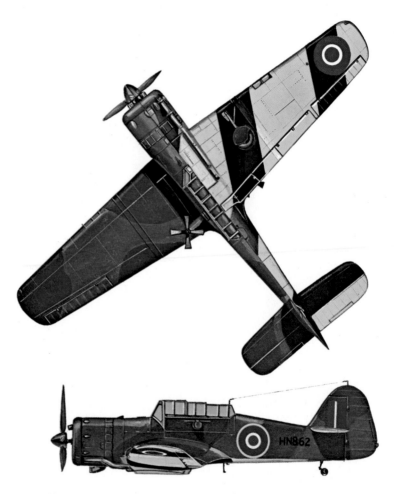

34

Miles Martinet TT I of the R.A.F. (unit unidentified), *ca.* late summer 1942. *Engine:* One 785/820 h.p. Bristol Mercury XX or 30 radial. *Span:* 39 ft. 0 in. (11·89 m.). *Length:* 30 ft. 11 in. (9·42 m.). *Height:* 11 ft. 7 in. (3·53 m.). *Normal take-off weight:* 6,680 lb. (3,030 kg.). *Maximum speed:* 237 m.p.h. (381 km./hr.) at 15,000 ft. (4,572 m.). *Normal range:* approximately 600 miles (966 km.). *Armament:* None.

JUNKERS Ju 87 (Germany)

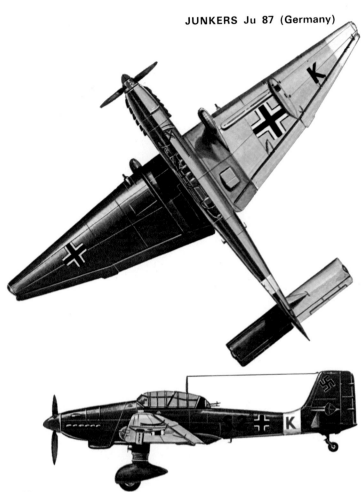

35
Junkers Ju 87D-3 of 2/St. G. 77, Eastern Front summer 1943. *Engine:* One
1,400 h.p Junkers Jumo 211J-1 inverted-Vee type. *Span:* 45 ft. 3¼ in.
(13·80 m.). *Length:* 37 ft. 8¾ in. (11·50 m.). *Height:* 12 ft. 9⅛ in. (3·89 m.).
Maximum take-off weight: 14,550 lb. (6,600 kg.). *Maximum speed:* 255 m.p.h.
(410 km./hr.) at 13,500 ft. (4,115 m.). *Operational ceiling:* 15,520 ft. (4,730 m.).
Maximum range: 954 miles (1,535 km.). *Armament:* One 7·9 mm. MG 17
machine-gun in each wing and two 7·9 mm. MG 81 guns in rear cockpit;
typical warload of one 1,102 lb. (500 kg.) bomb beneath fuselage and one
pack of ninety-two 4·4 lb. (2 kg.) SC-2 anti-personnel bombs beneath each
wing.

FAIRCHILD PT-19 (U.S.A.)

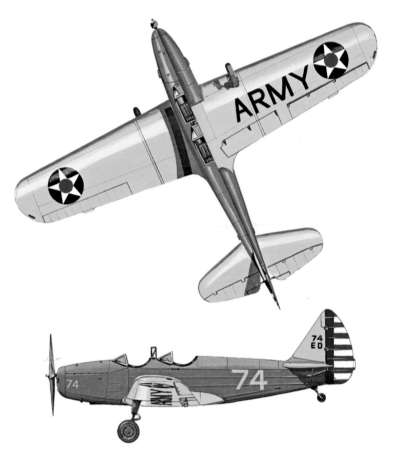

36

Fairchild PT-19A of the U.S.A.A.F., 1941–42. *Engine:* One 200 h.p. Ranger L-440-3 inverted in-line. *Span:* 35 ft. 11⅞ in. (10·97 m.). *Length:* 28 ft. 0 in. (8·53 m.). *Height:* 10 ft. 6 in. (3·20 m.). *Normal take-off weight:* 2,545 lb. (1,154 kg.). *Maximum speed:* 132 m.p.h. (212 km./hr.) at sea level. *Operational ceiling:* 15,300 ft. (4,663 m.). *Normal range:* 430 miles (692 km.). *Armament:* None.

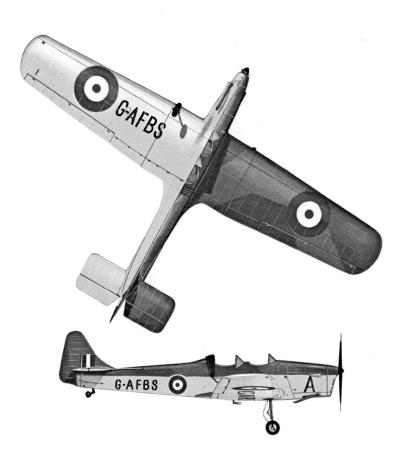

37

Miles Magister I (impressed civil aircraft) of the R.A.F. (unit unidentified), 1941.
Engine: One 130 h.p. de Havilland Gipsy Major 1 inverted-Vee type. *Span:*
33 ft. 10 in. (10·31 m.). *Length:* 24 ft. 7½ in. (7·51 m.). *Height:* 9 ft. 1 in.
(2·77 m.). *Normal take-off weight:* 1,863 lb. (845 kg.). *Maximum speed:*
132 m.p.h. (212 km./hr.) at 1,000 ft. (305 m.). *Operational ceiling:* 18,000 ft.
(5,486 m.). *Normal range:* 380 miles (612 km.). *Armament:* None.

ILYUSHIN II-2 (U.S.S.R.)

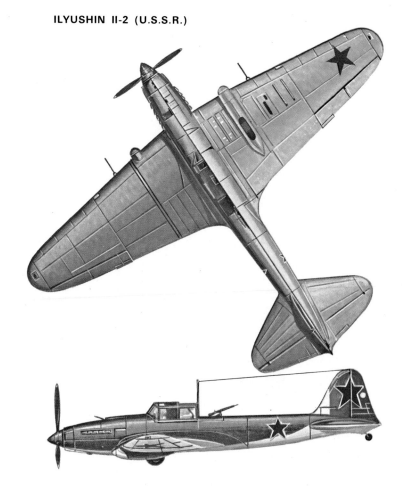

38

Ilyushin II-2m3 *Shturmovik* of the VVS-RKKA (Soviet Air Force), Eastern Front 1944. *Engine:* One 1,770 h.p. Mikulin AM-38F Vee type. *Span:* 47 ft. 10¾ in. (14·60 m.). *Length:* 38 ft. 2⅝ in. (11·65 m.). *Height:* 11 ft. 1⅞ in. (3·40 m.). *Normal take-off weight:* 12,147 lb. (5,510 kg.). *Maximum speed:* 251 m.p.h. (404 km./hr.) at 4,920 ft. (1,500 m.). *Operational ceiling:* 19,685 ft. (6,000 m.). *Normal range:* 373 miles (600 km.). *Armament:* One 23 mm. VYa cannon in each wing, two 7·62 mm. ShKAS machine-guns in upper front fuselage, and one 12·7 mm. UBT machine-gun in rear cockpit; provision for 882 lb. (400 kg.) of bombs internally and four 82 mm. RS-82 rocket projectiles or an additional 220 lb. (100 kg.) of bombs beneath each wing.

DEFIANT (U.K.)

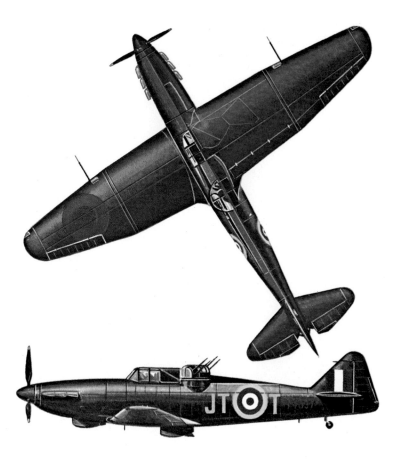

39

Boulton Paul Defiant I of No. 256 Squadron R.A.F., U.K. October 1941. *Engine:* One 1,030 h.p. Rolls-Royce Merlin III Vee type. *Span:* 39 ft. 4 in. (11·99 m.). *Length:* 35 ft. 4 in. (10·77 m.). *Height:* 12 ft. 2 in. (3·71 m.). *Normal take-off weight:* 8,318 lb. (3,773 kg.). *Maximum speed:* 304 m.p.h. (489 km./hr.) at 17,000 ft. (5,182 m.). *Operational ceiling:* 30,350 ft. (9,251 m.). *Normal range:* 465 miles (748 km.). *Armament:* Four 0·303 in. Browning machine-guns in dorsal turret.

DEWOITINE D. 520 (France)

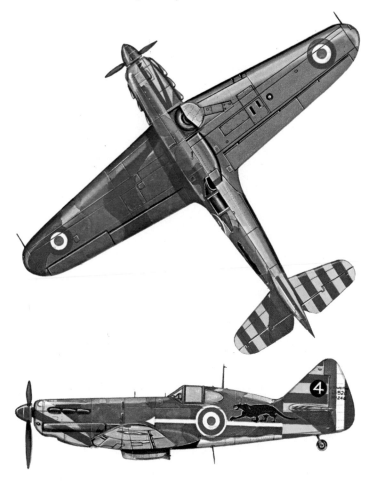

40

Dewoitine D. 520 of GC.II/7 (4th *Escadrille*), Vichy Air Force, Tunisia early 1942. *Engine:* One 930 h.p. Hispano-Suiza 12Y-45 Vee type. *Span:* 33 ft. 5⅝ in. (10·20 m.). *Length:* 28 ft. 8⅞ in. (8·76 m.). *Height:* 8 ft. 5⅛ in. (2·57 m.). *Maximum take-off weight:* 6,135 lb. (2,783 kg.). *Maximum speed:* 326 m.p.h. (525 km./hr.) at 19,685 ft. (6,000 m.). *Operational ceiling:* 36,090 ft. (11,000 m.). *Normal range:* 615 miles (990 km.). *Armament:* One 20 mm. Hispano HS 404 cannon mounted in the engine Vee and firing through the propeller hub, and two 7·5 mm. MAC 1934-M39 machine-guns in each wing.

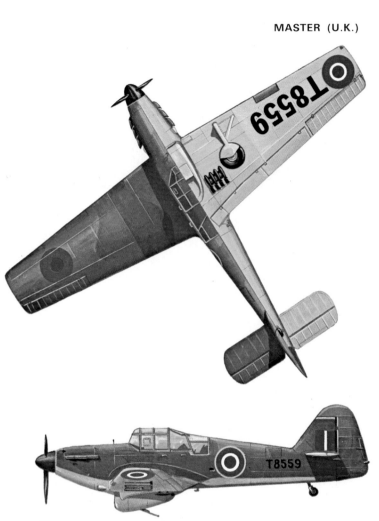

41

Miles Master I of the R.A.F. (unit unidentified), *ca.* early summer 1942. *Engine:* One 715 h.p. Rolls-Royce Kestrel XXX Vee type. *Span* (originally): 39 ft. 0 in. (11·89 m.). *Span* (as illustrated): 35 ft. 7 in. (10·85 m.). *Length:* 30 ft. 5 in. (9·27 m.). *Height:* 9 ft. 3 in. (2·82 m.). *Normal take-off weight:* 5,352 lb. (2,428 kg.). *Maximum speed:* 226 m.p.h. (364 km./hr.) at 15,000 ft. (4,572 m.). *Operational ceiling:* 28,000 ft. (8,534 m.). *Normal range:* 500 miles (805 km.). *Armament:* Provision for one 0·303 in. Vickers machine-gun in upper front fuselage and eight practice bombs beneath wing centre-section.

YAKOVLEV Yak-9 (U.S.S.R.)

42

Yakovlev Yak-9D of a Soviet Air Force Guards Fighter Regiment, Crimea, spring 1944. *Engine:* One 1,210 h.p. Klimov M-105 PF Vee type. *Span:* 32 ft. 9¾ in. (10·00 m.). *Length:* 28 ft. 0⅝ in. (8·55 m.). *Height:* 9 ft. 10⅛ in. (3·00 m.). *Normal take-off weight:* 6,867 lb. (3,115 kg.). *Maximum speed:* 373 m.p.h. (600 km./hr.) at 11,485 ft. (3,500 m.). *Operational ceiling:* 32,810 ft. (10,000 m.). *Normal range:* 808 miles (1,300 km.). *Armament:* One 20 mm. MPSh cannon mounted in the engine Vee and firing through the propeller hub, and one 12·7 mm. UBS machine-gun in port side of the upper front fuselage.

MIKOYAN-GUREVICH MiG-3 (U.S.S.R.)

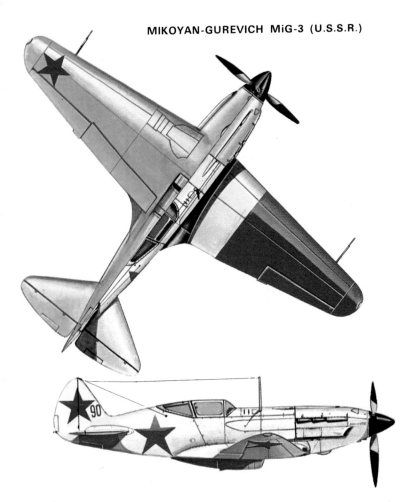

43

Mikoyan-Gurevich MiG-3 of the 12th Fighter Regiment Soviet Air Force,
Northern Front, winter 1941–42. *Engine:* One 1,350 h.p. Mikulin AM-35A Vee
type. *Span:* 33 ft. 9½ in. (10·30 m.). *Length:* 26 ft. 9 in. (8·155 m.). *Height:*
approximately 11 ft. 6 in. (3·50 m.). *Normal take-off weight:* 7,242 lb.
(3,285 kg.). *Maximum speed:* 398 m.p.h. (640 km./hr.) at 22,965 ft. (7,000 m.).
Operational ceiling: 39,370 ft. (12,000 m.). *Normal range:* 510 miles (820 km.).
Armament: One 12·7 mm. Beresin BS machine-gun and two 7·62 mm. ShKAS
machine-guns in upper front fuselage; provision for one 220 lb. (100 kg.) bomb,
two 55 lb. (25 kg.) bombs or three 82 mm. RS-82 rocket projectiles beneath
each wing.

MUSTANG (U.S.A.)

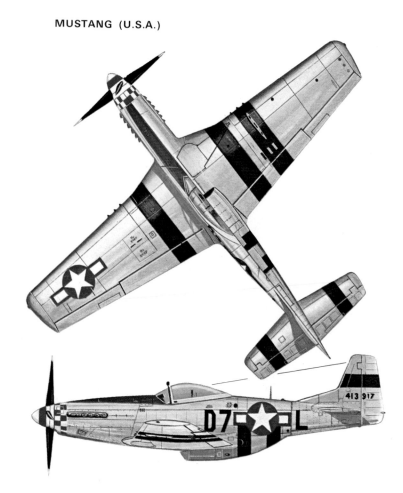

44

North American P-51D-5-NA of the 339th Fighter Group, 66th Fighter Wing
U.S. Eighth Air Force, interned in Sweden August 1944 and later purchased by
the R.Sw.A.F. *Engine:* One 1,490 h.p. Packard-built V-1650-7 (Rolls-Royce
Merlin) Vee type. *Span:* 37 ft. 0¼ in. (11·29 m.). *Length:* 32 ft. 3¼ in. (9·84 m.).
Height: 13 ft. 8 in. (4·16 m.). *Normal take-off weight:* 10,100 lb. (4,581 kg.).
Maximum speed: 437 m.p.h. (703 km./hr.) at 25,000 ft. (7,620 m.). *Operational
ceiling:* 41,900 ft. (12,771 m.). *Normal range:* 950 miles (1,529 km.). *Armament:*
Three 0·50 in. Browning MG 53-2 machine-guns in each wing; provision (with
two guns deleted) for one 1,000 lb. (454 kg.) bomb, five 5 in. rocket projectiles
or three bazooka-type rocket launching tubes beneath each wing.

KAWASAKI Ki-61 (Japan)

45

Kawasaki Ki-61-Ib Model 1B *Hien* of the 68th Fighter Group J.A.A.F., New Britain *ca.* spring 1944. *Engine:* One 1,175 h.p. Kawasaki Ha-40 inverted-Vee type. *Span:* 39 ft. 4½ in. (12·00 m.). *Length:* 28 ft. 8½ in. (8·75 m.). *Height:* 12 ft. 1⅝ in. (3·70 m.). *Normal take-off weight:* 6,504 lb. (2,950 kg.). *Maximum speed:* 368 m.p.h. (592 km./hr.) at 15,945 ft. (4,860 m.). *Operational ceiling:* 38,060 ft. (11,600 m.). *Normal range:* 373 miles (600 km.). *Armament:* Two 12·7 mm. Type 1 machine-guns in upper front fuselage and one in each wing.

HURRICANE (U.K.)

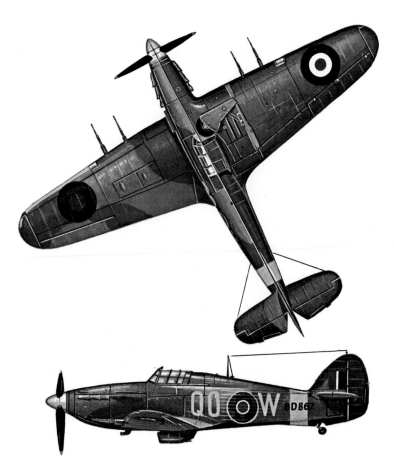

46

Hawker Hurricane IIC of No. 3 Squadron R.A.F., U.K. 1941. *Engine:* One 1,300 h.p. Rolls-Royce Merlin XX Vee type. *Span:* 40 ft. 0 in. (12·19 m.). *Length:* 32 ft. 2¼ in. (9·81 m.). *Height:* 13 ft. 1 in. (3·99 m.). *Normal take-off weight:* 7,544 lb. (3,422 kg.). *Maximum speed:* 329 m.p.h. (529 km./hr.) at 18,000 ft. (5,486 m.). *Operational ceiling:* 35,600 ft. (10,851 m.). *Normal range:* 460 miles (740 km.). *Armament:* Two 20 mm. Oerlikon or Hispano cannon in each wing; provision for one 250 lb. (113 kg.) or 500 lb. (227 kg.) bomb beneath each wing.

HURRICANE (U.K.)

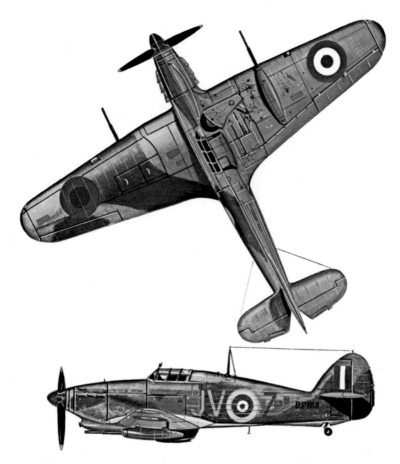

47

Hawker Hurricane IID of No. 6 Squadron R.A.F., Middle East 1942. *Engine:* One 1,300 h.p. Rolls-Royce Merlin XX Vee type. *Span:* 40 ft. 0 in. (12·19 m.). *Length:* 32 ft. 2¼ in. (9·81 m.). *Height:* 13 ft. 1 in. (3·99 m.). *Maximum take-off weight:* 8,100 lb. (3,674 kg.). *Maximum speed:* 316 m.p.h. (509 km./hr.) at 19,000 ft. (5,791 m.). *Operational ceiling:* 33,500 ft. (10,211 m.). *Range:* 480 miles (772 km.). *Armament:* One 0·303 in. Browning machine-gun in each wing and one 40 mm. Vickers S cannon in fairing beneath each wing.

MESSERSCHMITT Bf 109 (Germany)

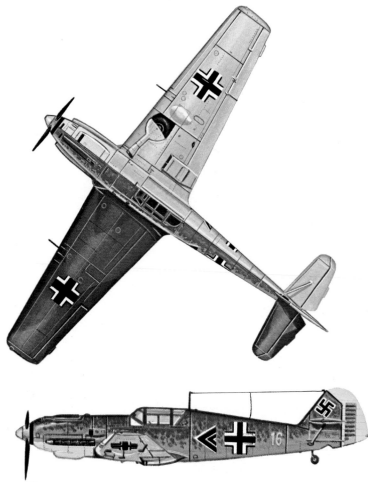

48

Messerschmitt Bf 109E-4 flown by Major Adolf Galland while commanding III/JG.26, France, June 1941. *Engine:* One 1,150 h.p. Daimler-Benz DB 601Aa inverted-Vee type. *Span:* 32 ft. 4½ in. (9·87 m.). *Length:* 28 ft. 4⅛ in. (8·64 m.). *Height:* 11 ft. 1⅞ in. (3·40 m.). *Normal take-off weight:* 5,523 lb. (2,505 kg.). *Maximum speed:* 357 m.p.h. (575 km./hr.) at 12,305 ft. (3,750 m.). *Operational ceiling:* 36,090 ft. (11,000 m.). *Normal range:* 413 miles (665 km.). *Armament:* Two 7·9 mm. MG 17 machine-guns in upper front fuselage and one 20 mm. MG FF cannon in each wing.

64

MACCHI C.202 (Italy)

49

Macchi C.202 *Serie* XI *Folgore* of the 353° *Squadriglia*, 20° *Gruppo*, 51° *Stormo C.T.,* Monserrato (Italy) *ca.* July 1943. *Engine:* One 1,075 h.p. Alfa Romeo R.A.1000 RC 41 (licence-built DB 601A-1) inverted-Vee type. *Span:* 34 ft. 8½ in. (10·58 m.). *Length:* 29 ft. 0⅜ in. (8·85 m.). *Height:* 9 ft. 11¼ in. (3·03 m.). *Normal take-off weight:* 6,459 lb. (2,930 kg.). *Maximum speed:* 370 m.p.h. (595 km./hr.) at 19,685 ft. (6,000 m.). *Operational ceiling:* 37,730 ft. (11,500 m.). *Normal range:* 475 miles (765 km.). *Armament:* Two 12·7 mm. Breda-SAFAT machine-guns in upper front fuselage and one 7·7 mm. Breda-SAFAT machine-gun in each wing.

KINGCOBRA (U.S.A.)

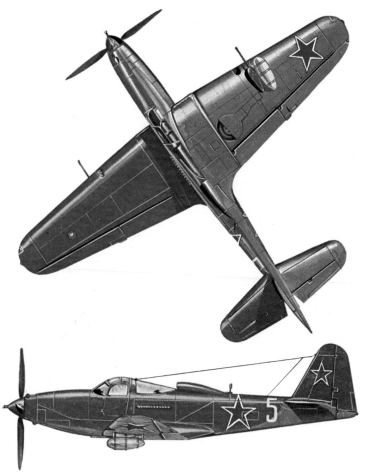

50

Bell P-63A-6 Kingcobra of the Soviet Air Force, *ca.* 1944. *Engine:* One 1,325 h.p. Allison V-1710-95 Vee type. *Span:* 38 ft. 4 in. (11·68 m.). *Length:* 32 ft. 8 in. (9·96 m.). *Height:* 12 ft. 7 in. (3·84 m.). *Normal take-off weight:* 8,800 lb. (3,992 kg.). *Maximum speed:* 408 m.p.h. (657 km./hr.) at 24,450 ft. (7,452 m.). *Operational ceiling:* 43,000 ft. (13,105 m.). *Typical range:* 450 miles (724 km.). *Armament:* One 37 mm. cannon firing through the propeller hub, two 0·50 in. machine-guns in upper front fuselage and one in each wing; provision for one 500 lb. (227 kg.) bomb beneath fuselage and one beneath each wing.

AIRACOBRA (U.S.A.)

51

Bell P-39D Airacobra of the 35th Fighter Group U.S.A.A.F., New Guinea 1942.
Engine: One 1,150 h.p. Allison V-1710-35 Vee type. *Span:* 34 ft. 0 in. (10·36 m.).
Length: 29 ft. 9 in. (9·07 m.). *Height:* 11 ft. 10 in. (3·61 m.). *Normal take-off
weight:* 7,650 lb. (3,470 kg.). *Maximum speed:* 368 m.p.h. (592 km./hr.) at
13,800 ft. (4,206 m.). *Operational ceiling:* 32,100 ft. (9,784 m.). *Normal range:*
800 miles (1,287 km.). *Armament:* One 37 mm. cannon firing through the
propeller hub, two 0·50 in. Browning M-2 machine-guns in upper front
fuselage and two 0·30 in. machine-guns in each wing; provision for one 500 lb.
(227 kg.) bomb beneath fuselage.

TYPHOON (U.K.)

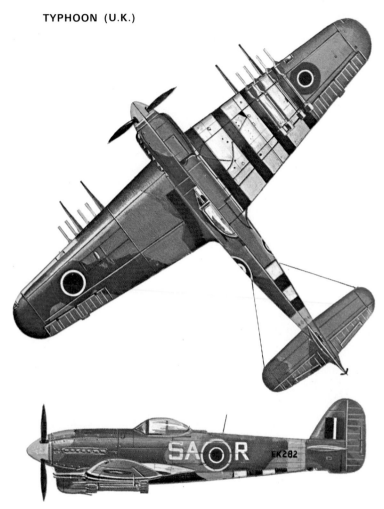

52

Hawker Typhoon IB of No. 486 Squadron R.N.Z.A.F., U.K. summer 1944.
Engine: One 2,200 h.p. Napier Sabre IIB in-line. *Span:* 41 ft. 7 in. (12·67 m.).
Length: 31 ft. 10¾ in. (9·72 m.). *Height:* 14 ft. 10 in. (4·52 m.). *Maximum take-off weight:* 12,905 lb. (5,853 kg.). *Maximum speed:* 409 m.p.h. (658 km./hr.)
at 10,000 ft. (3,048 m.). *Operational ceiling:* 34,000 ft. (10,363 m.). *Range with
underwing drop-tanks:* 910 miles (1,465 km.). *Armament:* Two 20 mm. Hispano cannon in each wing; provision for one 1,000 lb. (454 kg.) bomb or four
60 lb. (27 kg.) rocket projectiles beneath each wing.

TEMPEST (U.K.)

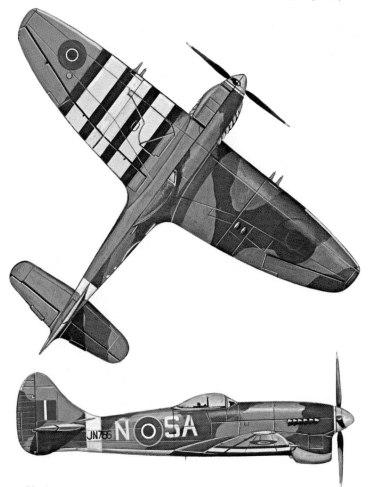

53

Hawker Tempest V Series 1 of No. 486 Squadron R.N.Z.A.F., U.K. *ca.* late spring 1944. *Engine:* One 2,180 h.p. Napier Sabre IIA in-line. *Span:* 41 ft. 0 in. (12·50 m.). *Length:* 33 ft. 8 in. (10·26 m.). *Height:* 16 ft. 1 in. (4·90 m.). *Normal take-off weight:* 11,500 lb. (5,217 kg.). *Maximum speed:* 436 m.p.h. (701 km./hr.) at 18,500 ft. (5,639 m.). *Operational ceiling:* 36,500 ft. (11,125 m.). *Normal range:* 740 miles (1,191 km.). *Armament:* Two 20 mm. Hispano Mk. II cannon in each wing; provision for one 1,000 lb. (454 kg.) bomb, four 60 lb. (27 kg.) rocket projectiles or other weapons beneath each wing.

FULMAR (U.K.)

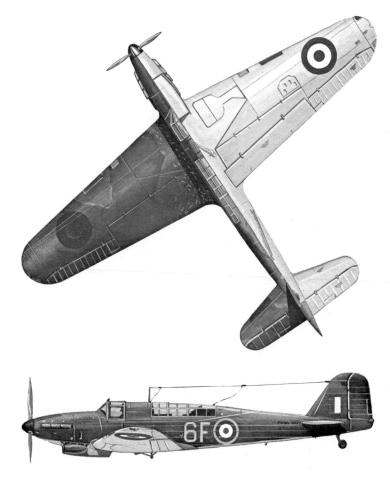

54

Fairey Fulmar II of No. 802 Squadron F.A.A., Malta theatre April 1942. *Engine:* One 1,300 h.p. Rolls-Royce Merlin 30 Vee type. *Span:* 46 ft. 4½ in. (14·14 m.). *Length:* 40 ft. 2 in. (12·24 m.). *Height:* 14 ft. 1¼ in. (4·30 m.). *Normal take-off weight:* 9,672 lb. (4,387 kg.). *Maximum speed:* 272 m.p.h. (438 km./hr.) at 7,250 ft. (2,210 m.). *Operational ceiling:* 27,200 ft. (8,291 m.). *Normal range:* 780 miles (1,255 km.). *Armament:* Four 0·303 in. Browning machine-guns in each wing and provision for one 0·303 in. Vickers K gun in rear cockpit; provision for one 100 or 250 lb. (45 or 113 kg.) bomb beneath each wing.

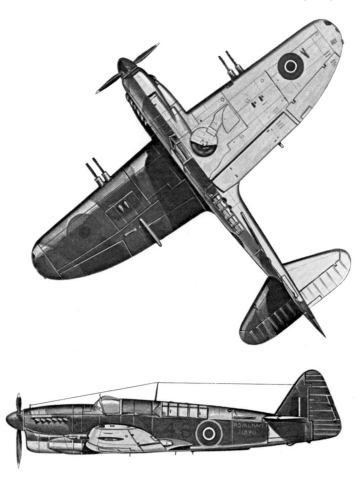

55

Fairey Firefly FR I of No. 1770 Squadron F.A.A., July 1944. *Engine:* One 1,730 h.p. Rolls-Royce Griffon IIB Vee type. *Span:* 44 ft. 6 in. (13·56 m.). *Length:* 37 ft. 7¼ in. (11·46 m.). *Height:* 13 ft. 7 in. (4·14 m.). *Maximum take-off weight:* 14,020 lb. (6,359 kg.). *Maximum speed:* 316 m.p.h. (509 km./hr.) at 14,000 ft. (4,267 m.). *Operational ceiling:* 28,000 ft. (8,534 m.). *Maximum range with auxiliary tanks:* 1,070 miles (1,722 km.). *Armament:* Two 20 mm. Hispano cannon in each wing; provision for one 1,000 lb. (454 kg.) bomb or four 60 lb. (27 kg.) rocket projectiles beneath each wing.

SPITFIRE (U.K.)

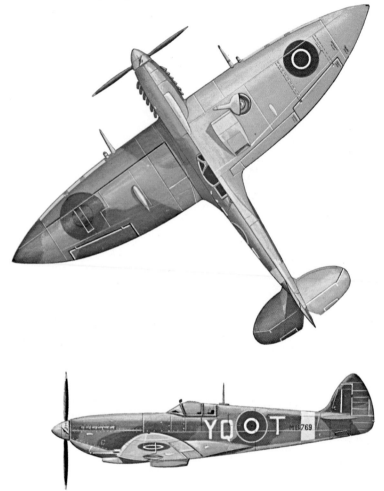

56

Supermarine Spitfire HF VII of No. 616 Squadron R.A.F., U.K. 1942. *Engine:* One 1,710 h.p. Rolls-Royce Merlin 64 Vee type. *Span:* 40 ft. 2 in. (12·24 m.). *Length:* 31 ft. 3½ in. (9·54 m.). *Height:* 12 ft. 7¼ in. (3·68 m.). *Maximum take-off weight:* 7,875 lb. (3,572 kg.). *Maximum speed:* 408 m.p.h. (657 km./hr.) at 25,000 ft. (7,620 m.). *Operational ceiling:* 43,000 ft. (13,106 m.). *Normal range:* 660 miles (1,062 km.). *Armament:* One 20 mm. Hispano cannon and two 0·303 in. Browning machine-guns in each wing.

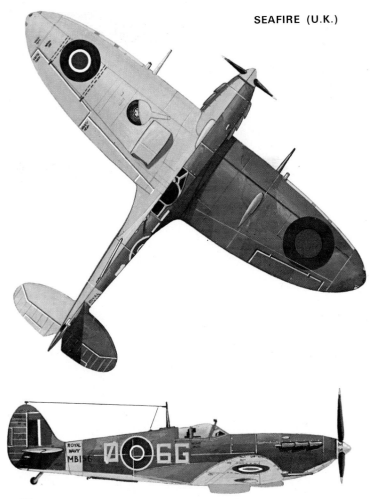

SEAFIRE (U.K.)

57

Supermarine Seafire F IIC of No. 885 Squadron F.A.A., H.M.S. *Formidable, ca.*
September 1942. *Engine:* One 1,470 h.p. Rolls-Royce Merlin 45 Vee type.
Span: 36 ft. 10 in. (11·53 m.). *Length:* 29 ft. 11 in. (9·12 m.). *Height:*
11 ft. 4¾ in. (3·47 m.). *Maximum take-off weight:* 7,100 lb. (3,220 kg.).
Maximum speed: 352 m.p.h. (566 km./hr.) at 12,250 ft. (3,734 m.). *Operational
ceiling:* 33,800 ft. (10,302 m.). *Normal range:* 465 miles (748 km.). *Armament:*
One 20 mm. Hispano cannon and two 0·303 in. Browning machine-guns in
each wing; provision for one 500 lb. (227 kg.) bomb beneath the fuselage or one
250 lb. (113 kg.) bomb beneath each wing.

WARHAWK (U.S.A.)

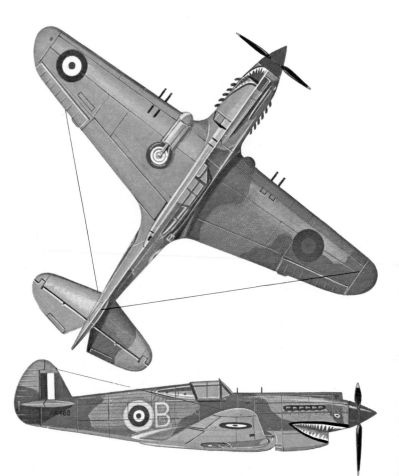

58

Curtiss P-40C Warhawk (Tomahawk IIB) of No. 112 Squadron R.A.F., Egypt autumn 1941. *Engine:* One 1,040 h.p. Allison V-1710-33 Vee type. *Span:* 37 ft. 3½ in. (11·37 m.). *Length:* 31 ft. 8½ in. (9·66 m.). *Height:* 12 ft. 4 in. (3·66 m.). *Normal take-off weight:* 7,549 lb. (3,424 kg.). *Maximum speed:* 345 m.p.h. (555 km./hr.) at 15,000 ft. (4,572 m.). *Operational ceiling:* 29,500 ft. (8,992 m.). *Normal range:* 730 miles (1,175 km.). *Armament:* Two 0·50 in. machine-guns in upper front fuselage and two 0·30 in. guns in each wing.

OXFORD (U.K.)

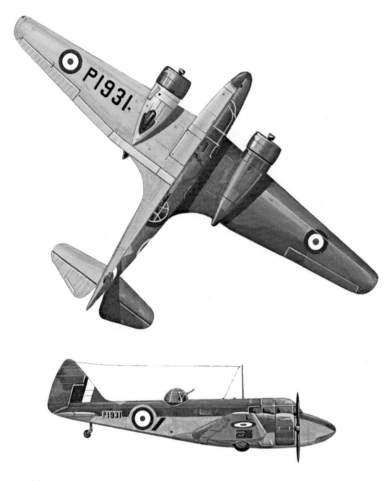

59

Airspeed Oxford I of the R.A.F. (unit unidentified), August 1940. *Engines:* Two 375 h.p. Armstrong Siddeley Cheetah X radials. *Span:* 53 ft. 4 in. (16·26 m.). *Length:* 34 ft. 6 in. (10·52 m.). *Height:* 11 ft. 1 in. (3·38 m.). *Normal take-off weight:* 7,500 lb. (3,402 kg.). *Maximum speed:* 185 m.p.h. (298 km./hr.) at 7,500 ft. (2,286 m.). *Operational ceiling:* 19,500 ft. (5,944 m.). *Normal range:* 960 miles (1,545 km.). *Armament:* None as trainer; some Oxfords on anti-submarine patrols carried 250 lb. (113 kg.) of bombs internally.

HENSCHEL Hs 129 (Germany)

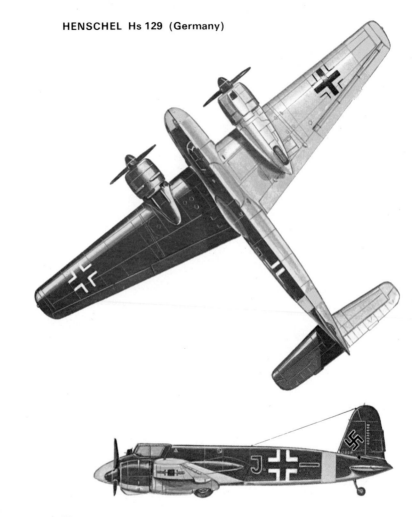

60

Henschel Hs 129B-2/R2 of an unidentified *Schlachtgeschwader*, Eastern Front, late summer 1943. *Engines:* Two 740 h.p. Gnome-Rhône 14M 04/05 radials. *Span:* 46 ft. 7 in. (14·20 m.). *Length:* 31 ft. 11¾ in. (9·75 m.). *Height:* 10 ft. 8 in. (3·25 m.). *Normal take-off weight:* 9,259 lb. (4,200 kg.). *Maximum speed:* 253 m.p.h. (407 km./hr.) at 12,500 ft. (3,810 m.). *Operational ceiling:* 29,530 ft. (9,000 m.). *Normal range:* 429 miles (690 km.). *Armament:* Two 20 mm. MG 151 cannon and two 7·9 mm. MG 17 machine-guns in fuselage nose, and one 30 mm. MK 101 cannon in ventral fairing.

BEAUFIGHTER (U.K.)

61

Bristol Beaufighter VIF of the R.A.F. Air Fighting Development Unit, U.K. May 1944. *Engines:* Two 1,670 h.p. Bristol Hercules VI or XVI radials. *Span:* 57 ft. 10 in. (17·63 m.). *Length:* 41 ft. 8 in. (12·70 m.). *Height:* 15 ft. 10 in. (4·83 m.). *Maximum take-off weight:* 21,600 lb. (9,797 kg.). *Maximum speed:* 333 m.p.h. (536 km./hr.) at 15,600 ft. (4,755'm.). *Operational ceiling:* 26,500 ft. (8,077 m.). *Normal range:* 1,480 miles (2,382 km.). *Armament:* Four 20 mm. Hispano cannon in fuselage nose and three 0·303 in. Browning machine-guns in each wing.

JUNKERS Ju 88 (Germany)

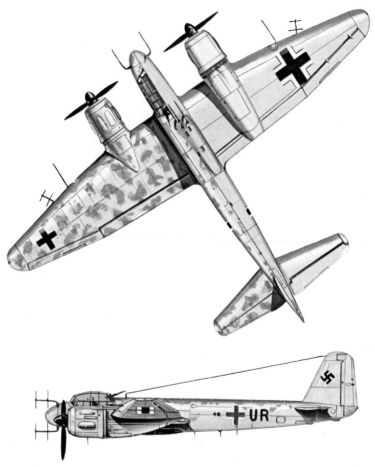

62

Junkers Ju 88G-1 of 7/NJG.2, which fell into Allied hands July 1944. *Engines:* Two 1,700 h.p. BMW 801D radials. *Span:* 65 ft. 7⅜ in. (20·00 m.). *Length:* 54 ft. 1½ in. (16·50 m.). *Height:* 15 ft. 11 in. (4·85 m.). *Normal take-off weight:* 28,880 lb. (13,100 kg.). *Maximum speed:* 342 m.p.h. (550 km./hr.) at 27,890 ft. (8,500 m.). *Operational ceiling:* 32,480 ft. (9,900 m.). *Typical range:* 1,553 miles (2,500 km.). *Armament:* Four 20 mm. MG 151 cannon in ventral pack and one 13 mm. MG 131 machine-gun in rear of cabin.

KAWASAKI Ki-45 (Japan)

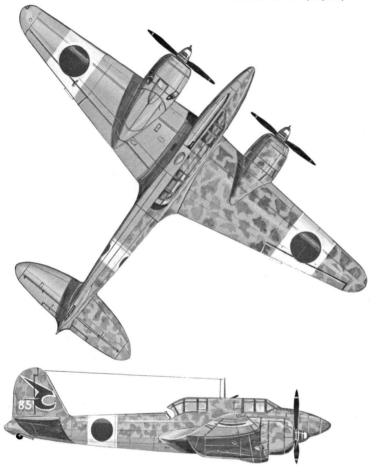

63

Kawasaki Ki-45-KAIc of the 2nd Squadron, 53rd Group J.A.A.F., Chiba Prefecture, home defence of Japan late 1944. *Engines:* Two 1,080 h.p. Mitsubishi Ha-102 radials. *Span:* 49 ft. 3⅜ in. (15·02 m.). *Length:* 36 ft. 1⅛ in. (11·00 m.). *Height:* 12 ft. 1⅝ in. (3·70 m.). *Normal take-off weight:* 12,125 lb. (5,500 kg.). *Maximum speed:* 340 m.p.h. (547 km./hr.) at 21,325 ft. (6,500 m.). *Operational ceiling:* 32,810 ft. (10,000 m.). *Maximum range:* 1,243 miles (2,000 km.). *Armament:* One 37 mm. Ho-203 cannon in ventral tunnel, two 20 mm. Ho-5 cannon in dorsal position and one 7·92 mm. Type 98 machine-gun in rear cockpit.

NAKAJIMA J1N (Japan)

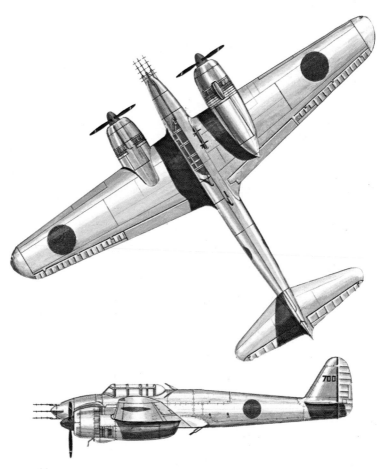

64

Nakajima J1N1-S, captured aircraft displayed in the U.S.A. *ca.* late 1945.
Engines: Two 1,130 h.p. Nakajima Sakae 21 radials. *Span:* 55 ft. 8½ in.
(16·98 m.). *Length* (excluding aerials): 39 ft. 11½ in. (12·18 m.). *Height:*
14 ft. 11½ in. (4·56 m.). *Normal take-off weight:* 15,212 lb. (6,900 kg.). *Maximum speed:* 315 m.p.h. (507 km./hr.) at 19,160 ft. (5,840 m.). *Operational ceiling:* 30,580 ft. (9,320 m.). *Normal range:* 1,584 miles (2,550 km.). *Armament:* Two 20 mm. Type 99-II cannon in dorsal position and two in ventral position.

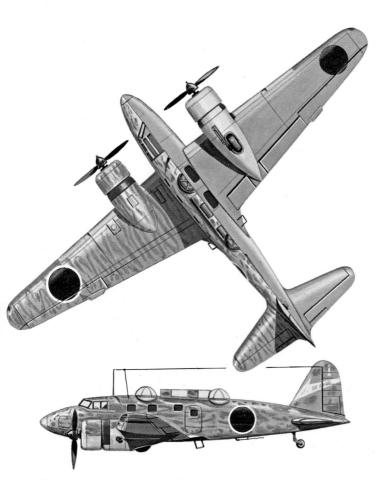

65

Tachikawa Ki-54 of the J.A.A.F. (unit unidentified), late 1944. *Engines:* Two
515 h.p. Nakajima Ha-13 Kotobuki radials. *Span:* 58 ft. 0$\frac{7}{8}$ in. (17·70 m.).
Length: 39 ft. 0$\frac{1}{2}$ in. (11·90 m.). *Height:* 11 ft. 9 in. (3·58 m.). *Normal take-off
weight:* 8,995 lb. (4,080 kg.). *Maximum speed:* 228 m.p.h. (367 km./hr.) at
6,560 ft. (2,000 m.). *Operational ceiling:* 19,390 ft. (5,910 m.). *Typical range:*
435 miles (700 km.). *Armament:* None.

POTEZ 63 (France)

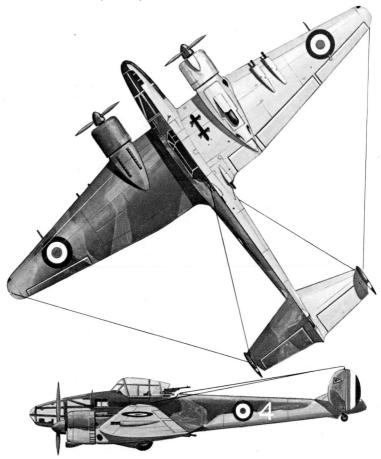

66

Potez P.63-11 of GR.II/39 (3rd *Escadrille*), Syria 1941. *Engines:* Two 700 h.p. Gnome-Rhône 14M series radials. *Span:* 52 ft. 5⅞ in. (16·00 m.). *Length:* 36 ft. 1¼ in. (11·004 m.). *Height:* 11 ft. 10½ in. (3·62 m.). *Normal take-off weight:* 9,773 lb. (4,433 kg.). *Maximum speed:* 264 m.p.h. (425 km./hr.) at 16,405 ft. (5,000 m.). *Operational ceiling:* 29,530 ft. (9,000 m.). *Maximum range:* 932 miles (1,500 km.). *Armament:* Two 7·5 mm. MAC 1934 machine-guns beneath each wing, one in rear cockpit and three in ventral position; provision for eight 22 lb. (10 kg.) bombs internally and two 110 lb. (50 kg.) bombs beneath each wing.

HEINKEL He 219 (Germany)

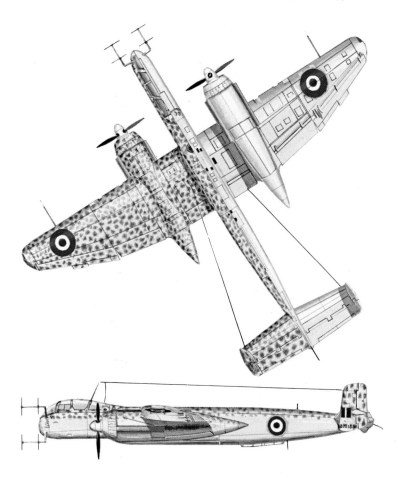

67

Heinkel He 219A-5/R2 *Uhu*, captured aircraft with R.A.F. markings super-imposed, *ca.* late autumn 1945. *Engines:* Two 1,800 h.p. Daimler-Benz DB 603E inverted-Vee type. *Span:* 60 ft. 8$\frac{3}{8}$ in. (18·50 m.). *Length:* 51 ft. 0$\frac{1}{4}$ in. (15·55 m.). *Height:* 13 ft. 5$\frac{3}{8}$ in. (4·10 m.). *Maximum take-off weight:* 33,730 lb. (15,300 kg.). *Maximum speed:* 416 m.p.h. (670 km./hr.) at 22,965 ft. (7,000 m.). *Operational ceiling:* 39,600 ft. (12,700 m.). *Maximum range:* 1,243 miles (2,000 km.). *Armament:* Four 20 mm. MG 151 cannon in ventral pack and one in each wing root.

DORNIER Do 217 (Germany)

68

Dornier Do 217N-1 of an unidentified *Nachtjagdgeschwader, ca.* spring 1943.
Engines: Two 1,750 h.p. Daimler-Benz DB 603A inverted-Vee type. *Span:*
62 ft. 4 in. (19·00 m.). *Length:* 58 ft. 9 in. (17·91 m.). *Height:* 16 ft. 3 in.
(4·95 m.). *Normal take-off weight:* 29,101 lb. (13,200 kg.). *Maximum speed:*
320 m.p.h. (515 km./hr.) at 18,700 ft. (5,700 m.). *Operational ceiling:* 29,200 ft.
(8,900 m.). *Maximum range:* 1,553 miles (2,500 km.). *Armament:* Four 20 mm.
MG 151 cannon and four 7·9 mm. MG 17 machine-guns in fuselage nose, one
13 mm. MG 131 machine-gun in turret aft of cabin and one in rear of ventral
cupola.

WHIRLWIND (U.K.)

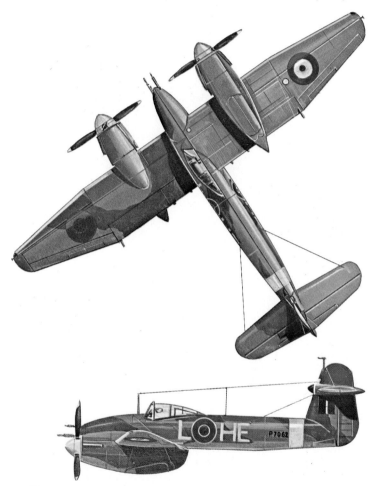

69

Westland Whirlwind I of No. 263 Squadron R.A.F., U.K. summer 1942. *Engines:*
Two 765 h.p. Rolls-Royce Peregrine I Vee type. *Span:* 45 ft. 0 in. (13·72 m.).
Length: 31 ft. 6 in. (9·60 m.). *Height:* 11 ft. 7 in. (3·53 m.). *Normal take-off
weight:* 10,356 lb. (4,697 kg.). *Maximum speed:* 360 m.p.h. (579 km./hr.) at
15,000 ft. (4,572 m.). *Operational ceiling:* 30,000 ft. (9,144 m.). *Maximum
range:* approximately 1,000 miles (1,610 km.). *Armament:* Four 20 mm. Hispano
cannon in fuselage nose; provision for one 250 or 500 lb. (113 or 227 kg.)
bomb beneath each wing.

MOSQUITO (U.K.)

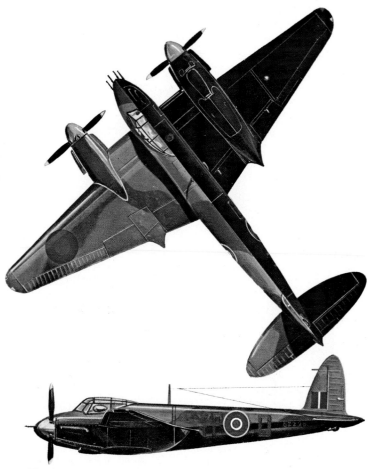

70

De Havilland Mosquito NF II of No. 23 Squadron R.A.F., Malta, January 1943. *Engines:* Two 1,460 h.p. Rolls-Royce Merlin 21/23 Vee type. *Span:* 54 ft. 2 in. (16·51 m.). *Length:* 40 ft. 4 in. (12·29 m.). *Height:* 15 ft. $3\frac{1}{2}$ in. (4·66 m.). *Normal take-off weight:* 18,100 lb. (8,210 kg.). *Maximum speed:* 354 m.p.h. (570 km./hr.) at 14,000 ft. (4,267 m.). *Operational ceiling:* 34,500 ft. (10,515 m.). *Normal range:* 1,520 miles (2,446 km.). *Armament:* Four 20 mm. Hispano cannon in lower front fuselage and four 0·303 in. Browning machine-guns in fuselage nose.

MESSERSCHMITT Me 410 (Germany)

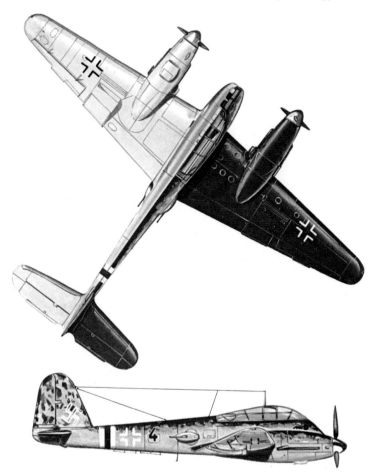

71

Messerschmitt Me 410A-1 *Hornisse* of III/ZG.1 *Wespen*, Germany 1944–45. *Engines:* Two 1,750 h.p. Daimler-Benz DB 603A inverted-Vee type. *Span:* 53 ft. 7$\frac{3}{4}$ in. (16·35 m.). *Length:* 40 ft. 11$\frac{1}{8}$ in. (12·48 m.). *Height:* 14 ft. 0$\frac{1}{2}$ in. (4·28 m.). *Maximum take-off weight:* 23,500 lb. (10,660 kg.). *Maximum speed:* 388 m.p.h. (625 km./hr.) at 21,980 ft. (6,700 m.). *Operational ceiling:* 32,810 ft. (10,000 m.). *Maximum range:* 1,448 miles (2,330 km.). *Armament:* Two 20 mm. MG 151 cannon and two 7·9 mm. MG 17 machine-guns in fuselage nose, and one 13 mm. MG 131 gun in each lateral barbette; provision for up to 4,409 lb. (2,000 kg.) of bombs internally, or 882 lb. (400 kg.) internally and two 110 lb. (50 kg.) bombs beneath each wing root.

MESSERSCHMITT Bf 110 (Germany)

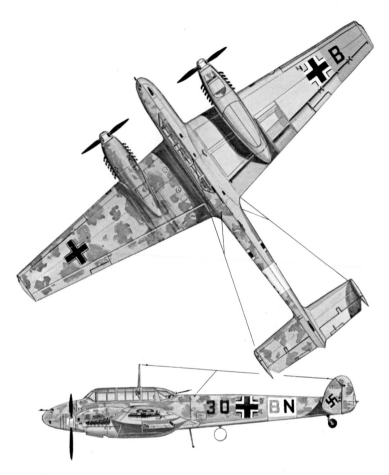

72

Messerschmitt Bf 110C-1 of 5/ZG.26, North Africa 1942. *Engines:* Two 1,100 h.p. Daimler-Benz DB 601A-1 inverted-Vee type. *Span:* 53 ft. 3¾ in. (16·25 m.). *Length:* 39 ft. 7¼ in. (12·07 m.). *Height:* 13 ft. 6⅝ in. (4·13 m.). *Normal take-off weight:* 13,289 lb. (6,028 kg.). *Maximum speed:* 336 m.p.h. (540 km./hr.) at 19,685 ft. (6,000 m.). *Operational ceiling:* 32,810 ft. (10,000 m.). *Maximum range:* 876 miles (1,410 km.). *Armament:* Two 20 mm. MG FF cannon and four 7·9 mm. MG 17 machine-guns in fuselage nose, and one 7·9 mm. MG 15 gun in rear cockpit.

SIEBEL Si 204 (Germany)

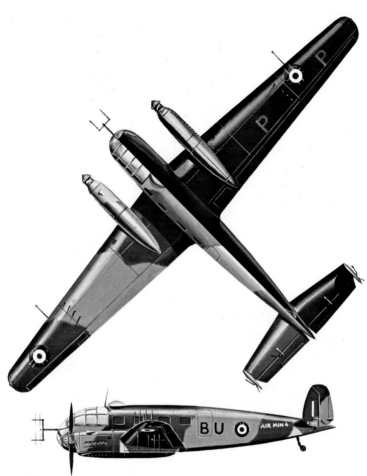

73

Siebel Si 204D-1, captured aircraft with manufacturer's flight test codes and R.A.F. markings superimposed, autumn 1945. *Engines:* Two 580 h.p. Argus As 411A-1 inverted-Vee type. *Span:* 69 ft. 10⅝ in. (21·30 m.). *Length:* 39 ft. 0½ in. (11·90 m.). *Height:* 14 ft. 5¼ in. (4·40 m.). *Maximum take-off weight:* 12,324 lb. (5,590 kg.). *Maximum speed:* 229 m.p.h. (368 km./hr.) at 7,610 ft. (2,320 m.). *Operational ceiling:* 24,605 ft. (7,500 m.). *Maximum range:* 932 miles (1,500 km.). *Armament:* None.

FOKKER G.I (Netherlands)

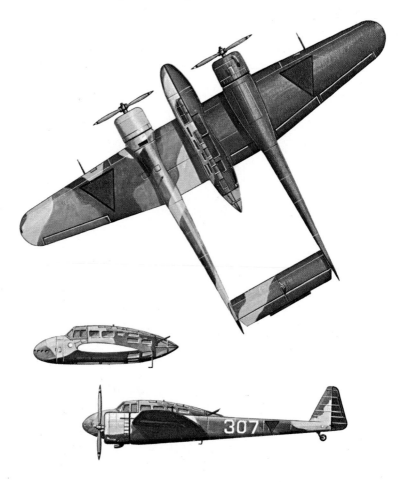

74

Fokker G.IA of the 3rd Fighter Group, 1st Air Regiment LVA, Waalhaven, late 1939. *Engines:* Two 830 h.p. Bristol Mercury VIII radials. *Span:* 56 ft. $3\frac{1}{4}$ in. (17·15 m.). *Length:* 37 ft. $8\frac{3}{4}$ in. (11·50 m.). *Height:* 11 ft. $1\frac{7}{8}$ in. (3·40 m.). *Normal take-off weight:* 10,582 lb. (4,800 kg.). *Maximum speed:* 295 m.p.h. (475 km./hr.) at 9,020 ft. (2,750 m.). *Operational ceiling:* 30,510 ft. (9,300 m.). *Normal range:* 876 miles (1,410 km.). *Armament:* Eight 7·9 mm. FN-Browning machine-guns in nose of nacelle and one in rear of nacelle; provision for up to 661 lb. (300 kg.) of bombs internally and externally.

LIGHTNING (U.S.A.)

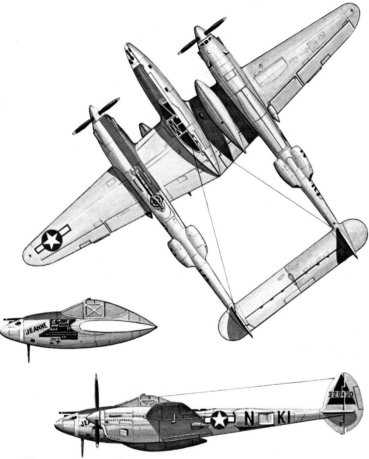

75

Lockheed P-38J-15-LO Lightning of the 55th Fighter Squadron, 20th Fighter Group, U.S. Eighth Air Force, U.K. early 1944. *Engines:* Two 1,425 h.p. Allison V-1710-89/91 Vee type. *Span:* 52 ft. 0 in. (15·85 m.). *Length:* 37 ft. 10 in. (11·53 m.). *Height:* 9 ft. 9¾ in. (2·99 m.). *Normal take-off weight:* 17,500 lb. (7,938 kg.). *Maximum speed:* 414 m.p.h. (666 km/hr.) at 25,000 ft. (7,620 m.). *Operational ceiling:* 44,000 ft. (13,410 m.). *Maximum range on internal fuel:* 1,175 miles (1,891 km.). *Armament:* One 20 mm. Hispano M2 cannon and four 0·50 in. Colt-Browning MG 53-2 machine-guns in nose of nacelle; provision for one bomb of up to 1,600 lb. (726 kg.) size beneath each inboard wing section or five 5 in. rocket projectiles beneath each outer wing section.

SAAB-21 (Sweden)

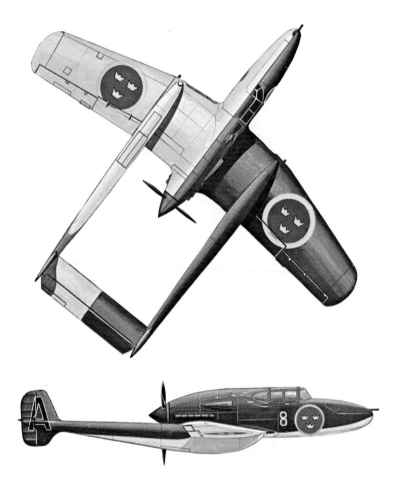

76

Saab J 21A-1 of the 1st Air Division, F 8 Wing Royal Swedish Air Force, Barkarby, *ca.* December 1945. *Engine:* One 1,475 h.p. SFA-built Daimler-Benz DB 605B inverted-Vee type. *Span:* 38 ft. 0⅝ in. (11·60 m.). *Length:* 34 ft. 3¾ in. (10·45 m.). *Height:* 13 ft. 0¼ in. (3·97 m.). *Normal take-off weight:* 9,149 lb. (4,150 kg.). *Maximum speed:* 398 m.p.h. (640 km./hr.) at 16,405 ft. (5,000 m.). *Operational ceiling:* 36,090 ft. (11,000 m.). *Armament:* One 20 mm. Hispano cannon and four 13·2 mm. Hispano machine-guns in nose of nacelle.

AIRACOMET (U.S.A.)

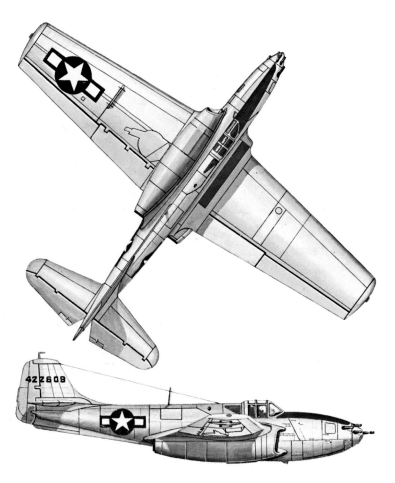

77

Bell P-59A (first production aircraft) of the U.S.A.A.F., Muroc Field late 1943. *Engines:* Two 2,000 lb. (907 kg.) st General Electric J31-GE-3 turbojets. *Span:* 45 ft. 6 in. (13·87 m.). *Length:* 38 ft. 1½ in. (11·62 m.). *Height:* 12 ft. 0 in. (3·66 m.). *Normal take-off weight:* 10,822 lb. (4,909 kg.). *Maximum speed:* 409 m.p.h. (658 km./hr.) at 35,000 ft. (10,668 m.). *Operational ceiling:* 46,200 ft. (14,082 m.). *Normal range:* 240 miles (386 km.). *Armament:* One 37 mm. M4 cannon and three 0·50 in. machine-guns in fuselage nose.

METEOR (U.K.)

78

Gloster Meteor III of No. 616 Squadron R.A.F., 2nd Allied Tactical Air Force, Germany, January 1945. *Engines:* Two 2,000 lb. (907 kg.) st Rolls-Royce Derwent 1 turbojets. *Span:* 43 ft. 0 in. (13·11 m.). *Length:* 41 ft. 3 in. (12·57 m.). *Height:* 13 ft. 0 in. (3·96 m.). *Maximum take-off weight:* 13,300 lb. (6,033 kg.). *Maximum speed:* 493 m.p.h. (793 km./hr.) at 30,000 ft. (9,144 m.). *Operational ceiling:* 44,000 ft. (13,410 m.). *Maximum range:* 1,340 miles (2,156 km.). *Armament:* Four 20 mm. Hispano Mk. III cannon in fuselage nose.

MESSERSCHMITT Me 262 (Germany)

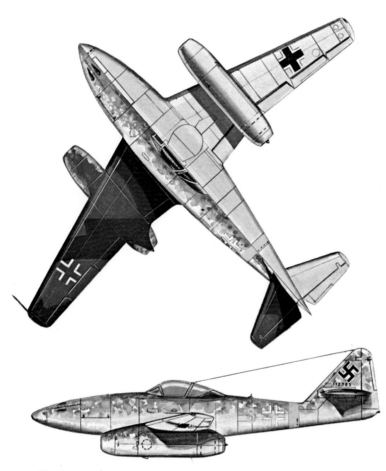

79

Messerschmitt Me 262A-1a *Schwalbe* of 3/JG.7 *Nowotny*, Brandenburg
March 1945. *Engines:* Two 1,984 lb. (900 kg.) st Junkers Jumo 004B series
turbojets. *Span:* 40 ft. 11½ in. (12·48 m.). *Length:* 34 ft. 9¾ in. (10·60 m.).
Height: 12 ft. 7 in. (3·835 m.). *Maximum take-off weight:* 14,101 lb. (6,396 kg.).
Maximum speed: 541 m.p.h. (870 km./hr.) at 19,685 ft. (6,000 m.). *Operational ceiling:* 37,565 ft. (11,450 m.). *Maximum range:* 652 miles (1,050 km.).
Armament: Four 30 mm. MK 108 cannon in fuselage nose.

MESSERSCHMITT Me 163 (Germany)

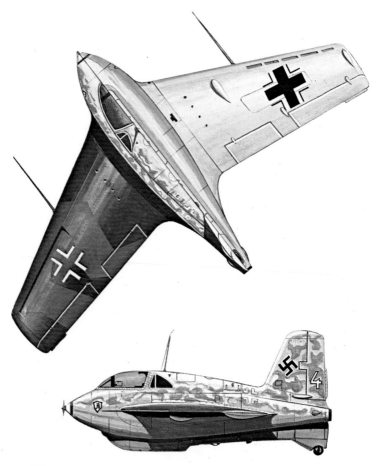

80

Messerschmitt Me 163B-1 *Komet* of 1/JG.400, Zwischenahn, summer 1944.
Engine: One 3,748 lb. (1,700 kg.) st Walter HWK 109-509A-1 liquid rocket
motor. *Span:* 30 ft. 7 in. (9·32 m.). *Length:* 18 ft. 8 in. (5·69 m.). *Height:*
9 ft. 0 in. (2·74 m.). *Normal take-off weight:* 9,502 lb. (4,310 kg.). *Maximum
speed:* 597 m.p.h. (960 km./hr.) at 29,500 ft. (9,000 m.). *Operational ceiling:*
39,370 ft. (12,000 m.). *Maximum endurance* (including climb): 8 minutes, after
which the aircraft returned to earth in a glide. *Armament:* One 30 mm. MK 108
cannon in each wing root, and four 5 cm. R4M rockets in each wing (firing
vertically upward) or twelve R4M rockets beneath each wing firing forward
conventionally

De Havilland Tiger Moth

A developed version of the D.H.60 Gipsy Moth, the prototype D.H.82 (G-ABRC) was flown on 26 October 1931, powered by a 120 hp Gipsy III inverted-Vee engine. It soon became the subject of RAF orders, to Specification T.23/31, for *ab initio* training. The initial batch of thirty-five aircraft were designated D.H.60T Tiger Moth I, being followed by an order for fifty aircraft, with 130 hp Gipsy Major 1 engines, designated D.H.82A Tiger Moth II, to Specification 26/33. The Tiger Moth entered service at the RAF Central Flying School in February 1932, and on 3 September 1939 the RAF had over five hundred Tiger Moth II's on strength, plus nearly three hundred examples of the Queen Bee, a radio-controlled target version. To these were soon added substantial numbers of civilian-owned Tiger Moths impressed for war service, and by the time World War 2 ended well over seven thousand Tiger Moths of all kinds had been built, nearly half of them by Morris Motors. Of the remainder, one hundred and fifty-one were built under licence in Norway, Sweden and Portugal, and two thousand nine hundred and forty-nine at factories in the British Commonwealth. Total wartime production for the RAF amounted to four thousand and five Tiger Moth II's, and both this and the Queen Bee were also used in small numbers by the Fleet Air Arm. Two hundred Canadian-built Tiger Moths were supplied in 1942 to the USAAF, by whom they were designated PT-24.

The Tiger Moth was one of the major types utilised in the huge Empire Air Training Scheme, but during the war it was also to be found on miscellaneous other duties that included casualty evacuation and even anti-submarine patrols. It served with the post-war RAF until 1947, and with the RAFVR for a further four years after this, large numbers being 'demobilised' and re-appearing in various civil guises from about 1950.

2 Boeing (Stearman) Kaydet series

Various biplanes emanating from the Stearman Aircraft Co (which later became the Wichita Division of the Boeing Aircraft Co) were employed as primary trainers by the US forces before and during World War 2. They stemmed from the 2-seat X70 evaluated by the US Army in 1934–35, after which an initial Army order for twenty-six examples of the Stearman Model 75 was placed in 1936. Delivery of these, under the designation PT-13, began later that year, and by 1942 a further one thousand one hundred and forty-two PT-13A/B/C/D had been delivered to the US Army. All were powered by variants of the Lycoming R-680 engine, apart from which they differed in minor detail only. The PT-13D was the first primary trainer to be standardised by both the USAAF and the US Navy, and eight hundred and seventy-three of this version were built for the Navy as the N2S-5. (The Navy had previously purchased sixty-one Whirlwind-engined Stearman 73's, which it designated NS-1.) A re-engined version, appearing in 1940 with a 220 hp Continental R-670 radial, was known as the PT-17. Three thousand seven hundred and sixty-nine PT-17's were built for the USAAF, and two thousand five hundred and eighty N2S-1/3/4 for the US Navy, making this the most widely used Kaydet variant. The Navy's N2S-2 (one hundred and twenty-five built) had the R-680 engine. A 225 hp Jacobs R-755-7 engine characterised the PT-18, which also appeared in 1940; one hundred and fifty were completed. The PT-27 was a 'winterised' version of the PT-17 with enclosed cockpits. Three hundred were built in 1942 for Canadian use as part of the Empire Air Training Scheme.

3 Henschel Hs 123

The Henschel Hs 123, the *Luftwaffe's* first production dive bomber (and also its last combat biplane), first flew in the spring of 1935, making its public debut on 8 May in the hands of General Ernst Udet, the man primarily responsible for its existence. Two of the first three prototypes broke up during high-speed diving tests, but the structural weaknesses were successfully eliminated in the Hs 123V4, which underwent service trials in the autumn of 1935. Apart from the substitution of the more powerful BMW 132Dc radial for the 650 hp BMW 132A-3 of the prototypes, the Hs 123A-1 production model differed little from the V4, and began to enter service with *Luftwaffe* units in mid-1936. In December, five Hs 123's were despatched to Spain to join the Condor

Legion and gain genuine battle experience. Others followed in 1938 and, in the event, were used in Spain more for ground-attack duties than for dive-bombing, proving notably successful in their changed role. The decision of the *Luftwaffe* to standardise on the Ju 87 for dive-bombing led to the cessation of Hs 123 production in the autumn of 1938 after only a comparatively small number (by current German standards) had been produced. By 1939 the Hs 123 was virtually obsolete by world standards, but in the early campaigns in Poland, France and the USSR, where the *Luftwaffe's* air superiority provided a protective umbrella for its activities, it continued to be used with marked success as a close-support aircraft and did not finally disappear from combat units until the summer of 1944; after this it was utilised chiefly for supply dropping or glider towing. Prototypes were flown before the war for proposed Hs 123B and C models, the former with a 960 hp BMW 132K engine and the latter a specialised ground-attack version with two extra guns mounted in the wings; but neither of these went into production.

4 Fiat C.R.42 Falco (Falcon)

The C.R.42 marked the culmination of the line of attractive and successful biplane fighters designed for Fiat by Ing Celestino Rosatelli during the 1920s and 1930s, and it was a tribute to their success that the prototype C.R.42 did not fly until early 1939, several years after most other major air forces had transferred their affections to monoplane fighters. Nor was the *Regia Aeronautica* its only supporter, for in 1939 thirty-four C.R.42's were ordered for the Belgian Air Force, and fifty exported to Hungary; and in 1940–41 seventy-two were delivered to the Royal Swedish Air Force. The fully retractable tail-wheel of the prototype C.R.42 was not retained in production aircraft, but otherwise the design remained basically unchanged. First deliveries were made during 1939, and when Italy entered the war in June 1940 the *Regia Aeronautica* had one hundred and ten Falcos in operational condition and thirty-three more at other bases in Italy. Fifty of these served briefly with the *Corpo Aereo Italiano* in the Brussels area late in 1940, and in their subsequent career the Falcos were employed not only as interceptors but as escort fighters and fighter-bombers in the Mediterranean, North Africa and Italy. Progressively improved versions included the C.R.42*bis*, with four 12·7 mm guns; the 'tropicalised' C.R.42 AS (*Africa Settentrionale* = North Africa); and a version fitted with two 20 mm cannon beneath the lower wings. When used for night fighting, equipped with twin searchlights and radio, the Falco was designated C.R.42 CN (*Caccia Nocturna*). Experimental versions included the twin-float IC.R.42 (I for *Idrovolante* = seaplane), and the C.R.42B which was fitted with a Daimler-Benz DB 601 Vee-type engine. Production of the C.R.42, which ended in 1942, amounted to one thousand seven hundred and

eighty-one aircraft. Despite their quite successful contribution to the Axis war effort, the high loss rate among Italian aircraft is highlighted by the figures for the C.R.42, for when the surrender came on September 1943 the total of Falcos still extant was one hundred and thirteen – thirty less than had been in service in June 1940. The Swedish Falcos (designated J 11) remained in service until 1945, after which a small number were used for a time on civilian target-towing duties.

5 Gloster Gladiator

The Gladiator single-seat fighter biplane – the last of its class to serve with the RAF – was evolved as a private venture to meet Air Ministry Specification F.7/30. The prototype, known as the S.S.37, was flown for the first time in September 1934 and handed over to the RAF in April 1935 for evaluation with the serial number K 5200. With a Mercury IXS engine replacing the prototype's 645 hp Mercury VIS engine, and an enclosed cockpit, the fighter was placed in production, to Specification F.14/35, as the Gladiator Mk I. The initial contract was for twenty-three aircraft, delivery of which began to No 72 Squadron in February 1937. On 3 September 1939 the RAF had two hundred and ten Gladiator I's on charge, and two hundred and thirty-four Gladiator II's, the latter figure including thirty-eight Sea Gladiators. The Gladiator II differed from the Mk I in having an 840 hp Mercury VIIIA engine, desert equipment and other detail improvements; the Sea

Gladiators were interim conversions from RAF machines, fitted with catapult points and an arrester hook, and a fairing between the undercarriage legs for attaching a collapsible dinghy. A further sixty Sea Gladiators were subsequently built as such for the Fleet Air Arm, and ultimate production for the RAF amounted to four hundred and forty-eight. Gladiators were also exported widely before World War 2, to Belgium (twenty-two), China (thirty-six), Eire (four), Greece (two), Latvia (twenty-six), Lithuania (fourteen), Norway (twelve), Portugal (fifteen), South Africa (eleven) and Sweden (fifty-five). In addition, ex-RAF machines were supplied to Egypt (forty-five), Finland (thirty), Greece (twenty-three) and Iraq (fourteen), although several of these aircraft were later returned to the RAF. Production of Gladiators finally ended in 1940, and despite their obsolescence they still equipped thirteen RAF fighter squadrons at the outbreak of war. By the Battle of Britain in the late summer of 1940, only one UK fighter squadron was still flying Gladiators, and they had virtually disappeared from British service by mid-1941. They continued to serve in North Africa and on the Eastern Front for a time beyond this, but eventually ended their days on miscellaneous second-line duties, particularly on meteorological flights.

6 PZL P.11

The P.11, basically a more powerful derivative of the earlier P.7 designed by Ing Zygmunt Pulawski, was brought to fruition by his successor, Ing Wsiewolod Jakimiuk, after Pulawski's death in March 1931. The P.11/I, flown in September 1931, was the first of six prototypes, the sixth machine being representative of the initial production series of thirty P.11a fighters, which were powered by Skoda-built Mercury IVS2 engines. Delivery of these to Polish Air Force units began in 1934, and in the following year the Rumanian Air Force ordered fifty similar aircraft which, with slightly modified tail surfaces and Rumanian-built 595 hp Gnome-Rhône K.9 engines, were designated P.11b. The next Polish variant was the P.11c, placed in production in 1935, which featured a redesigned front fuselage with the engine and cockpit both repositioned to give the pilot a better view forward. This became the standard Polish version, one hundred and seventy-five P.11c's being built and incorporating increased armament (on some aircraft), redesigned tail surfaces and various equipment and other changes. Twelve Polish Air Force squadrons were equipped with P.11c's at the outbreak of World War 2, the P.11a's having meanwhile been withdrawn to training schools. During the seventeen days fighting that followed the Nazi invasion of Poland, one hundred and fourteen P.11c's were lost, though not before they had accounted for over one hundred and twenty *Luftwaffe* aircraft and carried out extensive strafing of the advancing *Wehrmacht*. Known familiarly as the

Jedenastka (Eleventh), the P.11 was a versatile aeroplane, used for reconnaissance and liaison as well as for fighting, and its handling qualities made it popular with its pilots. It was, however, outclassed by its superior *Luftwaffe* opponents, although the Rumanian P.11's were also flown operationally during the Russo-German campaigns. Rumania remained the only non-Polish operator of the fighter, a Spanish order for fifteen having been frustrated in 1936. The proposed P.11d and P.11e export models did not materialise, but about eighty examples of the four-gun P.11f were built in Rumania in 1935-37. In July 1939 the PZL factories began production of the 4-gun P.11g, with a 840 hp Mercury VIII engine, but none had entered service before the invasion.

7 Chance Vought F4U Corsair

Originating with the Vought-Sikorsky Division of United Aircraft Corporation, the Vought V-166B prototype of the Corsair, designated XF4U-1, flew for the first time on 29 May 1940, becoming a few months later the first US warplane to fly faster than 400 mph (644 km/hr). This was the prelude to an 11-year production life, during which twelve thousand five hundred and seventy-one of these fighters were built, and a service career that lasted until the mid-1960s. The initial US Navy contract was for five hundred and eighty-four F4U-1's, delivery of which began in September 1942. Most of these went to Marine Corps or land-based Navy squadrons, due to early difficulties in operating the Corsair from aircraft carriers, and the first operational missions were flown by Squadron VMF-124 of the USMC in February 1943. The Corsair's gull-wing configuration was devised to avoid the excessively long undercarriage legs that would otherwise have been necessary to provide clearance for the large-diameter propeller; but the far-aft cockpit position gave the pilot a poor view forward when landing. Hence from the six hundred and eighty-ninth F4U-1 onward, a new, raised cockpit hood was introduced on the Corsairs being built by Vought and by the Brewster and Goodyear factories. The Vought F4U-1C, otherwise similar, was armed with four 20 mm wing cannon instead of the former six machine-guns, while the F4U-1D (Goodyear FG-1D) had an R-2800-8W water-injection engine and provision for eight underwing rocket projectiles or two 1,000 lb (454 kg) bombs. The Brewster production line closed in 1944 after manufacturing seven hundred and thirty-five F3A-1 Corsairs; Goodyear ultimately built four thousand and fourteen FG-1's and -1D's and Vought four thousand six hundred and sixty-nine F4U-1's to -1D's. One thousand nine hundred and seventy-seven were supplied to the Fleet Air Arm as Corsair Mks I to IV, and a further four hundred and twenty-five to the RNZAF. The British Corsair Mks II to IV had each wingtip clipped by 8 in (20·3 cm) to facilitate stowage aboard Royal Navy carriers, and preceded their

US counterparts into shipboard service, carrying out their first operational action in April 1944. In January 1943 Chance Vought became a separate division of UAC, and during that year twelve F4U-1's were modified to F4U-2's with four wing guns and radar in a fairing at the starboard wingtip. Others were converted to F4U-1P photo-reconnaissance aircraft. The next production model was the F4U-4 (Goodyear FG-4), with six 0·50 in guns in the wings and a 2,100 hp R-2800-1W engine. Delivery began toward the end of 1944, and despite cuts in orders at the end of the war, Chance Vought eventually completed two thousand three hundred and fifty-six F4U-4's and Goodyear two hundred FG-4's. These included batches of radar-equipped F4U-4E and -4N Corsairs for night fighting. Goodyear also built five F2G-1's and five F2G-2's, all with 3,000 hp R-4360-4 Wasp Major engines. During World War 2 the Corsairs in US service operated mostly from land bases in the Pacific theatre, where the distinctive note made by the airstream passing through their cooler inlets, allied to their eleven-to-one 'kill ratio' over their opponents, led the Japanese to refer to them by the grim but apt sobriquet 'Whistling Death'. Post-war production continued with the F4U-5 (which in its -5N version reached 470 mph = 756 km/hr), the AU-1 (originally F4U-6) and the F4U-7. These served with distinction in the Korean War and with the naval air arms of Argentina and France.

8 Grumman F4F Wildcat

Grumman's original proposals, which won a 1936 US Navy development contract, were for a biplane carrier fighter based on its earlier successful biplane types. This design, the XF4F-1, was then shelved in favour of a monoplane fighter whose prototype, the XF4F-2, was flown on 2 September 1937 powered by a 1,050 hp R-1830-66 Twin Wasp engine. The Navy decided to develop this still further, by ordering it to be rebuilt in a much-redesigned form as the XF4F-3, with an improved, supercharged XR-1830-76 engine. This aircraft flew on 12 February 1939, and was followed six months later by an initial production order for the F4F-3. Eventually, two hundred and eighty-five F4F-3's were built. Deliveries to the US Navy late in 1940 were preceded by an order from France for one hundred G-36A fighters, the export designation of the F4F-3 when fitted with a 1,200 hp Wright R-1820-G205A engine. This order, later reduced to eighty-one, was diverted to Britain in mid-1940 after the fall of France, these aircraft and nine others being employed by the Fleet Air Arm under the title Martlet I. Thirty G-36A's, ordered by Greece, were also diverted to Britain to become Martlet III's. Neither the F4F-3 nor the Martlet I embodied wing-folding, but this feature was incorporated in all but the first ten of an order for one hundred Martlet II (G-36B) fighters placed by Britain in 1940. (The other ten corresponded to the USN's sixty-five F4F-3A's, having non-folding wings and R-1830-90 engines.) The US Navy's first folding-wing Wildcat was the Twin Wasp-engined F4F-4, Grumman building one thousand three hundred and eighty-nine, including two hundred and twenty F4F-4B's with Cyclone engines as Martlet IV's for the Fleet Air Arm. The Eastern Aircraft Division of General Motors delivered eight hundred and thirty-nine similar (but four-gunned) aircraft, designated FM-1, to the US Navy and three hundred and eleven to the FAA as Martlet V's. Eastern also built the FM-2, production version of Grumman's XF4F-8, with a 1,200 hp Wright R-1820-56 Cyclone engine and taller fin and rudder. Four thousand four hundred and seven went to the US Navy, and three hundred and seventy to Britain; the latter were designated Wildcat VI, the FAA having by now adopted the US name for the fighter. Grumman's final production version (twenty-one were built) was the F4F-7, a heavier and slower unarmed version, with fixed wings, extra fuel and photo-reconnaissance cameras.

9 Grumman F6F Hellcat

The Hellcat, essentially a larger and more powerful development of the F4F Wildcat, flew in its original XF6F-1 form on 26 June 1942, with a 1,700 hp Wright R-2600-10 Cyclone engine. It was then re-engined with a 2,000 hp Pratt & Whitney R-2800-10 Double Wasp to become the XF6F-3, flying in this form on 30 July 1942. Production F6F-3's were virtually unchanged from this aircraft; they began to appear early in October 1942, making their operational debuts with the British Fleet Air Arm in July 1943 and with the US Navy a month later. Production for the US Navy totalled four thousand six hundred and forty-six F6F-3's, including eighteen F6F-3E and two hundred and five F6F-3N night fighters; a further two hundred and fifty-two were supplied to the British Fleet Air Arm as the Hellcat I. Aerodynamic and control-surface improvements were introduced on the F6F-5, which entered production in 1944 and was able to operate in the fighter-bomber role with under-wing weapons. The F6F-5 was powered by an R-2800-10W engine capable of 2,200 hp using water-injection, and was both the principal and the last production Hellcat model. By November 1945, when production ended, twelve thousand two hundred and seventy-two Hellcats had been manufactured. Of these, six thousand four hundred and thirty-six were of the F6F-5 model, nearly one-fifth of which were F6F-5N night fighters; and nine hundred and thirty others were essentially similar Hellcat II's for the Royal Navy. Whereas its predecessor, the Wildcat, had been widely used in both the Atlantic and Pacific war areas, the Hellcat operated (with the USN and the FAA) predominantly in the Pacific; it was in service with land-based Marine Corps units as well as carrier-based squadrons, and was officially credited with nearly five thousand victims – some eighty per cent of all the enemy aircraft destroyed in air-to-air combat by USN carrier pilots during the war.

10 Republic P-47 Thunderbolt

A revised requirement, following the early air fighting in Europe, necessitated an almost complete redesign by Alexander Kartveli of the XP-47 light fighter projected early in 1939. This resulted in the XP-47B, which was almost twice as heavy and had a Double Wasp radial engine instead of the Allison in-line previously envisaged. Orders were placed in September 1940 for one hundred and seventy-one P-47B's and six hundred and two P-47C's, and on 6 May 1941 the XP-47B made its first flight. The B and C models were basically similar, but the C was given a slightly longer fuselage to improve manoeuvrability. The first Thunderbolts entered USAAF service in 1942, becoming operational with Eighth Air Force units over Europe in April 1943 and in the Pacific theatre some two months later. By this time, huge orders had been placed for the P-47D, which initially was but a refined version of the C. To this configuration, Republic factories manufactured five thousand four hundred and twenty-three P-47D's and Curtiss a further three hundred and fifty-four which were designated P-47G. A major design change was then introduced, on the P-47D-25 and subsequent batches, in which the cockpit view was vastly improved by cutting down the rear fuselage and fitting a 'teardrop' canopy. The weight thus saved also allowed extra fuel to be carried, but production batches from P-47D-27 onward required a dorsal fin fairing to offset the 'missing' keel area of the slimmer rear fuselage. Eight thousand one hundred and seventy-nine bubble-canopied P-47D's were completed at Farmingdale and Evansville, and this model served widely both as a fighter and fighter-bomber, especially with the USAAF in Europe. The RAF received two hundred and forty Thunderbolt I's (early P-47D) and five hundred and ninety Mk II's (later P-47D), while two hundred and three were allocated to the Soviet Air Force under Lend-Lease and eighty-eight to Brazil. The next production model (intervening suffix letters denoting various experimental machines) was the P-47M; this utilised the 2,800 hp R-2800-57 engine (with which the XP-47J had flown at 504 mph = 811 km/hr), allied to the P-47D airframe. It was an improvised version, produced hastily to counter the V1 flying-bomb attacks on Britain, and only one hundred and thirty were built. The last – and, at a maximum gross weight of 20,700 lb (9,390 kg), the heaviest – production Thunderbolt, was the P-47N, a very long-range escort and fighter-bomber variant of which Republic built one thousand eight hundred and sixteen. Overall Thunderbolt production, which ended in December 1945, totalled fifteen thousand six hundred and sixty aircraft. About two-thirds of these survived the war, after which Thunderbolts found their way into numerous air forces; a few were still in service until the late 1960s.

11 Brewster F2A Buffalo

The F2A was the US Navy's first monoplane fighter, but so far as that service was concerned that was about its only distinction, and the aircraft's lack of favour is reflected in the small quantities that were built. Conversely, the export version in service with the Finnish Air Force was remarkably successful, the climate no doubt offsetting to some extent the overheating engines that were among the aircraft's early problems. Evolved as the Brewster Model 139, the prototype was completed to the designation XF2A-1 and flown for the first time in January 1938 with a 950 hp Wright Cyclone engine. In June fifty-four Model B-239's were ordered, as F2A-1's, with 940 hp R-1820-34 Cyclones. Eleven of these were delivered to the USN, nine of them joining Squadron VF-3 aboard the USS *Saratoga* from June 1939, and the remainder were released for export. These, plus one additional machine, were delivered to Finland (after reassembly by Saab in Sweden) by February 1940, and were fitted with four Browning machine-guns. They remained in front-line Finnish service until mid-1944. The US Navy, following flight trials of Brewster's XF2A-2 prototype (1,200 hp R-1820-40) in July 1939, ordered forty-three F2A-2's to replace the F2A-1's sent to Finland, and most of these followed the Finnish example by increasing the armament from two machine-guns to four. Foreign orders were received from Belgium (for the B-339) and the UK (B-339E). None

of the former machines reached Belgium, but twenty-eight from that order were eventually delivered to the British Fleet Air Arm, and the RAF received one hundred and seventy as Buffalo I's. Rejected for European service, the Buffalo was allocated to RAF, RAAF and RNZAF squadrons in Malaya, but after the fall of Singapore the type was soon withdrawn from front-line British service. The Netherlands East Indies Army Air Corps received seventy-two B-339D's, which served from spring 1941 in that theatre, and ordered a further twenty B-439's which, although completed, were never delivered. The F2A-3, ordered meanwhile for the US Navy, introduced so many equipment and structural changes and additions that its much higher gross weight severely affected both its performance and its controllability, and only one hundred and eight were built before production ended in March 1942.

12 Nakajima Ki-27

The Ki-27 was one of three contenders for a 1935 JAAF single-seat fighter requirement, the others being the Kawasaki Ki-28 and the Mitsubishi Ki-18. The Nakajima design was selected for its lightness and manoeuvrability, although the Japanese Navy also selected the Mitsubishi A5M1, the carrier-based counterpart of the Ki-18, for production. Three Ki-27 prototypes were ordered by the JAAF, the first of which was flown on 15 October 1936; all three were powered by 650 hp Nakajima Ha-1a radial engines and differed only in having wings of three different areas. The largest-area wings became the standard type, and with these a pre-series batch of ten Ki-27's was completed in 1936–37. Series production began, with the Type 97 Model A, or Ki-27a, in the summer of 1937, this version being powered by the 710 hp Ha-1b model of the Nakajima engine. Units of the JAAF in Manchuria began to receive the first Ki-27a fighters in 1938, making their combat debut against the Soviet Air Force in the Siberian border disputes of 1938–39. Here they proved successful against the opposing I-15 biplane fighters, though less so against the monoplane I-16's. Nevertheless, in service with the JAAF and the Manchurian air force, they accounted for more than twelve hundred and fifty enemy fighters for the loss of only a hundred of their own number. The Ki-27a gave way in 1939 to the Ki-27b, which differed only in having a modified cockpit hood and detail improvements, and an eventual total of three thousand three hundred and eighty-six Ki-27's of the two versions were built. One thousand three hundred and seven of these were completed by the Tachikawa Aircraft Co and the Manchurian Aircraft Co. Although virtually obsolete by the time of Pearl Harbor, the Ki-27 was still in fairly widespread JAAF service, and was later allotted the Pacific code name 'Nate' by the Allies. It was encountered in Burma, China and Malaya during the first six months of the Pacific war, but after this was gradually withdrawn for conversion to a 2-seat advanced training role with a 450 hp engine and the new designation Ki-79. Three examples were completed of the Ki-27-Kai in 1940, but this improved model was abandoned with the new Ki-43 Hayabusa became available.

13 **Mitsubishi A5M**

Designed by Jiro Horikoshi, who later designed the famous Zero-Sen, the single-seat A5M was the JNAF's first monoplane fighter, produced to meet a naval requirement issued in 1934. It was an all-metal aeroplane, with a flush-riveted skin and – for the first time on a Japanese combat aircraft – full-scale landing flaps. During its maiden flight on 4 February 1935 the prototype showed an excellent turn of speed, and within days had flown 61 mph (98 km/hr) faster than its specification required. Powerplant was a 550 hp Nakajima Kotobuki 5 radial, and an inverted gull wing was utilised to improve the downward view from the cockpit. Due to problems encountered with this wing, and with the original engine, the second prototype had a 560 hp Kotobuki 3 and a conventional straight-tapered wing instead of the previous semi-elliptical shape. The powerplant continued to give trouble, several alternatives being tested before the choice of the 585 hp Kotobuki 2-Kai-1 was made to power the A5M1 Model 11 initial production model. Manufacture of the A5M1 – now as a carrier-based rather than a land-based fighter – began in 1936, and thirty-six of this model were

ompleted. The A5M1 was then
upplanted by the A5M2a Model
21, featuring wingtip 'wash-out',
increased fin area and a 610 hp
Kotobuki 2-Kai-3 engine. Mit-
ubishi A5M's formed part of the 2nd
Combined Air Flotilla which embarked for Shanghai in September
1937, and carried out their first
operational mission later that
month. Flying both from carriers
and from land bases, they proved
remarkably successful against
Soviet-built I-16's. The A5M2b
Model 22 fighter-bomber proved
less popular in service, its enclosed
cockpit being heartily disliked by
Japanese pilots. The A5M3a Model
23 was an experimental version
fitted with a Hispano-Suiza *moteur-
canon* engine. The final variants, the
A5M4 Models 24 and 34, entered
production in 1938 and were the
principal JNAF versions at the time
of Pearl Harbor. They were employed as first-line fighters only for
the first six months of the Pacific
war, then being withdrawn to serve
as transition trainers for the A6M
Zero-Sen; some aircraft were built
from the outset as A5M4-K trainers.
Pacific code-name for the A5M was
'Claude'. Seven hundred and eighty-
two A5M's were built by Mit-
ubishi, and about two hundred by
the Kyushu Aircraft Co.

14 Vultee BT-13 and BT-15 Valiant

The Valiant originated in the
private-venture Model 51 prototype,
produced in 1939 and powered by a
500 hp R-1340-45 Wasp engine.
This was a 2-seat monoplane with a
retractable undercarriage, and was
accepted by the US Army in 1940 as
the BC-3; it was the last aircraft to
appear in the 'Basic Combat'
category, which was then reclassified
as AT (Advance Trainer). No
production was undertaken of the
Model 51, but substantial orders
were placed in 1940 for the Vultee
Model 54 basic trainer, under the
designation BT-13. The Model 54
had essentially the same airframe as
the Model 51, except for a slightly
shorter fuselage occasioned by the
use of the R-985-25 Wasp Junior
engine, but its landing gear was non-
retractable. Most of the USAAF's
Valiants differed in minor details
only, and the early contracts were,
for their time, among the largest to
be placed by the Army for any type
of military aircraft. Three hundred
examples were completed of the
original BT-13, followed in 1941 by
six thousand four hundred and seven
BT-13A's (R-985-AN-1 engine) and
one thousand one hundred and
twenty-five BT-13B's (24-volt electrical system). One BT-13A was rebuilt by Vidal in 1942 with an all-
plastic fuselage, being redesignated
XBT-16, but no production was
undertaken. Output of BT-13A airframes exceeded the available
supplies of Wasp engines, and so
in 1941 orders were also placed
for one thousand six hundred
and ninety-three examples of the
BT-15, which was the designation
of the BT-13A airframe fitted with a
450 hp Wright R-975-11 Whirlwind
engine. The US Navy was also a
large-scale user of Valiant trainers,
receiving one thousand three

hundred and fifty SNV-1's and six hundred and fifty SNV-2's corresponding respectively to the BT-13A and BT-13B. The Valiant did not remain long in US service after World War 2, but large numbers were sold abroad, notably in South America, where some were still in service in the early 1960s.

15 Blackburn Skua and Roc

When the Skua dive bomber entered service with the British Fleet Air Arm in November 1938 it was the first operational monoplane to be adopted by that service, and was also the first British combat aircraft designed specifically for the dive-bombing role. Two prototypes were ordered in 1935 to Specification O.27/34, and the first of these (K5178) was flown in 1937. Both were powered by 830 hp Bristol Mercury XII engines, but the similarly rated Perseus XII was chosen for the one hundred and ninety production aircraft ordered in July 1936. Delivery of these began in November 1938, the first recipient being No 800 Squadron aboard HMS *Ark Royal*. Two other squadrons were equipped with Skuas at the outbreak of World War 2, and one of No 803 Squadron's aircraft claimed the first *Luftwaffe* victim shot down in air combat on 25 September 1939, when it destroyed a Do 18 flying boat off the Norwegian coast. Carrying a 4-gun wing armament as well as a single rearward-firing gun, Skuas were employed as much as fighters as in their intended role, but their operational wartime career was comparatively

brief, Fulmars and Sea Hurricane replacing them during 1941. In 193 a production order was placed for fighter development of the Skua evolved to meet the requirements of Specification O.30/35. This aeroplane, the Blackburn Roc, followe the same tactical concept that produced the RAF's Defiant fighter and was similarly armed with fou machine-guns in a power-operate dorsal turret. This necessitated slightly wider fuselage than that of the Skua, and increased win dihedral replaced the upturne wingtips that characterised the earlier design; otherwise the two aircraft were substantially alike. A one hundred and thirty-six Roc were built by Boulton Paul; the initial three acted as prototypes, the first of them (L 3057) flying on 2 December 1938. The third wa fitted experimentally with twi floats. However, the concept of the 2-seat rear-turreted fighter, devoi of any forward-firing armament was quickly proved unsound durin the early fighting, and the Roc served only with two land-base squadrons of the FAA, betwee February 1940 and August 1941. I was then relegated to training o target towing duties, often with the turret removed.

16 Commonwealth Boomerang

Although only a 'stop-gap' fighter the Boomerang fulfilled an im portant role in the mid-war fightin in the Pacific theatre, more tha making up in ruggedness, manoeuv rability and climb what it lacke in speed and range. At the time of earl Harbor the Royal Australian ir Force's fighter force consisted ıly of two squadrons equipped ith American Buffalos, and in view ? the difficulty of obtaining rein-ırcements quickly from the UK it as decided to produce an interim ghter locally. This was done by asing the new design on the ommonwealth Wirraway general-urpose aeroplane already in pro-ıction in Australia, utilising as ıany of the latter's components as ossible. The resulting prototype, esignated CA-12 and serialled 46-1, flew on 29 May 1942 and was ut into production immediately fterwards to meet an initial order ır one hundred and five CA-12's laced in February 1942. These were ıllowed by ninety-five CA-13's and ırty-nine CA-19's before production :ased in January 1945, the later rpes differing in minor details only.)ne example was also completed f the CA-14 (later CA-14A) oomerang, with a turbo-super-harged engine, but production of ıis version was rendered unneces-ıry when the RAAF began to :ceive supplies of high-altitude pitfires from the UK The first .AAF unit to receive the Boomerang ʻas No 2 OTU, in October 1942, nd the fighter made its operational ebut with No 84 Squadron in the .ew Guinea battle area in April 943. It was also employed, latterly ı the ground-support role, in the orneo, Bougainville and New :ritain areas as well as in Australia.

7 **Polikarpov I-16**
'he I-16, known originally by the

Central Design Bureau designation TsKB-12, was evolved by a Soviet team under the direction of Nikolai Polikarpov, and made its first flight on 31 December 1933. The proto-type was powered by a 450 hp M-22 (licence-built Bristol Jupiter) radial engine and was armed with two machine-guns. A second proto-type (TsKB-12*bis*), with a 725 hp M-25 (Wright Cyclone) engine, was flown on 18 February 1934. With a 480 hp M-22 engine, the original version (designated I-16 Type 1) entered squadron service during the second half of 1934, and it was a group of these which first appeared in public at the May Day fly-past over Moscow in 1935. Later in 1935 the Type 1 was joined in service by the Types 4 and 6, with M-25 and 730 hp M-25A engines respectively, and by a 2-seat trainer variant of the Types 4 and 10 known as the I-16UTI or UTI-4. Successively improved production batches in-cluded the Type 10 (750 hp M-25B engine, four machine-guns and open cockpit), Type 17 (with 20 mm cannon replacing the two wing guns), Types 18 and 24 (1,000 hp M-62), and the Type 24B with a 1,100 hp M-63 engine and enclosed cockpit. With the M-63 engine the I-16's maximum speed rose to 323 mph (520 km/hr). In its earlier forms, the I-16 was a reasonably fast and swift-climbing fighter for its time, and was the world's first low-wing single-seat monoplane fighter with retractable landing gear to enter service. The various power-plant and armament changes, how-ever, increased the gross weight and power loading of the Soviet fighter to the detriment of its rate of climb and airfield performance. The early I-16's saw service in Mongolia, and during the Spanish Civil War the Type 10 could out-manoeuvre the German Bf 109B in most respects. It could not, however, match the much-improved Bf 109E, despite the increases in speed brought about by the M-62 or M-63 engines. Nevertheless, the stocky little I-16 remained in Soviet Air Force service throughout the initial German onslaught, until the spring of 1943; during its World War 2 career it was conspicuously successful as a ground-attack aircraft, carrying rocket projectiles beneath the wings. The I-16, during its service life, received no official name, but a host of nicknames; of these, its native sobriquet of *Ishak* (little donkey) summarised as aptly as any the many tasks it was called upon to undertake. It is not widely appreciated that the I-16 was one of the most extensively built Soviet fighters: nearly five hundred were involved in the Spanish conflict, and estimates of total production suggest an overall figure not far short of twenty thousand aircraft.

18 Macchi C.200 Saetta (Lightning)

The Saetta was the first single-seat fighter designed for Aeronautica Macchi by Ing Mario Castoldi, and was evolved as part of the *Regia Aeronautica* re-equipment programme that followed the Italian campaigns in East Africa during the mid-1930s. Its neat contours were spoiled only by the bulky 850 hp Fiat A.74 RC 38 radial engine tha powered the first prototype (MM 336) on its first flight on 24 December 1937. During 1938, after completion of the second prototype, an initial production order was placed for ninety-nine Saettas, these having enclosed cockpits and a higher powered version of the A.74 engine Delivery began in October 1939, and when Italy entered World War eight months later there were one hundred and fifty-six Saettas in service with the *Regia Aeronautica* Their first operational appearance of the war was over Malta and Saettas subsequently served in Greece, North Africa, Russia Yugoslavia and wherever th Italian forces were engaged. A tota of three hundred and ninety-seven C.200's were built by Macchi, in addition to which Breda completed approximately five hundred and SAI-Ambrosini about three hundred. Most of the wartime production aircraft reverted to open cockpits, which were much preferred by Italian pilots. Although not fast or well-armed by contemporary standards, the Saetta was a well-built and extremely manoeuvrable fighter, capable of withstanding considerable battle damage o climatic extremes. Toward the end of its career it was employed on escort or fighter-bomber duties, in the latter role carrying eight small or two larger bombs beneath th wings. In 1938 appeared the prototype Macchi C.201, with fuselage redesigned to take a 1,000 hp Fiat A.76 RC 40 radial, and in 1941 one C.200 was refitted with a Piaggio

P.XIX engine, but neither of these experiments reached production status, being discarded in favour of the much more promising C.202 powered by the Daimler-Benz inverted-Vee engine. The C.202 is described separately.

19 Fiat G.50 Freccia (Arrow)

The G.50, designed by Ing Giuseppe Gabrielli, was one of six designs (another being the Macchi C.200) submitted to the Italian Air Ministry in 1936 for an all-metal, single-seat fighter monoplane with retractable landing gear. The first prototype (MM 334) was flown on 26 February 1937, powered by an 840 hp Fiat A.74 RC 38 radial engine. An initial order for forty-five G.50's was given to the Fiat subsidiary CMASA, at Marina di Pisa, and delivery of these began in January 1938. Twelve of this batch were sent immediately to Spain to join the Italian *Aviazione Legionaria* fighting with the Republican forces under General Franco. Their participation was too short for a conclusive evaluation of the G.50's combat worth, but it was decided to maintain production as an insurance against possible difficulties in production of the Macchi C.200. A further two hundred G.50's were ordered, and a total of one hundred and eighteen G.50's were on *Regia Aeronautica* strength when Italy entered World War 2 in June 1940. Late in 1939 the Finnish government ordered thirty-five, most of which were delivered by the spring of 1940, and these gave excellent service until May 1944 before being withdrawn.

With the *Regia Aeronautica* the Freccia served in interceptor, ground-attack, convoy and bomber escort roles, and was employed in Belgium, Greece and the Balkan theatre as well as in the Mediterranean and North Africa during the first half of the war. Two hundred and forty-five examples of the original G.50 were built by Fiat-CMASA before this version was supplanted in production by the improved G.50*bis*, whose prototype was flown on 9 September 1940. This model had a refined fuselage design, modified canopy, a shorter and broader rudder, and increased fuel tankage and protective armour. Fiat's CMASA and Turin factories completed four hundred and twenty-one of this version. CMASA also designed and built one hundred and eight G.50B tandem 2-seat unarmed trainer models. Nine G.50*bis* were delivered to the Croatian Air Force. Experimental variants tested included the DB 601-engined G.50V of 1941, discarded in favour of the G.55 design, and the G.50*bis*-A, an enlarged 2-seat fighter-bomber with increased armament and bomb load, flown in 1942 but abandoned after the Italian Armistice. The proposed G.50*ter* was rendered abortive when the A.76 engine intended for it was abandoned before the aircraft's first flight in July 1941.

20 FFVS J 22

Before and immediately after the outbreak of World War 2, the *Flygvapnet* (Royal Swedish Air Force) had to face the prospect that orders placed abroad for combat aircraft either could not be fulfilled at all, because of the demands of war, or could be placed only for lesser types which would be no improvement over those already in service. With its major aircraft constructor, the Saab company, fully committed to production of bombers and reconnaissance aircraft, the *Flygvapnet* lacked any immediate prospect of an efficient, modern single-seat fighter available in sufficient quantity. Thus, in the autumn of 1940, the Royal Swedish Air Board set up a team, with Bo Lundberg as chief designer, to produce a stop-gap fighter, using wood and steel in its construction to conserve supplies of light alloys for more urgent needs. Design work began in January 1941, and on 1 September 1942 the prototype fighter made its first flight. It was powered by a Swedish-built 1,065 hp Pratt & Whitney Twin Wasp radial engine, and bore a superficial resemblance to the German Fw 190. An initial batch of sixty fighters, designated J 22, had been ordered in March 1942, and component manufacture was distributed among some five hundred companies – most of them outside the aviation industry. Assembly and flight testing of the completed aircraft was undertaken by the Flygförvaltningens Verkstad (FFVS) at Bromma, near Stockholm, which was ultimately responsible for one hundred and eighty J 22's. The *Flygvapnet*'s own workshop at Arboga completed a further eighteen. The first J 22 was completed in September 1943, and deliveries began two months later to

F9 Wing at Gothenburg. The fighter was produced in J 22A and J 22B versions: the former with two 13·2 mm M/39A and two 7·9 mm M/22F machine-guns and the latter with all four guns of the M/39A type. Some J 22's were still in service in 1952, although the type had by then been largely replaced by the Saab-21R jet fighter.

21 Focke-Wulf Fw 190

The Fw 190, indissolubly associated with the name of its designer, Dipl-Ing Kurt Tank, was technically one of the most advanced, and operationally one of the most eminent, fighters and fighter-bombers of 1939–45. One of two designs submitted by Focke-Wulf in response to an RLM specification of 1937, the prototype Fw 190V1 (D-OPZE) first flew on 1 June 1939, powered by a 1,550 hp BMW 139 radial engine. The second prototype was similarly powered, but in subsequent aircraft the larger and heavier 1,600 hp BMW 801 was substituted. Eighteen pre-production Fw 190A-0's were ordered in 1940, most of them having a 3 ft 3½ in (1·00 m) increase in wing span that became standard on production aircraft. These began with one hundred Fw 190A-1's, delivery of which started late in 1940, and continued with A-2 and A-3 subtypes with improved armament. This was increased to six guns in the Fw 190A-3, powered by a 1,700 hp BMW 801Dg engine. Early operational use was made of the Fw 190 in the low-altitude hit-and-run raids over southern England during

941–42, and by the end of the latter year nearly two thousand of these fighters had been built. New variants included the A-4 (BMW 801D-2, giving 2,100 hp with power boost), the A-4/U8 (reduced gun armament but carrying drop-tanks and a ,102 lb = 500 kg bomb load), and the rocket-carrying A-4/R6. By the end of 1942 the Fw 190 was also in widespread service in North Africa and on the Russian Front, in even greater numbers than in Europe. The Fw 190A-5 was produced primarily for night fighting and close-support duties; the A-6 and A-7 featured further improvements in firepower; the A-8, A-9 and A-10 were mostly fighter-bombers, with different versions of the BMW 801 engine, although some were utilised as all-weather fighters and others converted to tandem-seat trainers. A small number of Fw 190B and C prototypes were completed, with supercharged DB 603 inverted-Vee engines, but both models were discarded in favour of the long-nosed Fw 190D. This model evolved from tests with a few prototype aircraft fitted with the 1,776 hp Junkers Jumo 213A-1 engine, a liquid-cooled unit whose annular radiator duct presented a radial-engined appearance. The initial Fw 190D-0 and D-1 aircraft were delivered for evaluation in the spring and summer of 1943, and were characterised by their longer, newly contoured engine cowlings, lengthened rear fuselage and (on the D-1) increased in area. The first major production D model was the Fw 190D-9, which entered service with JG.3 in 1943.

This was an interceptor; subsequent versions, equipped for ground-attack, included the D-11 (two wing-mounted 30 mm MK 108 cannon), and the 2,060 hp Jumo 213F-engined D-12 and D-13 (single nose-mounted MK 108 or MK 103 respectively). Following the Fw 190D on the production line came another fighter-bomber, the Fw 190G. On this, the fixed armament was reduced to permit a single 3,968 lb (1,800 kg) bomb or its equivalent in smaller weapons to be carried externally. The Fw 190F, out of sequence, followed the G model into production. Both models were powered by the BMW 801D radial engine, but the Fw 190F had additional provision for twenty-four underwing rocket projectiles or a 3,086 lb (1,400 kg) armour-piercing bomb beneath the fuselage. Total Fw 190 production, excluding prototypes, amounted to twenty thousand and fifty-one machines, over six and a half thousand of which were fighter-bomber variants. The long-span, DB 603-engined Ta 152 developed by Dr Tank from the Fw 190D, succeeded it in production, but was in service only in comparatively small numbers when the war ended.

22 IVL Myrsky (Storm)

Finland's only nationally designed combat aircraft during World War 2 was the Myrsky, designed by Dr E. Wegelius and built by the Industria Valtion Lentokonetehdas (Finnish State Aircraft Factory) at Tampere. Like Sweden's J 22 fighter, the Myrsky was powered by the

Swedish-built Twin Wasp radial engine, and was flown for the first time in 1942. The first two aircraft (MY-1 and MY-2) acted as prototypes, but both of these and the first two production Myrsky I's were lost in a series of accidents which revealed numerous latent defects in the fighter's design and construction. The aircraft was unstable longitudinally; its landing gear was insufficiently strong, and so were the wing-root attachments; and the laminated plywood outer skin of the wings could not withstand the stresses of combat manoeuvres. A completely redesigned wing, strengthened undercarriage and other essential modifications were introduced from the fifth aircraft onward, and in 1944 forty-seven aircraft were completed in this form with the designation Myrsky II. Even with these improvements, the fighter was slow and poorly armed by contemporary standards; it was not popular with its pilots, and was used only in a limited role against the German forces during their withdrawal from Finland. Ten further aircraft, designated Myrsky III, had been partially completed before their production was halted by the Allied Control Commission late in 1944.

23 Bloch 151, 152 and 155

The Bloch 150-01 prototype which preceded this line of French single-seat fighters could scarcely have had a less auspicious start to its career, for twice, in July and August 1936, it failed to leave the ground during attempts to make its first flight. This was eventually accomplished, after much structural redesign and the substitution of a more efficient Gnome-Rhône engine, on 29 September 1937. Following yet further redesign, to make the aircraft suitable for mass production, it was ordered as the Bloch 151; but, instead of more than two hundred of these fighters scheduled for delivery to the *Armée de l'Air* by 1 April 1939, only one had actually been delivered by that date, and the type's disappointing performance, coupled with engine overheating and control problems, led to its relegation to a training role after modifications had been carried out. Only one hundred and forty Bloch 151's were completed. In April 1938 a contract had been placed for three more prototype aircraft, which emerged as the Bloch 152, 153 and 154, but only the 152 achieved production status. The Bloch 152-01, differing chiefly from its predecessor in having a 1,030 hp Gnome-Rhône 14N-21 engine, first flew on 15 December 1938. Production of the Bloch fighters was shared by the factories of the SNCA du Sud-Ouest, which by now had absorbed the Marcel Bloch company; initial orders for the Bloch 152 totalled two hundred and eighty-eight, but only one squadron was equipped with the type at the outbreak of war, and its 152's were non-operational. By January 1940 the *Armée de l'Air* had just over a hundred Bloch 152's in flyable condition, with nearly twice that number non-operational from lack of propellers. An eventual total of four hundred and eighty-two were taken on charge, only about two-thirds of which remained by the end of July 1940. Many of the survivors were used by the Vichy Air Force, and twenty were allocated by Germany to the Rumanian Air Force. At about the same time, the Royal Hellenic Air Force received nine Bloch 151's (of twenty-five ordered) from France. The Bloch 155 was a development of the 152 with a 1,180 hp Gnome-Rhône 14N-49 engine, flown for the first time on 3 December 1939. Production of this version began, but only nine had been accepted by the *Armée de l'Air* before the fall of France. Others were used by the Vichy forces until seized by the German authorities in 1942. The final development, the Bloch 157, promised to be far superior to its predecessors in every respect, but its evolution was forestalled by the German occupation of France. However, completion of the prototype was authorised, and this flew in March 1942, subsequently reaching a level speed of 441 mph (710 km/hr).

24 Fokker D.XXI

The Fokker D.XXI was designed in 1935 by E. Schatzki, initially for the Royal Netherlands East Indies Army Air Service. The prototype (FD-322), powered by a 645 hp Bristol Mercury VIS engine, made its first flight on 27 March 1936. The first contract was not placed until the early summer of 1937, when thirty-six of these fighters, powered by 830 hp Mercury VII or VIII engines, were ordered instead for the home air force. Delivery began in 1938, the prototype also being brought up to production standard and placed in service. Twenty-nine serviceable D.XXI's were available when Holland was invaded on 10 May 1940, divided between the 1st, 2nd and 5th Fighter Groups of the LVA at De Kooy, Schiphol and Ypenburg. After three day's fighting even these had to be grounded due to lack of ammunition, but in that short period they gave a good account of themselves against the faster and better-equipped *Luftwaffe* fighters, thanks to good handling qualities and a high degree of manoeuvrability. In 1937 seven Dutch-built D.XXI's were supplied to Finland, where the IVL (State Aircraft Factory) at Tampere built a further thirty-eight under licence for the 2nd Air Regiment of the Finnish Air Force during 1938. Finnish production of the D.XXI was then suspended until 1941, the Mercury VIII engines being more urgently needed for the Blenheim bombers being manufactured in the country. In 1940, however, a quantity of 825 hp Twin Wasp Junior engines was purchased from the USA, and the IVL produced fifty Wasp-powered D.XXI's in 1941 and a final five in 1944. These fought with distinction in the Russo-Finnish winter war of 1939–40 and in later campaigns, frequently with ski landing gear. A few were licence-built in Spain, before the Carmoli factory fell into Nationalist hands during the Civil War. In July 1937 two Dutch-built D.XXI's were bought by the Danish government, whose Naval Dockyard at Kløvermarken built ten more in 1939–40. These were serving with the Royal Danish Air Force's 2nd Eskadrille at Vaerløse when Denmark was invaded in April 1940. Contrary to popular belief, only one Danish-built D.XXI was fitted, experimentally, with 20 mm Madsen cannon in underwing blisters; standard armament of the remainder was two 8 mm DISA machine-guns in the upper front fuselage. Danish machines were also powered by the Mercury VIII engine, and not the Mercury VIS, as frequently stated.

25 Mitsubishi A6M Zero-Sen

The exacting terms of the 12-*Shi* (1937) JNAF specification to which Jiro Horikoshi designed the celebrated Zero fighter resulted in the most widespread service career ever enjoyed by a Japanese combat aircraft. Two A6M1 prototypes were built, each with a 780 hp Zuisei 13 radial engine, and the first flight was made on 1 April 1939. Production began in 1940 with the A6M2 Model 11, the only major change being the adoption of the more powerful Sakae 12 engine. Following operational evaluation of fifteen Zeros in China, the JNAF officially accepted the type at the end of July 1940. Sixty-four Model 11's were completed, the Model 21 with folding wingtips following these into production in November 1940. This was the major JNAF version at the time of Pearl Harbor, although in mid-1941 the A6M3 Model 32 made its first appearance. Similar at first to the A6M2, except for its 1,300 hp supercharged Sakae 21 engine, the

A6M3's performance was later improved by removing the foldable tip section of each wing. This, however, reduced the Zero's manoeuvrability, and the full-span wing, in non-folding form, was restored in the A6M3 Model 22. In the air fighting over Guadalcanal early in 1943 it began to be apparent that the Zero was no longer maintaining its early superiority over its Allied opponents. Hence the A6M5 Model 52 was developed, retaining the Sakae 21 engine but having a shorter-span wing which was, in essence, that of the Model 32 with the square tips rounded off. Sub-types produced included the A6M5a Model 52A (strengthened wings and increased ammunition), A6M5b Model 52B (increased armament and armour protection), and A6M5c Model 52C (further protective armour, two 20 mm and three 13 mm guns), all of which appeared in 1944. The Model 52C was produced primarily to offset the non-availability of Mitsubishi's new A7M1 carrier fighter, but its higher gross weight had such a penalising effect upon performance that comparatively few were built. The A6M6c Model 53C had a Sakae 31 engine with methanol injection, bullet-proof fuel tanks and underwing rocket rails. When supplies of Sakae engines were compromised by continued Allied air attacks, there appeared the A6M8c Model 54C, with a 1,500 hp Mitsubishi Kinsei 62 and armed only with four wing guns. In 1945 Mitsubishi built four hundred and sixty-five examples of a special *Kamikaze* version, the A6M7 Model 63, and several hundred more

Zeros of all versions were also expended in suicide attacks. A total of ten thousand nine hundred and thirty-seven Zeros of all versions was built by VJ-day. Mitsubishi built three thousand eight hundred and seventy-nine of these, but the principal manufacturer was Nakajima, whose factories produced six thousand two hundred and seventeen landplane Zeros and three hundred and twenty-seven examples of a twin-float version designated A6M2-N. In addition, five hundred and eight A6M2-K 2-seat conversion trainers were built by Hitachi and Sasebo Naval Air Arsenal, and six A6M5-K's by Hitachi and Omura Naval Arsenal.

26 Reggiane Re 2000 Falco I (Falcon)

Reggiane SA, a Caproni subsidiary, produced during the late 1930's a series of compact single-seat fighters whose merits were greater than their production or extent of service might suggest. The line began with the Re 2000, designed in 1938 by Ings Antonio Alessio and Roberto Longhi, whose prototype (MM 408) first flew on 24 May 1939. It could out-manoeuvre both the Macchi C.200 and the Messerschmitt Bf 109E, against which it was flown in comparative trials, but its less robust construction led the *Regia Aeronautica* to cancel its original intent to order two hundred production machines. The Re 2000 met with greater success in the export market, however, which accounted for most of the one hundred and seventy that were eventually built. Sixty, ordered by

Sweden in 1940, served as the J 20 with the *Flygvapnet* from 1941 to 1945; while seventy more were delivered to the Hungarian Air Force, in 1940–41. In addition, the MAVAG company in Hungary built a further one hundred and ninety-two under licence, most of them with locally built Gnome-Rhône 14K engines and Gebauer machine-guns. The Hungarian Re 2000 was known as the *Héja*, and was employed chiefly on the Russian Front. Other prospective customers whose intentions were forestalled by the war included Finland, Spain, Switzerland, the UK and Yugoslavia. Some twenty-eight Re 2000's, taken out of the export lines, were evaluated by the Italian government, as a result of which ten aircraft were 'navalised' in 1940–41 to serve with the *Regia Marina* as catapult fighters aboard Italian warships; but these saw no operational service. Meanwhile a strengthened prototype (MM 454) with 1,175 hp Piaggio P.XIX RC 45 engine, produced originally to overcome the Italian Air Ministry's reservations about the Re 2000's structural weaknesses, became instead the prototype for the Re 2002 *Ariete* (Ram) fighter-bomber and ground attack aircraft. Less than fifty Re 2002's were built, but these did enter service, in 1942, with the *Regia Aeronautica*. Armed with two 12·7 mm and two 7·7 mm guns, the *Ariete* could carry a useful load of up to 1,433 lb (650 kg) of bombs, and was also tested as a torpedo carrier. It took part in the defence of Sicily during the Allied landings. The basic Re 2000 airframe was also utilised in the development of two variants powered by Daimler-Benz liquid-cooled inverted-Vee engines: the Re 2001 *Falco* II and the Re 2005 *Sagittario* (Archer).

27 Lavochkin La-5 and La-7

The La-5 came into being early in 1942 primarily as a developed version of the LaGG-3 single-seat fighter which had entered service a year or so earlier. Although following a substantially similar structural layout, the prototype La-5 featured improved armament and an all-round-vision cockpit canopy, and was powered by a 1,330 hp Shvetsov M-82F radial engine. Following successful completion of its flight trials programme, the La-5 entered production in mid-summer 1942 and was in service by the autumn. Early combat encounters showed it to be a better all-round performer than the Bf 109G which was its most formidable opponent, although the La-5's climb rate was inferior to the German fighter. Attempts to improve this aspect of the Soviet fighter's performance resulted in 1943 in the La-5FN, a reduced-weight version with a 1,510 hp M-82FN direct-injection engine, which exhibited greater climbing power and manoeuvrability than either the Bf 109G or the Fw 190A-4. Its flying qualities were reportedly excellent, and the La-5FN proved as popular as it was efficient. A 2-seat trainer version, the La-5UTI, was also produced in quantity. The La-7, similarly powered to the La-5FN, featured a revised engine cowling

and other aerodynamic refinements, and improved further upon its predecessor's combat performance at some cost in fuel load and range. This type entered Soviet Air Force service in mid-1944, production being maintained in parallel with that of the La-5FN. The basic design was taken a stage further in the La-9, with redesigned wingtips, tail surfaces and cockpit, and a 1,850 hp ASh-82FNV engine. Although this began to enter service late in 1944, it saw little or no war-time action, but remained to become a standard post-war fighter with Soviet bloc air forces. The line ended with the La-11, first evolved in 1945 as a long-range escort development of the La-9 and later used in the Korean War of 1950–53. Operating as low-altitude fighters, fighter-bombers and ground-attack aircraft, the La-5 and La-7 had few, if any, equals on the Eastern Front. Both types also served with a Czechoslovak Air Division of the Soviet forces during 1944–45. No precise account of overall production is available, but the total built is thought to have been between fifteen and twenty thousand.

28 Nakajima Ki-43 Hayabusa (Peregrine Falcon)

The Ki-43 was designed by Dr Hideo Itokawa in 1938 as a potential replacement for the JAAF's Ki-27 fighter, and the first of three prototypes was flown early in January 1939. Despite excellent speed and range qualities, the aircraft was somewhat heavy on the controls, and the first of the ten pre-production aircraft, which appeared in November 1939, was a lighter aeroplane with increased wing area and 'combat flaps' that vastly improved its handling characteristics. It was quickly ordered in quantity and was to remain in production throughout the Pacific war, by which time five thousand seven hundred and fifty-one had been delivered. The initial version, the Ki-43-Ia Model 1A, entered production in March 1941. Fire-power was improved in later versions, the major early version being the Ki-43-Ic Model 1C with two fuselage-mounted 12·7 mm guns. At the time of Pearl Harbor about forty Ki-43's were in JAAF service and, although extremely popular as flying machines, combat experience soon revealed a need for greater armour protection and increased engine power. These appeared in the Ki-43-IIa Model 2A, built by Tachikawa factories in 1942–43, which was powered by the 1,105 hp Sakae Ha-115 engine and could carry two 551 lb (250 kg) underwing bombs. This was succeeded in November 1943 by the Ki-43-IIb Model 2B, a clipped-wing variant of the Model 2A with greater manoeuvrability. Joint production by Nakajima and Tachikawa from December 1944 yielded the Ki-43-IIIa Model 3A (1,250 hp Kasei Ha-112 engine), the last production version. Two prototypes were completed of the Tachikawa-developed Model 3B, with two 20 mm cannon, but no production was achieved before VJ-day. The Hayabusa was encountered in particularly strong numbers during the battle for Leyte Island, and in the defence of the Kurile Islands north of Japan, but it served widely throughout all the mainland and island battle areas of south-east Asia, in suicide attacks during 1944–45, and in the final defence of the Japanese homeland. The Hayabusa (Pacific code name 'Oscar') was an excellent and versatile fighter, its only serious drawback being its lack of adequate armament.

29 Nakajima Ki-44 Shoki (Demon)

The Ki-44, a contemporary of the Nakajima Ki-43, was designed in response to a 1938 JAAF requirement for a short-range interceptor capable of defending Japanese home targets. The first of ten prototypes was flown in August 1940, and some aircraft from this batch were placed temporarily in operational service during the early part of the Pacific war. The 4-gunned *Shoki* proved to be a fast-climbing and highly manoeuvrable fighter, but its bulk and high take-off and landing speeds created an initial resistance to its introduction among JAAF pilots. Once its different handling requirements were mastered, however, the Ki-44 became more readily accepted for the effective fighter that it undoubtedly was. Production began with forty Ki-44-Ia Model 1A's, delivery of which began in the summer of 1942. The Model 1A was powered by a Nakajima Ha-41 engine, but the five subsequent production versions all had the 1,450 hp Nakajima Ha-109. The Ki-44-Ib and -Ic (Models 1B and 1C), which entered service in 1943, each had four 12·7 mm guns, as did the Ki-44-IIb Model 2B; the Ki-44-IIc Model 2C had a pair of 40 mm cannon replacing the wing guns; while the lighter-weight Ki-44-III Model 3 had these replaced in turn by 20 mm weapons. Comparatively few Model 3's were completed, but the *Shoki* Model 2C performed particularly well against high-flying formations of US Liberator bombers. Code-named 'Tojo' by the Allies, the *Shoki* operated chiefly over its native terrain, although small numbers were encountered in Burma and New Guinea during the later war years. A total of one thousand two hundred and thirty-three, in all versions, were manufactured.

30 Nakajima Ki-84 Hayate (Gale)

Despite a superficial likeness to the Ki-43 and Ki-44 fighters, the Ki-84 Hayate was an entirely new single-seater, designed under the direction of T. Koyama from April 1942 to succeed its stablemates in service. Greater attention was given, following combat experience in earlier fighters, to such features as armour protection and self-sealing fuel tanks, and the Ki-84 was also more sturdily built than its forebears. But for a series of difficulties encountered with its Homare powerplant, much more would doubtless have been heard of the Hayate in the Pacific air fighting, for it could match most of the best US fighters at heights of up to 30,000 ft (9,000 m). The first of two Ki-84 prototypes was flown in April 1943, and these two aircraft were soon followed by an initial

batch of eighty-three for service evaluation. Delivery of production aircraft to the JAAF started in April 1944, and the fighter (code-named 'Frank' by the Allies) was first met in action five months later, operating from Chinese bases near Hangkow. All three variants of the Ki-84-I were similarly powered, differing chiefly in the armament installed. The Model 1A had 12·7 mm nose and 20 mm wing guns; in the Model 1B all four were of 20 mm calibre; while in the Model 1C the wing guns were 30 mm calibre. The Hayate was employed as a day and night fighter, dive bomber and ground-attack aircraft, but was hampered operationally by faults in the insufficiently developed Homare engine, which restricted its performance capabilities above 30,000 ft, and to some weakness in the main landing gear. The latter created several attempts to evolve a lighter-weight version of the Hayate, most of which eventually proved to be heavier than the original! They included the all-wood Ki-106, the mainly steel-built Ki-113 and the mixed construction Ki-84-II. Projects incomplete when the war ended included the supercharged Ki-84-III and Ki-84R, and the Ki-84P with increased wing area and 2,500 hp Ha-219 engine. Most promising of all was the Ki-114, developed by Mansyu and tested briefly before VJ-day. This had a Ha-112-II engine, yet in spite of increased length and enlarged tail surfaces was some ten per cent lighter than the Ki-84-Ia. Total number of Hayates delivered to the JAAF was three thousand four hundred and seventy: Mansyu Hikoki built about a hundred, but most were manufactured at Nakajima's Ota and Utsonomiya factories.

31 Mitsubishi J2M Raiden (Thunderbolt)

The Raiden was the first JNAF aircraft designed specifically for interception, regarded prior to 1938 strictly as a function of the Army Air Force. Proposals were submitted in April 1940, and the first of three J2M1 prototypes was flown on 20 March 1942, powered by a 1,430 hp Kasei 13 radial engine. Tests revealed that performance was below specification, the landing gear retraction mechanism unreliable, the engine far from satisfactory and the cockpit view, particularly during landing, extremely poor. A deeper cockpit hood, a 1,820 hp Kasei 23a engine and other improvements were incorporated from the fourth machine, and this – designated J2M2 Model 11 – was eventually accepted for production in October 1942. One hundred and fifty-nine Model 11's were built, entering service in December 1943 despite continuing engine troubles and the breaking up of several aircraft while on test. The next and most widely used models (two hundred and eighty-one built by Mitsubishi) were the J2M3 and J2M3a Models 21 and 21A. One of the latter was given an even deeper cockpit hood in mid-1944, being redesignated J2M6a Model 31A. In May 1944 the first example was completed of the J2M5 Model 33, with a 1,820 hp Kasei 26a and the wing

armament reduced to two 20 mm cannon. This version proved to be one of the best high-altitude Japanese interceptors of the war, and post-war US test reports spoke of its 'splendid climbing performance' and 'fine controllability'. The design was now vindicated, but supply shortages of the Kasei 26a engine which was the key to its success prevented more than thirty-five J2M5's being completed, and proposals to re-engine the J2M3 and J2M3a with this unit had to be forsaken. Two J2M4's were built to study the possible advantages of fitting engine turbo-superchargers, but this project was abandoned. The Raiden (Allied code name 'Jack') was used almost exclusively for home defence, but was also encountered in the Marianas campaign in September 1944.

32 Kawanishi N1K Shiden (Violet Lightning)

The Shiden was unique among World War 2's landplane fighters in being evolved from a floatplane fighter, the N1K1 Kyofu (Mighty Wind). The result proved, in the end, to be among the finest fighter aircraft to operate in the Pacific theatre. Adaptation of the original Kyofu design by Dr Kikuhara had already begun in April 1942, four months before the floatplane's first flight, and the first landplane N1K1-J made its maiden flight on 24 July 1943. A problem was created by the 1,990 hp Homare 21 engine, which required a large-diameter propeller and hence (because of the mid-wing configuration) an unusually stalky main landing gear, with associated problems of retraction. The Homare in any case was a troublesome engine, pressed into production without sufficient development, and production of the Model 11 Shiden, which began in August 1943, was thus subject to constant interruption for modifications found necessary as the flight trials progressed. A second N1K1-J production line was established, but in the meantime a major redesign had been initiated in the autumn of 1943, aimed at simplifying production. The redesigned fighter, known as the N1K2-J Model 21 Shiden-Kai, required only about two-thirds of the airframe parts of its predecessor, and by adopting a low-wing configuration successfully overcame the landing gear retraction problem as well. Aerodynamic refinements included a slightly longer fuselage and redesigned vertical tail surfaces, but the problematical Homare powerplant was retained. The first N1K2-J flew on 3 April 1944, and by the middle of the year the Shiden-Kai had entered production. Inevitably, output continued to be hampered by modifications, as well as by Allied air attacks on the factories concerned. Thus, compared with one thousand and eleven N1K1-J's built (including prototypes), only four hundred and six N1K2-J's were completed by Kawanishi. To the latter were added a further twenty-three completed in small quantities by the Aichi, Mitsubishi and Showa companies and by the Naval Air Arsenals at Hiro and Omura. Several versions, with alternative engines or increased armament, were tested or projected before the war ended, but none reached production status. Both operational models of the Shiden received the Allied code name 'George', and were prominent in the Philippines, around Formosa and over the Japanese island of Honshu among other Pacific battle areas.

33 North American AT-6 Texan

The original NA-16 design, which ultimately gave rise to one of the most famous training aeroplanes ever built, was entered in modified form, as the NA-26, in a USAAC competition of March 1937 for an aircraft in what was then known as the 'Basic Combat' category. One hundred and eighty similar aircraft were eventually ordered by the US Army as BC-1's, and a further four hundred produced for the RAF as the Harvard I. Sixteen of an improved model for the US Navy were designated SNJ-1. North American built ninety-two BC-1A's and three BC-2's, but the new 'Advance Trainer' classification then replaced the former BC category, and nine of the BC-1A's were delivered under the trainer's new designation AT-6, being followed by a further eighty-five aircraft ordered as AT-6's. The BC-1A/AT-6 differed from the original BC-1/Harvard I primarily in its squared-off wingtips and new straight-edged rudder, which remained the standard appearance of the Texan/Harvard throughout the rest of its considerable production life. Purchases and Lend-Lease upplies of the AT-6 to the RAF (as he Harvard II) totalled one housand one hundred and seventy-three, the majority being used at ZATS airfields in Canada. The US Navy's sixty-one SNJ-2's resembled the SNJ-1, except for an engine change and detail differences. The next large-scale model was the NA-77, one thousand five hundred and forty-nine being built as AT-6A's for the US Army and two hundred and seventy as SNJ-3's for the Navy. Four hundred AT-6B's for the USAAF were basically similar, but were specially equipped for gunnery training and utilised the R-1340-AN-1 Wasp engine in place of the AT-6A's R-1340-49. The former engine became standard for all subsequent Texans, the next basic model of which was the NA-88. This was built with a 12-volt electrical system (two thousand nine hundred and seventy AT-6C's and two thousand four hundred SNJ-4's) and with a 24-volt system three thousand seven hundred and thirteen AT-6D's and one thousand three hundred and fifty-seven SNJ-5's). Seven hundred and twenty-six AT-6C's were supplied to the RAF as the Harvard IIA; the RAF received three hundred and fifty-one AT-6D's, and the Fleet Air Arm five hundred and sixty-four, as the Harvard III. Final American-built model was the NA-121, twenty-five of which became the USAAF's AT-6F and nine hundred and thirty-one the USN's SNJ-6. Noorduyn in Canada built a version, similar to the AT-6A except for its R-1340-AN-1 engine: fifteen hun-

dred went to the USAAF with the designation AT-16, and two thousand four hundred and eighty-five to the RAF as the Harvard IIB. A small number of Harvard IIB's also served with the Royal Navy. Most of the RAF's Harvard IIA's and III's were utilised in Southern Rhodesia, where, like their counterparts in Canada, they played a leading role in the giant Empire Air Training Scheme.

34 **Miles Martinet**

First British service aircraft designed specifically for a target-towing role, the M.25 Martinet was based upon the radial-engined Master II trainer, many components of which were utilised in its design. The first of two Martinet prototypes (LR 241) was flown on 24 April 1942, and one thousand seven hundred and twenty-four production aircraft were subsequently built to Specification 12/41 for the RAF and Fleet Air Arm. Main external differences from the Master included a lengthened nose, raised cockpit for the two-man crew, and increased wing span. The airframe was strengthened to compensate for the additional equipment and the stresses imposed by drogue towing. The towing gear and targets were stowed in a flat rectangular fairing beneath the centre fuselage, with a wind-driven external winch just beneath the cockpit canopy on the port side. Production continued until 1945, and during the war Martinets were used for communications and air/sea rescue duties in addition to their target-towing activities. In 1943 Martinet PW 979 became the prototype for the M.50 Queen Martinet radio-controlled target drone aircraft. A further seventeen Martinets were similarly converted, and sixty-five more built later from the outset to this configuration. The M.37 Martinet Trainer, with raised rear cockpit, was a development begun during the war, but it was not flown until 1946 and only two conversions were made. After the end of World War 2, small numbers of Martinets were sold to the air forces of Belgium and Eire, and five to a Swedish commercial operator.

35 **Junkers Ju 87**
The Ju 87 was designed initially as a dive bomber, and first flew in 1935. Early development and production of the Ju 87A, B, C and R bomber variants are described in the *Bombers, Patrol and Transport Aircraft 1939–45* volume in this series. The next major variant to enter production was the Ju 87D, whose evolution had begun in 1940. Several sub-types of this model were built, their chief characteristics being the use of a more powerful Jumo engine, increased fuel tankage similar to that of the Ju 87R, and a considerably refined airframe with reinforced armament and extra armour protection for the crew. Most D variants were evolved for a ground-attack role, and could carry a variety of different weapon loads ranging from a single 3,968 lb (1,800 kg) bomb beneath the fuselage to a pair of underwing pods each containing six 7·9 mm machine-

guns. The dive brakes fitted to the earlier Ju 87's were usually omitted. The Ju 87D-5 introduced an extended wing of 49 ft 2½ in (15·00 m) span, and the D-7 was a specialised night-attack version. Variants of the Ju 87D served in the Mediterranean, North Africa and on the Eastern Front, equipping units of the Hungarian and Rumanian air forces as well as those of the *Luftwaffe*. Proposals to replace the D model by developments of it designated Ju 87 and Ju 187 were abandoned in 194, but one other variant was encountered operationally. This was the Ju 87G, which entered service in 1943 as an anti-tank aeroplane with a 37 mm BK 37 cannon mounted in a streamlined fairing attached beneath each wing. These could be replaced by bombs for more general ground attack missions. The Ju 87G was essentially a conversion of the long-span D-5, and aircraft of this type were quite successful in knocking out Soviet tanks along the Eastern Front until the appearance of better-class Soviet fighter opposition in the autumn of 1944. Operational trainers for pilots engaged in ground-attack work were produced, under the designation Ju 87H, by converting various D sub-series to have dual controls and modified cockpit hoods. When production of the Ju 87 series finally ended in September 1944, more than five thousand seven hundred of these aircraft had been built.

36 **Fairchild PT-19, PT-23 and PT-26**
Originating as the Fairchild M-62

is monoplane primary trainer was contemporary of the Boeing-Stearman Kaydet biplane, and was ultimately built in almost as great a quantity. First purchases were made 1940 as part of the US Army Air Corps expansion programme, the initial model having open tandem cockpits and a 175 hp Ranger L-440-1 engine. Two hundred and twenty-five of this model, designated PT-19, were delivered during FY 1940. Mass production then began in 1941 of three thousand one hundred and eighty-one PT-19A's, with 200 hp L-440-3 engines, by Fairchild, with an additional four hundred and seventy-seven by Aeronca and forty-four by the St Louis Aircraft Corporation. Nine hundred and seventeen PT-19B's, built by Fairchild and Aeronca, differed only in being equipped for blind-flying training and having a collapsible canvas hood for the front cockpit. The PT-23, introduced to avoid delays in the supply of sufficient Ranger engines, was essentially the same airframe mounting an uncowled Continental R-670 engine of 220 hp. Eight hundred and sixty-nine PT-23's were completed by Aeronca, Fairchild, Howard Aircraft Corporation and St Louis in the USA and by Fleet Aircraft Corporation in Canada. Howard and St Louis also produced two hundred and fifty-six PT-23A's with blind-flying equipment. For use in Canada in the Empire Air Training Scheme, a variant of the PT-19A was evolved with a fully-enclosed canopy for the two occupants. Fairchild contributed six hundred and

seventy, with L-440-3 engines, to the RCAF under Lend-Lease, and production of eight hundred and seven PT-26A's and two hundred and fifty PT-26B's by Fleet, with L-440-7 engines, was also financed by US funds. The Canadian-built PT-26 and PT-26A aircraft were designated Cornell I and II, and were used at RAF flying schools in Southern Rhodesia as well as in Canada.

37 Miles Magister
The Tiger Moth and the Magister elementary trainers may be regarded as the British counterparts of the Kaydet and the Fairchild PT-19 series, although the Magister was built in by no means the quantity of the American monoplane. Nevertheless, what it lacked in numbers the 'Maggie' more than made up for in appeal, and many hundreds of British and Commonwealth pilots remember their training on Magisters with something akin to affection. The Magister was first introduced into RAF service in October 1937, a descendant of the civil Hawk Major (an example of which had undergone service evaluation in 1936) and other members of the Hawk family. It was the first monoplane *ab initio* trainer to be accepted for RAF service, and later served extensively with the Fleet Air Arm as well. To Specification 37/37, production was initiated early in 1937, and continued until 1941, when one thousand two hundred and three Magisters had been built. About three-fifths of this total were already in service by 3 September 1939.

After the outbreak of World War 2 these were augmented by many more Magisters, and other Miles two-seaters, impressed from the British Civil Register, and the type was employed at most RAF Elementary Flying Training Schools. The Magister was a fully aerobatic aeroplane, and could be equipped for blind-flying training, when a canvas hood was provided for the rear cockpit. Most of those in war-time service dispensed with the mainwheel 'spat' fairings to facilitate maintenance. Substantial numbers returned to civilian flying in the UK after the war, when the type was renamed Hawk Trainer III, and many others were exported.

38 Ilyushin Il-2

Probably the most advanced and most effective ground-attack air-craft to see service during World War 2, the Il-2 *Shturmovik*, like the Junkers Ju 87 before it, introduced a new word into the terminology of combat aircraft. After extensive study of several proposals by a number of design teams, those of the Ilyushin bureau were accepted, and materialised in the BSh-2 (or TsKB-55) prototype, which flew for the first time on 30 December 1939. About fifteen per cent of its total weight consisted of armour-plate protection for the engine, fuel and cooling systems and the two-man crew, and tests with the first two prototypes indicated insufficient engine power and a lack of longi-tudinal stability. The original 1,370 hp AM-35 engine was therefore replaced, in a modified prototype

(TsKB-57), by the new 1,680 h AM-38 which offered much greate power for take-off and low altitud flying. The TsKB-57 was a single seater, with improved armamen and capable of carrying severa alternative external warloads; flew for the first time on 12 Octobe 1940. This version entered pro duction, as the Il-2, in the followin spring, and carried out its firs operational engagements in th summer of 1941. Output of aircra and engines increased rapidly, th number of Il-2's in service bein quadrupled by mid-1943. By thi time a modified version was in pro duction, in which a second cre member was restored to man a rear firing gun, and which had improve take-off performance, manoeuvra bility and anti-tank weapons. Thi model, designated Il-2m3, entere production in mid-1942 and becam operational in the following Octobe By early 1943 the 2-seat version wa scoring heavily in air-to-air comba even against the German Bf 109' and with masterly understatemen the official trials report declared tha it could 'be introduced with ad vantage into ground-attack units The improved anti-tank weapon and 37 mm cannon carried b later-production Il-2m3's main tained the aircraft's effectivenes even against the new Germa Panther and Tiger tanks in th summer of 1943, and flying per formance was sustained by intro duction of the 1,750 hp AM-48 engine in later production batche The total quantity built – estimate at about thirty-five thousand – woul alone make the Il-2 an outstanding aeroplane, but its intrinsic merits had no need of academic support, and its achievements were their own recommendation.

39 Boulton Paul Defiant

The Defiant was designed to Air Ministry Specification F.9/35, which called for a 2-seat fighter in which the entire armament was concentrated in a power-operated, centrally mounted turret permitting a 360° radius of fire in the hemisphere above the aeroplane. The theory was that such a fighter would be useful for attacking enemy bomber formations from below: how it was to defend itself in the event of similar attack is apparently not recorded! The first of two prototypes (K 8310) was flown – minus the turret – on 11 August 1937, and the Boulton Paul design was selected in preference to its only remaining competitor, the Hawker Hotspur; indeed, the initial order for eighty-seven was placed before either type had flown. Despite excellent flying characteristics, the Defiant's early trials programme was protracted, and only three had been delivered by the outbreak of war, although orders by then had increased to well over four hundred. The first RAF squadron to equip with Defiant I day fighters (1,036 hp Merlin III engine) was No 264 in December 1939, which carried out its first operational sorties on 12 May 1940. The next day, five out of a flight of six were destroyed by Bf 109E's that had attacked them in their weakest quarters – from ahead and below.

Then, by flying mixed formations of Defiants and Hurricanes – to which the Defiant bore a considerable resemblance – enemy pilots were for a while deceived into diving from behind on to what they believed to be defenceless Hurricanes, only to be met by a stream of fire from the Defiant's four Browning guns. However, the effectiveness of this chase-me-so-I-can-hit-you policy was short-lived, and soon the Defiant was transferred to night-fighting operations, equipped with the newly developed airborne interception radar. The Defiant II, with AI Mk IV radar, and Merlin XX engine, entered squadron service in September 1941, though in comparatively small numbers, but the night-fighter Defiants were appreciably more successful than the type had been on daytime operations, accounting for more enemy aircraft during the winter *blitz* of 1940–41 than any other type. Two hundred and seven Defiant II's were built, compared with seven hundred and thirteen Mk I's. In 1942, however, the Defiant's role as a fighter ended. A number were transferred to air/sea rescue, training and other second-line duties, but the main task ahead of the aircraft was now that of a target tug. One hundred and forty Defiant III's were manufactured (without turrets) for this role, in addition to which many more ex-fighter Mks I and II were converted to similar configuration. Defiant DR 994 had the distinction of being fitted with the first-ever Martin-Baker ejection seat, with which the first dummy ejection trials were carried out in May 1945, and one other machine was later used for similar trials.

40 Dewoitine 520

Design of the D.520, by Robert Castello, was initiated by Dewoitine in mid-1936 as a private venture. After some initial lack of enthusiasm, the French ordered two prototypes of a modified version in April 1938 from the SNCA du Midi, which by then had absorbed the Dewoitine company. The first of these was flown on 2 October 1938, powered by an 860 hp Hispano-Suiza 12Y-21 engine, and in later trials with a 12Y-29 engine it attained its design speed of 373 mph (520 km/hr). The second prototype carried armament and incorporated a number of structural and aerodynamic improvements, including redesigned tail surfaces. An initial order was placed in April 1939 for two hundred D.520's, and successive orders (and cancellations) up to April 1940 required a total of two thousand two hundred to be built for the *Armée de l'Air* and one hundred and twenty for the *Aéronavale*. Production aircraft, with a slightly longer fuselage, increased fuel tankage and armour protection for the pilot, were powered by Hispano-Suiza 12Y-45 engines, and began to be delivered to an experimental flight at Bricy in January 1940. When the German offensive in France began on 10 May 1940, only thirty-six D.520's were in service, with *Groupe de Chasse* I/3. These fought their first actions against the *Luftwaffe* on 13 May. In all, D.520's served with five *Groupes*

de Chasse during the May–June fighting, destroying well over a hundred enemy aircraft for a loss of fifty-four of their own number due to enemy action. After 25 June 1940, well over three hundred D.520's (of four hundred and thirty-seven then built) survived either in unoccupied France or in North Africa, and the latter were utilised by four *Groupes* of the Vichy French Air Force and one *Escadrille* of the *Aéronavale*. In 1941 the German authorities ordered the production of five hundred and fifty more D.520's, although only three hundred and forty-nine of these were actually completed. In 1943–44, following the occupation of the remainder of France and the disbandment of the Vichy Air Force, the SNCA du Sud-Est completed a further quantity for German use, bringing overall production of the D.520 to nine hundred and five aircraft. In addition to the *Luftwaffe*, the air forces of Bulgaria, Italy and Rumania were also supplied with quantities of the French fighters. Aircraft recaptured by the Allies, as France was progressively liberated, fought with the *Forces Françaises de l'Interieur* during the final months of the war in Europe.

41 Miles Master

The Master was evolved from the Miles Kestrel trainer which, when it made its public debut at Hendon in July 1937, attracted considerable attention on account of its clean, fighter-like lines and the maximum speed of 295 mph (475 km/hr) which it could reach with its 745 hp

Rolls-Royce Kestrel XVI engine. The production Master I, ordered in June 1938, incorporated detail modifications to the airframe, but was a heavier aeroplane and powered by the lower-rated 715 hp Kestrel XXX. Nevertheless it remained one of the fastest trainers of its time anywhere in the world, was sturdily built and fully aerobatic. The first production Master I (N 7408) was flown on 31 March 1939, and deliveries to the RAF began just before the outbreak of war. Nine hundred Mks I and IA were built, the latter version having a slightly modified windscreen. This total also included twenty-five aircraft completed as M.24 emergency fighters during the Battle of Britain, and several Master I's for the Fleet Air Arm. Cessation of Kestrel engine production, coupled with the ever-increasing numbers of radial-engined aircraft entering British service, led to large orders for the Master II, whose prototype (N 7422) had flown on 30 October 1939. This was essentially a Mk I airframe adapted to take an 870 hp Bristol Mercury XX air-cooled radial, and production of the Master II eventually totalled one thousand seven hundred and ninety-nine. This version was used for general training duties, many later being converted as glider tugs. The prevalence of US Lend-Lease aircraft in British service led to the third basic model, first flown on 27 November 1940. This was the Master III, which differed from the Mk II primarily in having an 825 hp Pratt & Whitney R-1535-SB4-G Twin Wasp Junior engine. The American engine, although a two-row radial and heavier than the single-row Mercury, was of smaller diameter; hence the extra weight was offset by a reduction in drag, and performance remained virtually unaffected. Six hundred and two Master III's were completed before production ceased in favour of the Martinet in 1942. During the early months of 1942 the original duo-curved wingtips of all Master variants were clipped by 20·5 in (0·52 m) on each side and squared off, to relieve stress on the centre-section occasioned by the gull-wing configuration. Manoeuvrability was slightly increased as a result, at little cost to the aircraft's ceiling and rate of climb.

42 Yakovlev Yak-9

The Yak-9, which itself was produced in a number of variants, represented the culmination of a highly successful line of single-engined fighters and trainers from the Yakovlev design bureau whose combined production total was in the region of thirty thousand aircraft. It stemmed from the I-26 prototype of 1938 (which became the Yak-1 in production two years later), via the Yak-7, and the machines which acted as Yak-9 prototypes were originally designated Yak-7DI, signifying that they were designed as long-range fighters. They appeared in the first half of 1942, differing from the standard Yak-7B fighter chiefly in making greater use of light alloys in their construction. Production began in the autumn of 1942, and the Yak-9 was in operational service by the turn of the year in the fighting around Stalingrad. In 1943 the Yak-9 began to be used as an anti-tank aircraft, being modified for this purpose as the Yak-9T to carry a 37 mm cannon or a lighter weapon in the forward part of the fuselage. This was followed in 1944 by the Yak-9K, mounting a 45 mm cannon that fired through the propeller shaft. The Yak-9B was a fighter-bomber version equipped to carry a 992 lb (450 kg) bomb internally, and in 1943–44 the Yak-9D and Yak-9DD emerged as variants with their range further increased to proved fighter cover for advancing troops and for bombing raids over enemy-held territory. One squadron of these, flying from southern Italy after the Italian armistice, provided support for the partisan forces in Yugoslavia, and other Yak-9 variants served with Polish and French units (including the celebrated Normandie-Niemen group) fighting in the USSR. The last major version to serve during the war period was the all-metal Yak-9U, which flew in prototype form in January 1944. This became operational during the second half of that year and was characterised chiefly by further aerodynamic refinements and the adoption of the new 1,600 hp VK-107A engine which raised the fighter's top speed to 435 mph (700 km/hr). The Yak-9U could climb from sea level to 16,400 ft (5,000 m) in nearly half a minute less than the Messerschmitt Bf 109G. The final Yak-9 variant (originally

known briefly as the Yak-11) wa the Yak-9P, which appeared ir 1945. This saw comparatively littl service in World War 2, but was a standard post-war fighter and fighter-bomber with Soviet and satellite air forces, including the North Korean Air Force during 1950–53.

43 Mikoyan & Gurevich MiG-3
The first fighter aeroplane to be produced by the now-famous Mikoyan-Gurevich design bureau originated under the designation I-200. Work on this project, which was for a high-altitude fighter, began late in 1939, and the prototype was flown on 5 April 1940, powered by a 1,200 hp (at altitude) Mikulin AM-35A engine. The aircraft was of mixed metal and wood construction, and lightly armed with one 12·7 mm and two 7·62 mm machine-guns. It entered production, as the MiG-1, late in 1940, but in the following year the design was modified to become the MiG-3. The redesigned fighter featured a sliding canopy for the previously open cockpit, improved rearward vision for the pilot, extra internal tankage, increased outer-wing dihedral and the radiator bath extended further forward under the fuselage. Production was extremely modest by Soviet war-time standards – only some two thousand one hundred MiG-1's and MiG-3's were built – and, despite an excellent high-altitude performance, the MiG-3's effectiveness as a combat machine was limited. At lower altitudes, although manoeuvrable, it could not fly or climb as

fast as its *Luftwaffe* opponents, and it was lacking in firepower. The latter weakness was recognised later by equipping the fighter with an additional 12·7 mm gun beneath each wing, but the extra weight of these and the increased armour protection added simultaneously served only to detract still further from the MiG-3's performance. Production of the MiG-3 ceased, with that of the AM-35A engine, at the end of 1941.

44 North American P-51 Mustang

The Mustang was first conceived to meet a British requirement for a high-speed fighter posed in April 1940, and was evolved by a design team led by Raymond Rice and Edgar Schmued. With the manufacturer's designation NA-73, the prototype (registered NX 19998) made its first flight on 26 October 1940 powered by a 1,100 hp Allison V-1710-F3R engine. The initial British orders were for six hundred and twenty Mustang I's, the first of which reached the UK in November 1941. Two similar aircraft were evaluated by the US Army as XP-51's, after which one hundred and fifty P-51's were ordered for Lend-Lease to the RAF as Mustang IA's. In the event, fifty-five of these were repossessed by the USAAF and converted to F-6A photo-reconnaissance aircraft, while two others became XP-78's (later XP-51B's) when fitted in 1942 with Packard-built Merlin engines. (This followed similar British experiments with Merlin 60 series engines fitted in four Mustang I's.) The Merlin was to become the Mustang's standard powerplant on both sides of the Atlantic, but before this the USAAF received five hundred examples of an Allison-engined ground-attack variant, the A-36A, and three hundred and ten P-51A's, also Allison-powered. The RAF received fifty P-51A's (Mustang II), and thirty-five others were converted to F-6B's. The A-36A was briefly named Invader (and the P-51 named Apache), but the British name Mustang was later adopted for all P-51 variants. One A-36A was evaluated by the RAF, but no production aircraft were received. First Merlin-engined production models were the P-51B and P-51C (RAF Mustang III), the combined US production of which totalled three thousand seven hundred and thirty-eight. The nine hundred and ten supplied to the RAF were fitted with bulged cockpit hoods to improve visibility. Ninety-one US conversions of P-51B/C Mustangs into F-6C's were carried out. A major design change appeared with the P-51D, in which the rear fuselage was cut down to permit the fitting of a 'teardrop' cockpit canopy affording all-round vision. Production totalled nine thousand two hundred and ninety-three of this model and the basically similar P-51K. Eight hundred and seventy-six became Mustang IV's with the RAF, and two hundred and ninety-nine became reconnaissance F-6D's or F-6K's. Next production model was the P-51H, five hundred and fifty-five of which were completed in 1945 before outstanding contracts for more than another three thousand Mustangs were cancelled at the war's end. The first RAF Mustangs became operational, in an armed tactical reconnaissance capacity, in July 1942, while from December 1943 P-51B's of the USAAF flew in increasing numbers as escorts to Eighth Air Force bombers during raids over Europe. The Mustang also figured largely in the Allied campaigns in North Africa, against V1 flying bombs over Britain in 1944 and as escort during the B-29 bombing raids of 1944–45 against Japan. Unquestionably, it was one of the greatest and most versatile fighters ever built, and a firm favourite with all who flew it; as the British journal *The Aeroplane* commented in July 1942: 'Pilots who fly the Mustang praise it so lavishly that they exhaust their superlatives before they have finished their eulogies.'

45 Kawasaki Ki-61 Hien (Swallow)

Two designs were formulated by Dr Takeo Doi to meet a February 1940 fighter requirement of the JAAF: the Ki-60 'heavy' fighter and the lightweight Ki-61. Three prototypes of the former were completed, but the Ki-60 was then discarded for the more conventional Ki-61 design. Twelve Ki-61 prototypes were built, all similar in their essential features, and the first of them was flown in December 1941. It was powered by a 1,100 hp Ha-140 liquid-cooled engine, evolved in Japan from the German DB 601A, and this later gave rise to the erroneous assumption that the Ki-61 was a licence-built development of the Messerschmitt Bf 109. The initial production model, delivery of which began in August 1942, was the Ki-61-I Model 1, which was armed with two 12·7 mm and two 7·7 mm guns. Successive improvements in armament led to the Model 1A (two 7·7 mm fuselage guns and two 20 mm wing-mounted Mauser cannon), Model 1B (four 12·7 mm guns), Model 1C (two fuselage 12·7 mm and two 20 mm Ho-5 in the wings) and Model 1D (two fuselage 12·7 mm and two 30 mm in the wings). Total production of the Ki-61-I series fighters amounted to two thousand seven hundred and thirty-four. Following its first operational appearance in New Guinea in April 1943, the Hien (Allied code name 'Tony') was encountered in virtually all battle areas of the Pacific war. It was particularly prominent around Rabaul, in the battle for Leyte Island, and in the home defence of Japan. In September 1942, to offset certain maintenance difficulties encountered with the Ha-40 engine, Kawasaki began to evolve the Ki-61-II, utilising the new Ha-140 which promised to develop 1,450 hp. The first Ki-61-II Model 2, completed in August 1943, featured a lengthened fuselage, modified canopy and a ten per cent increase in wing area. However, difficulties with the Ha-140 engine and associated structural problems prevented more than another seven from being completed by January 1944. Attention was then devoted to the Ki-61-IIa Model 2A, with strengthened airframe and the wings and armament of the Ki-61-Ic. The Model 2B was similar except in having four 20 mm guns. However, after only thirty-one Model 2A's and 2B's had been completed, output was slowed down because it was fast outpacing that of the necessary powerplants. Another three hundred and seventy-four Ki-61 airframes were completed, but only ninety-nine of them received their intended powerplants and more than one-third of those were destroyed in air attacks before delivery. The remainder were eventually fitted with 1,500 hp Mitsubishi Ha-112-II radial engines to become Ki-100's, and in this form were so successful that further development of the proposed Ki-61-III was rendered unnecessary.

46 & 47 **Hawker Hurricane**
The first monoplane in an historic cavalcade of Hawker fighters, the Hurricane, perhaps more than any other type, is indissolubly associated with the name of its designer, Sydney Camm. Its evolution began in 1933 as a monoplane development of the Fury biplane fighter, to have a fixed landing gear and a Rolls-Royce Goshawk engine. Early in 1934, however, significant improvement of the design included a fully retractable main undercarriage, provision for eight wing-mounted machine-guns and the decision to use the new Rolls-Royce PV-12 engine that later became the Merlin. To Specification F.36/34, Hawker completed an unarmed prototype (K 5083), powered by a Merlin C engine, which flew for the first time

on 6 November 1935. In March 1936, anticipating the first RAF orders by some three months, Hawker began to prepare for an initial production of one thousand of the fighters – a piece of foresight whose value was emphasised when the Battle of Britain was fought some four years later. The initial RAF order was for six hundred Hurricane I's, and delivery of these began, to No 111 Squadron, in October 1937. On 3 September 1939 there were three hundred and fifteen Hurricanes on the fully operational strength of fourteen RAF squadrons, plus others in reserve, and total orders stood at three thousand five hundred. Eventual production of the Hurricane I, shared between Hawker and Gloster factories in the UK and the Canadian Car and Foundry Co of Montreal, amounted to three thousand nine hundred and fifty-four. Powerplant was originally the Merlin II, later the Merlin III; the Canadian-built machines were later redesignated Mk X. Unlike the Spitfire, the Hurricane became operational with the Advanced Air Striking Force in France at the outset of World War 2, and it outnumbered the Spitfire by about two to one in the Battle of Britain in August–October 1940. During the second half of 1940 the Hurricane I began to appear in the Middle East, following the entry of Italy into the war; these aircraft (and later Hurricanes serving in North Africa) were characterised by the distinctive Vokes sand filter beneath the nose. In 1942, Hurricanes also made their operational appearance in the Far

East, in Singapore, the Netherlands East Indies and Burma, and were operating also in the fighter-bomber role. Meanwhile, on 11 June 1940, Hurricane P 3269 had flown with a 1,185 hp supercharged Merlin XX engine to serve as prototype for the Mk II. Early production aircraft, retaining the standard 8-gun wings, were designated Mk IIA; with twelve machine-guns the designation became Mk IIB, while the Mk IIC had a wing armament of four 20 mm cannon. Acknowledgment that the Hurricane was becoming outclassed as a fighter came in 1942 with the increasing use of the aircraft for ground-attack duties. Several Hurricane IIC's were equipped to carry underwing rocket projectiles, and the Mk IID was a special anti-tank version with two 40 mm underwing cannon and two Brownings in the wings. The only other British production model, the Mk IV, was also a ground-attack type, with a variety of possible weapon arrangements and a 1,620 hp Merlin 24 or 27 engine. The other major operational form of the aircraft was the Sea Hurricane, equipped with catapult spools and (except for the first fifty Mk IA's) an arrester hook. This first appeared in 1941 as an interim step to protect convoys from the attentions of U-boats and prowling Fw 200 maritime patrol bombers, and the Sea Hurricanes were carried on board CAM ships (Catapult Aircraft Merchantmen). Once launched, they had to 'ditch' in the sea after an engagement in the hope of the pilot being picked up by another ship in the convoy.

Conversion of existing Hurricanes resulted in Sea Hurricanes Mks IA, IB, IC and XIIA. The Mk IIC had a 1,460 hp Merlin XX and full Fleet Air Arm radio and other equipment, but no catapult spools. The total number of Sea Hurricanes built or converted was about eight hundred. Overall Hurricane production in the UK was thirteen thousand and eighty by Hawker, Gloster and Austin Motors; the Canadian Car and Foundry Co built additional Mk X, as well as Mks XI, XII and XIIA, with various armaments and Packard-Merlin engines, to a total of one thousand four hundred and fifty-one, making a grand total of fourteen thousand five hundred and thirty-three Hurricanes of all kinds. Two thousand nine hundred and fifty-two Hurricanes were allocated to the Soviet Air Force during the early years of the war, although many of these were lost en route.

48 Messerschmitt Bf 109

The Bf 109 was designed in response to a 1933 RLM specification by the Bayerische Flugzeugwerke, the original concept being based on the use of the 610 hp Junkers Jumo 210A engine, which was then the most powerful developed in Germany. An example of this engine was not available in time for the first flight of the prototype (D-IABI), which flew instead in September 1935 with a Rolls-Royce Kestrel V. In January 1936 the second machine was flown with the Jumo engine, and by then ten aircraft had been ordered by the RLM for evaluation. The proposed two-gun Bf 109A did not go into production, the first series model being the Bf 109B-1 (635 hp Jumo 210D) armed either with three MG 17 guns or two MG 17's and an MG FF, the latter firing through the propeller shaft. A team of Bf 109's scored several successes at Zürich in 1937, and on 11 November that year the Bf 109V13, with a specially boosted DB 601 engine, established a new world landplane speed record of 379·38 mph (610·55 km/hr). Twenty-four Bf 109B-2's were despatched in 1937 to join the *Luftwaffe*'s Condor Legion in Spain, followed soon after by others of the same model. The Bf 109C-1, which joined them in 1938, had the number of guns increased to five. Some B-2 aircraft were converted to Bf 109D-0's by the installation of DB 600A engines, and small numbers of the similarly powered D-1 were exported to Hungary and Switzerland. By this time five other German manufacturers had joined the production programme, and two hundred and thirty-five Bf 109D series fighters were in *Luftwaffe* service at the outbreak of World War 2. They were already being replaced in increasing numbers, however, by the Bf 109E series which first appeared in 1938. This series proved to be superior in performance and manoeuvrability to virtually every type of fighter opposed to it during the advances through Poland, Czechoslovakia, France, Belgium and Holland, and Bf 109E production mounted so rapidly that Germany could afford to export substantial numbers of the Bf 109E-3 in 1939–40 to Bulgaria (nineteen), Hungary

(forty), Japan (two), Rumania (sixty-nine), Slovakia (sixteen), Switzerland (eighty), the USSR (five) and Yugoslavia (seventy-three). Despite these claims on the numbers built, the Bf 109E remained the principal *Luftwaffe* version in service throughout the Battle of Britain. The E series extended to the E-9, and included models built as fighters, fighter-bombers and reconnaissance aircraft. In July 1940 Fieseler began converting ten E-3's to Bf 109T (*Träger* = carrier) configuration for operation from the proposed aircraft carrier *Graf Zeppelin*, but this project proved abortive and they were restored to their original configuration late in 1941. The finest model of the Bf 109 was the Bf 109F, the first version capable of out-manoeuvring the Spitfire V and a much cleaner design aerodynamically. The F series were powered by either 1,200 hp DB 601N or 1,300 hp DB 601E engines, with neater nose contours, the tail assembly redesign included a cantilever tailplane and retractable tailwheel, and the increased-span wings had rounded-off tips. By the late summer of 1942, however, the F series had been supplanted in production and service by the Bf 109G, familiarly known as the 'Gustav'. This was the last major production model, and was intended to be an improved version of the Bf 109F. In fact, the heavier DB 605 engine and extra equipment installed brought an inevitable drop in performance; but despite this, the production rate actually increased, and the Bf 109G was widely employed in Europe, North Africa and on the Russo-German front. More than fourteen thousand Bf 109's – nearly half of the total German production of the type – were built in 1944 alone, and G models were exported to Bulgaria (one hundred and forty-five), Finland (one hundred and sixty-two), Hungary (fifty-nine), Japan (two), Rumania (seventy), Slovakia (fifteen), Spain (twenty-five) and Switzerland (twelve). The Bf 109H was an extended-span high-altitude version built only in small numbers, and the Bf 109K (a refined version of the G) likewise saw only limited service. Projected versions included the Bf 109L and Bf 109S, neither of which reached production status. Licence production of the German fighter continued after the war in Czechoslovakia and Spain, and when this too came to an end an approximate total of thirty-five thousand Bf 109-type fighters had been built; between 1936 and 1945, production of this aircraft represented nearly two-thirds of Germany's entire output of single-seat fighters.

49 Macchi C.202 Folgore (Thunderbolt)

Attempts to improve the performance of the C.200 Saetta fighter (q.v.) began as early as 1938, when Macchi evolved the C.201 by redesigning the fuselage with the object of installing a 1,000 hp Fiat A.76 RC 40 radial engine. When development of this engine was abandoned the C.201 was testflown with a standard Saetta engine,

but the project was then discarded in favour of the more promising C.202. This resulted from the acquisition in 1940 of a specimen of the German Daimler-Benz DB 601A-1 liquid-cooled inverted-Vee engine, which was installed in a C.200 airframe (MM 445) to create the prototype of the C.202. This machine flew for the first time on 10 August 1940, and the advance over the C.200, both aerodynamically and in terms of performance, was such that immediate production of the new fighter was authorised. Initially, production C.202's were powered by DB 601 engines imported from Germany, but soon these engines began to be licence-built in Italy for the Folgore as the Alfa Romeo RA.1000 RC 41. Production of the C.200 and C.202 continued in parallel, and the first examples of the Folgore began to enter service with the *Regia Aeronautica* in the summer of 1941. At first, they carried similar armament to the Saetta, but later batches had two additional 7·7 mm wing guns, and one was tested with a 20 mm Mauser MG 151 cannon in a fairing beneath each wing. The Folgore is generally considered the most effective Italian fighter of the war period, and served in the Mediterranean, North Africa and on the Eastern Front. It remained in production until the Italian armistice in September 1943, though the quantity manufactured was somewhat restricted by the output rate of the engines to power it. Macchi built three hundred and ninety-two, and about eleven hundred more were completed by Breda. The C.205V Veltro (Greyhound) was a much-improved development with a 1,475 hp DB 605A engine, but became available too late to take any major part in the war.

50 Bell P-63 Kingcobra

The Kingcobra, developed from the P-39 Airacobra, originated in April 1941 when three XP-39E prototypes were ordered, utilising the P-39D fuselage allied to new, angular tail surfaces, an Allison V-1710-47 engine and a completely redesigned laminar-flow wing. Two months later two additional prototypes, designated XP-63 (Bell Model 33) were ordered; these incorporated further modifications, and the first of them (41-9511) made its maiden flight on 7 December 1942. A third prototype (XP-63A) was flown in April 1943, and in the following October delivery began of the first of one thousand seven hundred and twenty-five production P-63A's, in several sub-series which differed chiefly in their armament or other equipment. Provision was made for various external stores, including bombs, rocket projectiles or auxiliary fuel tanks. The XP-63B was a proposed version (subsequently cancelled) with a Packard-built Merlin engine, but the next to go into production was the P-63C, which had additional fin area beneath the rear fuselage and a V-1710-117 engine; one thousand two hundred and twenty-seven P-63C's were completed. One P-63D, thirteen P-63E's (increased wing span) and one P-39F were completed in 1945,

and the final total of all P-63 variants built by 1946 was three thousand three hundred and three. None are known to have served operationally with the USAAF, but two thousand four hundred and twenty-one P-63A's and P-63C's were allocated under Lend-Lease arrangements to the Soviet Air Force, with whom they rendered excellent service, chiefly as ground-attack aircraft. Three hundred P-63C's were supplied to the Free French Air Force (FAFL), and more than three hundred others were used in the USA as armoured target aircraft.

51 Bell P-39 Airacobra

Originating as the Bell Model 12, the Airacobra was designed by Robert J. Woods primarily as a vehicle for a heavy-calibre cannon. Installation of this gun in the optimum firing position – in the nose, along the aircraft's centre line – dictated the fighter's radical configuration whereby the engine was installed amidships, aft of the cockpit, to drive the propeller by means of a long extension shaft. When one XP-39 prototype was ordered in October 1937 the Bell fighter achieved the further distinction of becoming the first single-engined fighter ordered by the USAAC to be fitted with a tricycle landing gear. The XP-39 flew for the first time on 6 April 1938, a contract for thirteen YP-39 test aircraft being awarded in April 1939. These were based on the prototype, after its modification to XP-39B standard without the engine supercharger originally fitted. The first production version was the P-39C, but only twenty of these were completed. In the P-39D, the 37 mm cannon and twin 0·50 in guns in the nose were supplemented by four 0·30 in wing-mounted machine-guns and provision was made for an external bomb or fuel tank to be carried. Four hundred and four P-39D's were built for the US Army, delivery beginning in April 1941. A further four hundred and ninety-four P-39D-1 and D-2 Airacobras (Bell Model 14) were built for Lend-Lease allocations, these having a nose cannon of lighter (20 mm) calibre. Plans by Britain to buy six hundred and seventy-five Airacobras were by no means fully realised: many were lost during delivery and more than two hundred were instead made available to the Soviet Air Force, while the USAAF, after Pearl Harbor, repossessed a similar quantity which it designated P-400. Only one RAF squadron (No 600) became operational with the Airacobra, but those of the USAAF were soon in action against the Japanese in theatres as far afield as Alaska, Hawaii, Panama and the south-west Pacific. During the latter half of 1942 they also became operational over Europe and in North Africa, and were particularly effective in the latter theatre in the ground-attack role. Numerous further variants appeared, the differences between which principally concerned the variant of V-1710 engine and type of propeller fitted; they included the P-39F, J, K, L, M, N and Q. The last of these introduced a change of armament, replacing the four 0·30 in wing guns by two of 0·50 in calibre. The two most widely built models were the P-39N (two thousand and ninety-five) and the P-39Q (four thousand nine hundred and five). Entire production of the Airacobra, ending in 1944, was undertaken by Bell, who built a total, including experimental machines, of nine thousand five hundred and fifty-eight. Well over half this total, mostly P-39N's and P-39Q's, were allocated to the Soviet Union; nearly two hundred of these were lost en route, but four thousand seven hundred and fifty-eight arrived safely to render excellent service on the Eastern Front between 1942 and 1945.

52 Hawker Typhoon

The Typhoon was evolved by Sydney Camm's design staff at Hawker Aircraft in response to Air Ministry Specification F.18/37, which was for an interceptor capable of combating such heavily armed and armoured escort fighters as the Messerschmitt Bf 110. Such an aeroplane was inevitably heavier than either the Hurricane or the Spitfire, and to provide a comparable performance the powerplants selected were the new Napier Sabre H-type in-line engine and the X-type Rolls-Royce Vulture, both of which promised to develop some 2,000 hp. Prototypes were completed with both types of engine: the Vulture-engined design, named Tornado, was later abandoned when Vulture production was curtailed.

With the Sabre engine, the aircraft was named Typhoon, and the first of two prototypes (P 5212) was flown on 24 February 1940. Early service trials and squadron experience were far short of being satisfactory, and it is conceivable that the Typhoon's future career might soon have ended but for the appearance in 1941 of the Focke-Wulf Fw 190 in hit-and-run raids across the English Channel. The Fw 190 could out-manoeuvre all other British fighters, including the Spitfire V, and the Typhoon was the only effective means of stopping it. The early Typhoon IA's carried six 0·303 in Browning guns in each wing, but these were replaced in the Mk IB by four wing-mounted 20 mm cannon, which became the Typhoon's regular fixed armament. The fighter was unspectacular at altitude, but its clashes with the Fw 190 had revealed outstanding strength and agility at low level, and from this stemmed the type's widespread use – and success – as a ground-attack aircraft. After extensive weapons trials during 1942, Typhoons began to be fitted for operational use in the following year with underwing rails for eight rocket projectiles, the chief weapon employed by the type. Before and after the invasion of Europe, rocket-armed Typhoons attacked land and sea targets in the Channel and in Belgium, France and the Netherlands. A total of three thousand three hundred and thirty Typhoons were built, all by Gloster except for the two proto-types, five Mk IA's and ten Mk IB's. The Typhoon IB represented the

major version, over three thousand being completed with Sabre IIA, IIB or IIC engines, some sixty per cent of this total having bubble-type canopies in place of the original frame-type cockpit hood and car-type access door.

53 Hawker Tempest
The Tempest, originating as the P.1012, was originally given the name Typhoon II, but despite a certain external similarity to the Typhoon IB the P.1012 was virtually a new design, evolved specifically to overcome the performance difficulties of its predecessor. Two prototypes were built to Specification F.10/41, and the first of these (HM 595) was flown on 2 September 1942 with a Napier Sabre V engine. A Sabre IV powered the second machine, but contracts for four hundred similarly powered Tempest I's were later amended to a Sabre II-engined version, which as the Tempest V was the first to enter production. This proved to be the only Tempest to see operational wartime service, designated Mk V Series I with a Sabre IIA and Mk V Series IIB with a Sabre IIB and fully buried guns. The first Tempests were delivered to No 3 Squadron RAF and No 486 Squadron RNZAF in April 1944, and flew many cross-Channel sorties before and after the invasion of Normandy. Soon after the invasion, they rapidly became one of the principal fighters employed to combat the VI flying bombs over southern England, accounting for more than one-third of those destroyed. Eight hundred

Tempest V's were built. The Mk VI (one hundred and forty-two built) was an improved model with Sabre V engine, but did not see service until after the war. Neither did the Tempest II, chronologically the last serving version, which was powered by a 2,520 hp Bristol Centaurus V or VI radial engine. Four hundred and seventy-two Tempest II's were completed, this model remaining in RAF service until 1951 and with the Indian and Pakistan air forces until 1953. The Tempest V and VI were relegated to target-towing duties in the early post-war period.

54 Fairey Fulmar

This 2-seat carrier-borne fighter, the first eight-gun combat aeroplane to serve with the British Fleet Air Arm, was adapted from a lightweight variant of the Battle day bomber produced by Fairey in 1936. Specification O.8/38 was issued to cover a fighter version of this design, but no separate prototype was built. The first flight was made on 4 January 1940 by N 1854, which was the first aircraft of the initial production order. The first squadron to receive the Fulmar I was No 806, in July 1940 – after an uncommonly rapid service trials programme – and a month or two later this squadron had become operational aboard HMS *Illustrious* in the Mediterranean. In all, the Fulmar served with fourteen FAA squadrons, despite the modest numbers built. These comprised two hundred and fifty Mk I's with 1,080 hp Merlin VIII engines, and three hundred and fifty Mk II's powered by the 1,300 hp

Merlin 30 and incorporating equipment for operation in tropical climates. Despite a useful armament and range, the Fulmar's performance was well below that of contemporary land-based fighters. It was used with some success on night convoy escort and night intruder duties during the middle war years, but was superseded in the carrier-based day fighter role by Seafires and other single-seat types from 1942 onward.

55 Fairey Firefly

Conceived early in 1940 as an extremely advanced 2-seat Fleet fighter, the Fairey Firefly saw comparatively little of its total squadron service during World War 2, but it was to remain a standard FAA type, in much-altered form, until the late 1950s. The Fairey design, evolved under H. E. Chaplin, received official Admiralty approval in June 1940, when two hundred Fireflies were ordered to Specification N.5/40. The prototype (Z 1826) was flown on 22 December 1941, was armed with four 20 mm cannon and, despite being nearly two tons heavier than the earlier Fulmar, was some 40 mph (64 km/hr) faster, thanks to its superior aerodynamic qualities and a 1,730 hp Griffon IIB engine. Three further prototypes were completed, and deliveries of production Firefly F Mk I's began in March 1943, although it was July 1944 before the type became operational, with No 1770 Squadron (HMS *Indefatigable*), in the attacks upon the German battleship *Tirpitz*. Four undred and twenty-nine F Mk I's, built by Fairey and General Aircraft Ltd, were followed by three hundred and seventy-six FR Mk I's, officially designated as fighter-reconnaissance aircraft and carrying ASH detection radar. During production of the Mk I series, modifications introduced included a revised front cockpit hood, fully faired gun barrels and, from the four hundred and seventy-first aircraft onward, substitution of the 1,765 hp Griffon XII engine. Meanwhile, thirty-seven examples had been completed of a night fighter model, the NF Mk II, with twin leading-edge fairings housing the scanners of their AI radar, and a slightly longer fuselage. They were superseded by the NF Mk I, with an improved radar carried in a single under-nose pod but otherwise structurally similar to the other Mk I's. The proposed Firefly III was abandoned, after one aircraft had been tested with a Griffon 61 series engine, in favour of the Mk IV which, with a 2,330 hp Griffon 72, was flown in 1944. This version was further modified in 1945, but did not enter service until after the war had ended.

56 & 57 Supermarine Spitfire and Seafire

One of the select few combat aeroplanes to become a legend in its own lifetime, the Spitfire and its naval counterpart, the Seafire, appeared in more than forty major variants* during its service career,

* The various Mk numbers were not always built in chronological order, and some changes in Mk number

and remained in continuous production throughout the entire period of World War 2 – the only Allied warplane to do so. The Spitfire's designer, Reginald J. Mitchell, had ideas of his own regarding the ideal configuration for a single-seat fighter, and his design, which was to become the Spitfire, was so clearly superior to the F.5/34 Specification to which it had been submitted that an entirely new Specification (F.37/34) was drafted to cover the prototype's manufacture. This machine (K 5054), powered by a 990 hp Rolls-Royce Merlin C engine, flew for the first time on 5 March 1936, and two substantial contracts for the fighter were placed in 1936–37. Delivery of the first Spitfire I's, to No 19 Squadron, began in August 1938, and by 3 September 1939 nine squadrons were fully equipped with Spitfires and the total orders were in excess of two thousand. One thousand five hundred and sixty-six Spitfire I's (1,030 hp Merlin II or III) were eventually built, this being the principal model in service during the Battle of Britain. It was during the career of this version that two of the three basic Spitfire wing configurations became established. The original wing, mounting eight 0·303 in Browning machine-guns, became known as the 'A' wing; the 'B' wing mounted four Brownings with two 20 mm Hispano cannon. The 'C' wing, first introduced into ser-

occurred; the description here has therefore been somewhat simplified, for reasons of space, to avoid unnecessary confusion.

vice on the Mk VC, was a 'universal' wing capable of mounting four machine-guns, two cannon, or one cannon and two machine-guns in each half. The Spitfire II, with 1,175 hp Merlin XII, entered service late in 1940; nine hundred and twenty were built, some of which were later converted to Mk V's. Only one experimental Mk III (1,280 hp Merlin XX) was completed, the chronology then continuing with two hundred and twenty-nine Mk IV's (actually produced after the Mk V) equipped for photographic reconnaissance. The first really large-scale model was the Spitfire V, which began to enter service in March 1941. Six thousand four hundred and seventy-nine examples of this version were completed. In addition to the standard elliptical-pattern wings, Spitfires were modified for low-level fighting with 'clipped' wingtips, and for high-altitude roles with pointed tip extensions. First in the latter category were the pressurised Mk VI (one hundred built) and Mk VII interceptors (one hundred and forty built), the Mk VII having a redesigned fuselage and a 1,710 hp Merlin 64 engine. The Mk VII was the first variant to exceed 400 mph (644 km/hr) in level flight. The Spitfire VIII appeared in 1943 in high-, intermediate- and low-level forms, a total of one thousand six hundred and fifty-eight being completed, but it was preceded in 1942 by the Mk IX. This was, in essence, the Spitfire VC airframe with a Merlin 60-series engine installed. Production of the Mk IX totalled five thousand six hundred and sixty five. The Mk IX appeared wit standard, clipped and extende wings, and introduced a fourt variation: the 'E' wing, with on Hispano and one 0·50 in Brownin in each half. The sixteen Mk built, and four hundred and seventy one Mk XI, were photo-reconnai sance variants. Another major stag in the Spitfire's evolution came i 1943 with the Mk XII (one hundre built), in which the Merlin engin was replaced by a 1,735 hp Griffo III or IV and the vertical tail are was increased. The Mk XIV including the clipped-wing FR M XIVE (total of nine hundred an fifty-seven completed), were base upon the Mk VIII, locally strength ened to take a 2,050 hp Griffon 6 engine. This model was use successfully against the V1 flyin bombs in 1944, and was also th first aircraft to destroy one of th new Me 262 jet fighters in aeri combat. The Spitfire XVI, whic entered service in 1944, was ground-attack model basically sim lar to the earlier Mk IX, except tha it employed a Packard-built Merli 266 engine; one thousand and fifty four were built. The Spitfire XI was an unarmed photo-reconnais sance derivative of the Mk XIV wit a Griffon 65 or 66 engine; tw hundred and forty-five were buil serving both in Europe and in th Far East. Variants which did no become operational before the war end, but which kept productio going until October 1947, include the Mks XVIII, 21, 22 and 24 Overall Spitfire production totalle twenty thousand three hundred and thirty-four. In addition to their service with the RAF and Commonwealth air forces, many other Spitfires, of various marks, were supplied during the war years to the USAAF, the Soviet Air Force, and the air arms of Egypt, Portugal and Turkey. The Spitfire also enjoyed a successful career at sea. Following the adaptation of the Hurricane (q.v.) for shipboard operation, deck-landing trials were conducted aboard HMS *Illustrious* late in 1941 with a standard Spitfire VB equipped with catapult points and an arrester hook. An order was then placed for some one hundred and sixty-six similar conversions, which were named Seafire IB. The first of these entered Fleet Air Arm service (with No 807 Squadron) in mid-1942, to be followed by three hundred and seventy-two Seafire IIC's – built from the outset as Seafires and based on the Spitfire VC. A considerable improvement over these interim versions was evident in the Mk III of 1943, powered by various marks of Merlin engine and the first Seafire to incorporate wing folding. One thousand two hundred and twenty Seafire III's were completed, many of them fitted with photo-reconnaissance cameras. Installation of the Griffon engine was pursued under Specification N.4/43, the first variant with this powerplant (a 1,850 hp Griffon VI) being the Seafire XV which appeared in 1944. Three hundred and ninety Seafire XV's were completed, entering service in May 1945; but this model was still

working up for employment in the Pacific theatre when the war in the Far East ended. Post-war Seafires in service included the Mks XVII, 45, 46 and 47, some of which were operational during the Korean War of 1950–53.

58 Curtiss P-40 Warhawk

Although not an outstanding combat aeroplane, the Curtiss P-40 served with the USAAF and other Allied air forces in every operational theatre of World War 2, was built in considerable numbers and proved to be highly adaptable to a variety of tasks. Moreover, it had the added advantage of being available in quantity at a time when more sophisticated and more famous wartime fighters were still in the early stages of development or production. Its design originated in 1937, as a development of the radial-engined P-36 (Hawk 75), powered by the new Allison V-1710 Vee-type engine. The prototype XP-40, a converted P-36A airframe, was flown in October 1938, and in April 1939 an order was placed for five hundred and twenty-four production P-40's. This was later reduced to two hundred, to permit Curtiss to meet an order for one hundred and forty similar machines placed by the French government. In the event, the French aircraft were diverted to the RAF in 1940, who named them Tomahawk I. Most of these, due to their poor armament (two 0·30 in guns) were relegated to the Middle East or to Army Co-operation units. The RAF's Tomahawk IIA (one hundred and ten received) corresponded with the P-40B for the USAAF (one hundred and thirty-one) and had two additional wing-mounted guns, self-sealing fuel tanks and extra armour protection. One hundred P-40B's were diverted from a British order to supply the American Volunteer Group in China. Two more wing guns, making six guns in all, characterised the P-40C, the USAAF receiving one hundred and ninety-three and the RAF nine hundred and thirty as the Tomahawk IIB. The first substantial redesign appeared in the P-40D of 1941, which had a shorter nose, minus the nose guns, and a deeper radiator beneath an Allison V-1710-39 engine. The four wing guns were raised to 0·50 in calibre, and provision existed for bombs to be carried beneath the fuselage and wings. Only twenty-two P-40D's went to the USAAF, but five hundred and sixty were allocated to the RAF, which gave them the new name Kittyhawk I. The USAAF preferred the P-40E, with six wing guns; it ordered eight hundred and twenty of this model, and another fifteen hundred became Kittyhawk IA's. Several were also delivered to the RAAF and RCAF. Installation of Packard-built Merlin engines produced the P-40F, one thousand three hundred and eleven of which were built; one hundred were supplied to the USSR and others to the Free French Air Force (FAFL), but planned delivery of P-40F's to the RAF as Kittyhawk II's did not materialise. The RAF was, however, allocated twenty-one P-40K's and six hundred P-40M's (Kittyhawk III) and five hundred and eighty-six P-40N's (Kittyhawk IV). US production included thirteen hundred P-40K's, with slightly increased fin area; seven hundred P-40L's (similar to the F but with only four guns); and four thousand two hundred and nineteen P-40N's. The N model had the four guns and other weight-saving attributes of the F and L, combined with a 1,360 hp V-1710-81 engine. In 1944, many former F and L models had their Merlin engines replaced by Allisons and were converted as P-40R advanced trainers. Production ended in December 1944 after a grand total of thirteen thousand seven hundred and thirty-eight P-40 series aircraft had been produced.

59 **Airspeed Oxford**
The origin of the Oxford twin-engined trainer lay in the 8-passenger Envoy III, which served with the King's Flight of the RAF in the mid-1930s. From this was developed a version known as the Convertible Envoy, seven of which were built for the South African Air Force with a hand-operated dorsal turret mounting a single machine-gun. Major differences discernible in the Oxford I, which first flew in January 1937, were wings of increased span and area, a modified fuselage nose and fully cowled Cheetah IX engines. Delivery of the Oxford I, to the Central Flying School, began in November 1937, and some three hundred were in RAF service by the outbreak of World War 2. Initially, the Oxford I was equipped to provide training in navigation,

bombing and gunnery; the advent of powered turrets in wartime combat aircraft rendered the Oxford's hand-operated turret extinct, although it normally remained in position on most Oxford I's in service. By 3 September 1939 there were also in service over seventy examples of the Oxford II, produced for pilot training and lacking the dorsal turret. Several Oxford II's were later used for ambulance duties. The Oxford III and the Gipsy Queen-engined Oxford IV were projects only. The final production model was the Oxford V, whose performance was somewhat improved by the introduction of 450 hp Pratt & Whitney R-985-AN-6 Wasp Junior engines. Total Oxford production, by Airspeed, de Havilland, Percival and Standard Motors, reached eight thousand seven hundred and fifty-one. Among these, the Mks I and II predominated, although many of them were later converted to Mk V standard with American engines. Oxfords were used as trainers in every major Commonwealth country, and as ambulances in the Middle East.

60 Henschel Hs 129

The 1938 RLM specification that resulted in the Hs 129 was prompted by the need, revealed during the Spanish Civil War, for a specialised close support and ground-attack aeroplane. Dipl-Ing Nicholaus of Henschel designed the Hs 129 around the use of twin Argus As 410 engines, three prototypes being completed. The first of these was flown in the spring of 1939, and

in 1940 a small pre-series batch of Hs 129A-0's were sent to a *Luftwaffe* trials unit for evaluation. Pilots' reports were highly unfavourable, chiefly due to the aircraft's inadequate power, and were sufficiently damning to prevent the Argus-engined Hs 129A from entering production. The existing Hs 129A-0's were not, evidently, too unsatisfactory to pass on to the Rumanian Air Force, which used them for some months on the Russian Front. Meanwhile, Herr Nicholaus's team produced an alternative design, known originally by the project number P.76, but this was rejected by the RLM, which directed instead that the Hs 129A be adapted to take captured French Ghome-Rhône 14M radial engines. Thus re-engined, and with cockpit and other internal modifications, the type became known in 1941 as the Hs 129B. The Hs 129B-1, following a batch of seven pre-series Hs 129B-0's, entered production in autumn 1941, and became operational with *Luftwaffe* units in the Crimea early in 1942. Later, the Hs 129B appeared in numbers in North Africa, being employed primarily as an anti-tank aircraft in both theatres. Several B-1 sub-types were produced, with various combinations of armament. Standard equipment, as installed in the B-1/R1, comprised two 20 mm MG 151 cannon and two 7·9 mm MG 17 machine-guns, with provision for a small external bomb load. Without bombs, and with a fixed ventral 30 mm MK 101 cannon, it was designated B-1/R2; the B-1/R3 had the big cannon replaced by a ventral tray of four more MG 17's; the B-1/R4 and B-1/R5 each carried the standard quota of guns, but with a more varied bomb load and photo-reconnaissance camera respectively. The B-1/R2 was notably successful in the anti-tank role, and prompted the evolution of the all-gun B-2 series. The B-2/R1 was similar to the B-1/R1 except that 13 mm MG 131's replaced the MG 17's; to this the B-2/R2 added a 30 mm MK 103 cannon; while the B-2/R3 discarded the two MG 131's in favour of two more MG 151's (making four in all) and a 37 mm cannon. Final version was the B-2/R4, with a huge 75 mm ventral cannon whose muzzle projected nearly 8 ft (2·4 m) ahead of the aircraft's nose. A total of eight hundred and sixty-six Hs 129B's were built before production ceased in the summer of 1944.

61 Bristol Beaufighter

The Beaufighter originated in 1938 as a private-venture design, based upon the wings, rear fuselage and tail unit of the Beaufort torpedo bomber. The prototype (R 2052) first flew on 17 July 1939, by which time Specification F.17/39 had been issued to cover a handsome initial order for three hundred of these pug-nosed fighters. By the end of May 1940 three other prototypes were flying, and the first small batch of Mk IF production aircraft was accepted by the RAF in 1940; first combat success was by aircraft of No 640 Squadron in November 1940. With their 10-gun armament and airborne interception

radar, the early Beaufighters were the most potent night fighters in production and service, and by the end of 1940 they were performing also as day fighters in the Western Desert. In the spring of 1941, No 143 Squadron of Coastal Command became the first unit to operate the Mk IC, a coastal protection and anti-shipping version otherwise similar to the Mk IF and also powered by 1,590 hp Hercules XI engines. Nine hundred and fourteen Beaufighter I's were built. To avoid undue drain on the output of Hercules engines, orders were also placed for the Merlin-engined Mk II, two prototypes of which had been flown in 1940. Four hundred and fifty production Mk IIF's were built, with the 1,280 hp Merlin XX as their standard powerplant. Most of them served as night fighters in the UK, but a number were delivered to the Fleet Air Arm. A slight tendency toward instability, already noticed in the Beaufighter I, became even more noticeable in the Mk II with its longer Merlin nacelles. It was cured, after some experiment, by giving the tailplane 12 degrees of dihedral, a modification that became standard on all aircraft of the type. The Mks III, IV and V were experimental variants, the next large-scale model being the Mk VI, produced, like the Mk I, as the VIF and VIC for Fighter and Coastal Command respectively. The main difference was the return to a more powerful Hercules engine, giving the Beaufighter enhanced performance, including the ability to carry a small bomb load. The dorsal

Vickers K gun for the observer first appeared on this version, one thousand eight hundred and thirty of which were built. (Sixty of these were completed as ITF = Interim Torpedo Fighters. The torpedo-carrying Beaufighters are described in the *Bombers, Patrol and Transport Aircraft 1939–45* section). A number of Beaufighter VIF's served with the USAAF in 1943, and others were fitted with the AI radar nose 'thimble' that later characterised the TF Mk X. British production of Beaufighters (all variants) totalled five thousand five hundred and sixty-two, and ended in September 1945.

62 Junkers Ju 88

In parallel with the Ju 88A bomber series (see *Bombers, Patrol and Transport Aircraft 1939–45*), Junkers also pursued the development of the basic airframe as a 'heavy' fighter, for which its speed and sturdy construction rendered it particularly suitable. This emerged as the Ju 88C, of which the first version was the C-2, a conversion of the Ju 88A-1, with a 'solid' nose mounting three MG 17 machine-guns and a 20 mm MG FF cannon, and a single aft-firing MG 15 gun. It entered service with NJG.1 late in 1940, being followed by small batches of the C-4, which utilised the extended-span wings of the Ju 88A-4 bomber, and the C-5. Nose armament was increased by two more cannon in the C-6, with Jumo 211J engines and the rear-firing MG 15 replaced by an MG 131 gun. Final C sub-type was the C-7 which, like the C-6, operated as

both a day and a night fighter. The next night-fighter model was the Ju 88G, which utilised the same angular vertical tail as the Ju 188 bomber and carried improved Lichtenstein radar. The G series appeared from mid-1944, principal sub-types being the G-1 (BMW 801D engines), G-6a and G-6b (BMW 801G), G-6c (Jumo 213A) and G-7 (Jumo 213E-1). A small batch of H-2 'heavy' fighters was built, and the Ju 88 fighter variants then came to an end with the Ju 88R, produced in R-1 and R-2 forms for day and night fighting respectively. A specialised version also appeared, for service primarily on the Russian Front, in general ground-attack/anti-tank configuration. This variant was the Ju 88P, with either a 75 mm cannon (in the P-1) or two 37 mm cannon (in the P-2) mounted in the nose. Of the overall Ju 88 production total of fourteen thousand six hundred and seventy-six aircraft (not counting prototypes), slightly over three thousand nine hundred were completed as fighter or ground-attack variants.

63 Kawasaki Ki-45 Toryu (Dragon Killer)

The Ki-45, known by the Allied wartime code name 'Nick', originated in the earlier Kawasaki Ki-38 evolved to a 1937 JAAF requirement for a long-range escort fighter. However, so extensive were the modifications required by the JAAF that a new designation was allotted. Six Ki-45 prototypes were built initially, the first being flown in January 1939. Due to problems encountered with both the landing gear and the Ha-20B engines during trials, three of the prototypes resumed flight testing in July 1940 re-engined with Mitsubishi Ha-25's. In slightly enlarged and modified form, the fighter eventually entered production in September 1941 as the Ki-45-Kai. A second Kawasaki factory joined the production programme in August 1942, by which time the Ha-162 engine had become the standard powerplant. With this engine and the original armament the fighter was now designated Ki-45-Kai-A; the Kai-B initially had one 12·7 mm and one 37 mm gun in the front fuselage; the Kai-C and -D differed in internal equipment only. The Ki-45 was by now being used increasingly as a night fighter, and some mounted a 50 mm or 75 mm weapon for anti-shipping missions. An eventual fourteen prototypes and one thousand six hundred and eighty-seven production Toryus were completed by Kawasaki between 1939 and 1945, the type becoming operational early in 1942 as escort fighter, patrol and anti-shipping aircraft. The Ki-45 was used extensively in the suicide role, being the first JAAF type to figure in this form of warfare during World War 2. It was also one of the most effective night fighters used in the home defence of Japan in 1944–45. The projected Ki-45-II, with 1,500 hp Ha-112-II engines, was converted from December 1942 to become the single-seat Ki-96, three prototypes of which were completed. The first of these was flown in September 1943, but the project was later abandoned by the JAAF and several Ki-96 components were later used in completing prototypes of the Kawasaki Ki-102.

64 **Nakajima J1N**
The Nakajima J1N was evolved originally as a multi-seat escort fighter and attack aircraft, and was entered, together with a Mitsubishi design, to meet a JNAF requirement issued in June 1938. The Mitsubishi entry was later withdrawn, and the Nakajima prototype, designed by K. Nakamura, flew for the first time in May 1941. The J1N proved somewhat difficult to handle and manoeuvre, and the remote control mechanism for the rear gun barbettes gave trouble, but its general performance was satisfactory enough, and the JNAF decided to adopt it instead for a reconnaissance role. With the rear guns deleted, and powered by 1,130 hp Sakae 21 engines, it entered production in the summer of 1942 as the J1N1-C Model 11, and began to reach JNAF units in the Solomon Islands toward the end of the year. Requests from the combat areas led the Japanese Navy to agree in March 1943 to the modification of two J1N1-C's as night fighters, with two pairs of 20 mm cannon aft of the cockpit, to fire at a 30-degree angle above and below the rear fuselage. Following the successful operational use of these two machines, the 2-seat J1N1-S Model 11 night fighter entered production, this receiving the name Gekko (Moonlight). The Allied code name, for both J1N models, was 'Irving'.

Some Ji N1-C's were converted, as an interim measure, to Ji N1-F fighters with one 20 mm cannon in a hand-operated dorsal turret. Later Gekkos were equipped with airborne interception radar and deployed against the B-29's attacking Japanese targets, but they lacked the speed or performance at altitude to be fully effective. Some, with an underwing bomb load, were used in the attack role, and the Ji N was also proposed (though never used) as a torpedo carrier. Including prototypes, Nakajima built a total of four hundred and seventy-seven of all versions.

65 Tachikawa Ki-54
The Ki-54, which appeared in prototype form in the summer of 1940, was employed as a civilian transport by several Japanese commercial operators before the beginning of the war in the Pacific. It possessed a better performance than other Japanese aircraft in its class by virtue of its clean lines, fully retractable main landing gear and variable-pitch propellers, although it exhibited a tendency toward nose-heaviness when landing. The type was produced as an advanced trainer for the JAAF, being equipped to provide instruction in bombing and gunnery techniques as well as pilot and navigator training. Later in the war a version known as the Model C appeared for the troop transport role, being furnished with seats for up to nine passengers. In many respects the career of the Ki-54 (code named 'Hickory' by the Allies) paralleled that of the Air-speed Oxford, although it was built in considerably smaller numbers; about one thousand two hundred were completed by Tachikawa prior to the end of the war. Many of these were used in the suicide role during 1944–45.

66 Potez 63
Evolved to a 1934 specification for a 3-seat strategic fighter, the Potez 63 was designed by MM Coroller and Delaruelle, the -01 prototype flying for the first time on 25 April 1936. In general appearance it bore a superficial resemblance to its German contemporary, the Messerschmitt Bf 110, a fact which contributed to the loss of many Potez fighters during combat in World War 2. The Hispano-Suiza-engined first prototype was later redesignated Potez 630-01, to distinguish it from the second machine (631-01), which had Gnome-Rhône engines. In May 1937 the French Air Ministry ordered ten evaluation machines which included representatives of both types, together with examples of the Potez 633 (light bomber configuration), 637 (reconnaissance and Army co-operation) and 639 (attack bomber). In June 1937 the Potez company became part of the new SNCA du Nord, from which was ordered eighty Potez 630's and ninety Potez 631's, the latter figure including ten with dual controls for conversion training. Orders were placed in 1938 for one hundred and twenty-five Potez 633's for the *Armée de l'Air*, plus export batches for Greece (twenty-four) and Rumania (forty); a manufacturing

licence was also granted to Avia in Czechoslovakia, but none were built in that country. Only eleven of the Greek and twenty-one of the Rumanian 633's had been delivered by August 1939, when delivery of the remainder was halted by the French government. Production of the Potez 631 by this time had reached two hundred and ten for the *Armée de l'Air*. Also completed were sixty Potez 637's, but this was essentially an interim service model pending availability of the Potez 63.11, a much-redesigned development which was first flown on 31 December 1938. This differed principally in the design of the front fuselage, and an initial order had been placed for one hundred and forty-five for the armed reconnaissance role. Nearly seventeen hundred more were ordered in 1939. Production continued under German direction after the occupation of France, and the eventual total of Potez 63.11's completed appears to have been in the region of nine hundred. Variants of the Potez 63 series served with units of the *Luftwaffe* and the Vichy Air Force, as well as with the FAFL, in Europe and North Africa.

67 Heinkel He 219 Uhu(Owl)

After an initial lack of interest when proposals for this multi-purpose fighter were first submitted to it in August 1940, the RLM authorised Heinkel, late in 1941, to begin detailed design work on the project. The first He 219 prototype was flown on 15 November 1942, powered by two 1,750 hp DB 603A engines, and underwent armament trials during the following month. An initial order was placed for one hundred production aircraft, and this figure was increased to three hundred by the time tooling-up began in April 1943. About twenty pre-series He 219A-0's had been completed by the summer, and were followed by forty examples of the He 219A-2 (the A-1 having been abandoned). The A-2 was a 2-seat model; proposals for the 3-seat A-3 bomber and the high-altitude reconnaissance A-4 sub-types were not adopted. Production thus continued with the A-5, A-6 and A-7; most of these were powered by variants of the DB 603 engine, but Jumo 213E's were installed in the A-7/R5 and Jumo 222's in the A-7/R6. The A-5 was a 3-seater and carried additional internal fuel. Total production of the He 219A-series aircraft was two hundred and sixty-eight, and these, together with some twenty prototype or pre-production machines and a few 2-seat He 219B-2's (developed from the A-6) were the only models to serve operationally with the *Luftwaffe*. Prototype airframes were completed of the He 219C-1 night fighter and C-2 fighter-bomber, but when VE-day arrived these still awaited delivery of their Jumo 222 engines. The C series were to have carried a 4-man crew, the additional member manning a tail turret with four MG 131 machine-guns.

68 Dornier Do 217

In an attempt to overcome a severe shortage of specialised night fighters, the *Luftwaffe* in 1942 initiated the conversion of large numbers of Dornier 217 bombers to fulfil this function. Fundamentally, the airframe conversion entailed replacing the bulbous, glazed nose of the bomber with a more streamlined 'solid' fairing containing additional guns. First version selected for conversion was the Do 217E-2. A total of one hundred and fifty-seven E-2's underwent modification, after which they were redesignated Do 217J-1 or J-2. The former was an intruder version, retaining a reduced bomb-carrying capability, while the J-2 night fighter had the bomb bay faired over and was equipped with Lichtenstein airborne interception radar. Both mounted four 20 mm cannon and four 7·9 mm machineguns in the nose, and had provision for one 13 mm gun in a ventral position, in addition to the dorsal armament. In 1943 the J series began to be replaced by the Lichtenstein-equipped Do 217N series, powered by DB 603A in-line engines and converted from the M series bombers. The N-1 and N-2 were both night fighters, and were otherwise generally similar to the J-2 except that the N-2 had no ventral gun. Fifty conversions from M to N were carried out. The non-fighter Do 217 models are described in the *Bombers, Patrol and Transport Aircraft 1939–45* section of this book.

69 Westland Whirlwind
The Whirlwind was one of several British wartime aircraft to fall victim to the vicissitudes of the Rolls-Royce Peregrine engine; but for this its service career might well have been more significant, for it was a fast, well-armed design with excellent manoeuvrability and first-class flying qualities. It was designed by William Petter to Specification F.37/35, the first of two prototypes (L 6844) being flown on 11 October 1938. Production was ordered three months later, but delays in the supply of Peregrine engines caused the first deliveries of Whirlwind I fighters (to No 263 Squadron) to be put back until July 1940. Several accidents, due to rather poor forward vision in the landing attitude and the fighter's high landing speed, delayed the equipment of the second Whirlwind squadron (No 137) until November 1941, and these remained the only two RAF squadrons to employ the type. The Whirlwind's performance was particularly good at low altitude, a factor that contributed to its employment during the latter half of 1942 in the fighter-bomber role; previously it had been employed as an interceptor or escort fighter. But in January 1942, following the abandonment of Peregrine production, manufacture of the Whirlwind also ceased. One hundred and sixteen were built, including the two prototypes.

70 De Havilland Mosquito
Although conceived as a fast day bomber, the D.H.98 Mosquito had too good a turn of speed for its potential as a fighter to pass unnoticed, and the third of the three prototypes (W 4052), which first flew on 15 May 1941, was completed to a night-fighter configuration with AI Mk IV radar in a 'solid' nose.

Four hundred and sixty-six Mosquito Mk II's were subsequently built, the first deliveries being made to No 157 Squadron in January 1942 as replacements for the Douglas A-20 Havoc. Ninety-seven Mk II's were later converted to NF Mk XII's with centrimetric AI Mk VIII radar, followed by two hundred and seventy NF XIII's, the production counterpart of the Mk XII. On these subsequent radar-carrying night fighters the nose machine-guns were omitted. Other specialist night fighter models included the Mks XV, XVII (one hundred conversions from Mk II), and XIX (two hundred and twenty built), the two last-named having AI Mk X radar of US manufacture. The most numerous version of all, however, was the Mosquito Mk VI, of which two thousand seven hundred and eighteen were built during and after the war. The first Mk VI was a converted Mk II (HJ 662), first flown in its new form in February 1943. Carrying the standard fighter armament, the Mk VI was able to carry two 250 lb or 500 lb (113 or 227 kg) bombs in the rear of the bomb bay, with two additional bombs or auxiliary fuel tanks beneath the outer wing sections. It entered service with No 418 Squadron in the spring of 1943. An alternative load comprised eight 60 lb (27 kg) rocket projectiles, and Mk VI's so equipped entered service with Coastal Command early in 1944 for anti-shipping strike duties. They had actually been preceded by a small batch of twenty-seven FB XVIII's produced by converting the standard FB VI to mount a 57 mm cannon in the nose. Principal Canadian and Australian counterparts to the FB VI were the FB 26 and FB 40 with Packard-built Merlin engines. Whether as a bomber, day or night fighter, reconnaissance or intruder, the Mosquito in its many guises served in all operational theatres of the war, including the Pacific area from early 1944. Three hundred and forty-eight examples were also built of a trainer variant, the T Mk III; most of these were delivered to the RAF, but some were sold abroad and a few were also supplied to the Fleet Air Arm. The other non-fighter variants are described in the *Bombers, Patrol and Transport Aircraft 1939–45* section.

71 Messerschmitt Me 210 and Me 410 Hornisse (Hornet)

The Me 210 was designed as a potential successor to the Bf 110, and RLM approval of the project in 1937 was followed on 2 September 1939 by the first flight of the twin-finned Me 210V1 prototype. This aircraft showed marked instability in flight, and attempts to remedy this resulted in a large-area single fin and rudder being introduced on the second machine. This still did not eliminate all the Me 210's control problems, but the RLM had committed itself to a substantial order for one thousand aircraft of this type before the first prototype had flown. The three production models – the Me 210A-1, A-2 and B-1, were all similarly powered, with 1,395 hp DB 601F engines; the A-2 was fitted with external bomb racks, while the B-1 had the two MG 17 guns deleted and carried two aerial reconnaissance cameras. In April 1942, however, the RLM halted production of the Me 210. It was later resumed for a brief period, but the final total completed in Germany was only three hundred and fifty-two, plus one hundred and eight built under licence in Hungary with DB 605 engines. In the search for a replacement type, the RLM passed over the pressurised Me 310 project in favour of a simpler derivative, the Me 410, which was also powered by DB 603A engines. Known as the *Hornisse*, the Me 410 entered production late in 1942. By 1944 a total of one thousand one hundred and twenty-one had been manufactured. Several A and B sub-types were produced, with armament or equipment variations, for service as 'heavy' fighters, bomber destroyers and photographic reconnaissance aircraft. The Me 410A-3 and B-3 had bulged bomb-bay fairings containing three aerial cameras.

72 Messerschmitt Bf 110

The Bf 110 was the second production warplane designed by Prof Willy Messerschmitt after joining the Bayerische Flugzeugwerke AG, and was evolved in response to an RLM specification of early 1934 for a long-range escort fighter and *Zerstörer* (destroyer) aircraft. Three prototypes were completed with DB 600 engines, and the first of these was flown on 12 May 1936. The second, delivered early in the next year to the *Luftwaffe* for service

trials, was received with mixed feelings. It was fast for a relatively heavy twin-engined machine, but was also heavy on the controls and less manoeuvrable than was desired. Four pre-series Bf 110A-0's were ordered, and these, due to the comparative scarcity of DB 600 engines, were fitted instead with 610 hp Jumo 210B units. These proved clearly inadequate, and were succeeded in the spring of 1938 by two Bf 110B-0 aircraft with 690 hp DB 600A engines to carry out trials for the initial Bf 110B-1 production series. Plans to evaluate the B-1 operationally in the Spanish Civil War were forestalled when that conflict was resolved before it was ready for service. Thus, the first model to go into active service was the Bf 110C, in which increased power was provided by the use of DB 601A engines. Other refinements appearing in the C model included squared-off wingtips to improve the manoeuvrability, and a modified crew enclosure. The Bf 110C entered service in 1939, over five hundred of this model being on the *Luftwaffe*'s strength by the end of that year. Some were produced for the fighter-bomber and reconnaissance roles, and the Bf 110 was employed primarily in ground-attack manoeuvres during the invasion of Poland. Hence it was not until it was fully exposed as a fighter, in the Battle of Britain, that its shortcomings in that capacity became apparent. Losses then became so heavy that the Luftwaffe was obliged to send Bf 109's with the bomber formations to protect their Bf 110 escorts. Production of the C model continued, latterly with 1,200 hp DB 601N engines, but many of the earlier machines were withdrawn to such second-line duties as glider towing. Attempts to boost the aircraft's range resulted in the Bf 110D, produced both as a fighter (D-0 and D-1) and as a fighter-bomber (D-2 and D-3), but by mid-1941 most of the C and D versions were operational only in the Middle East or on the Eastern Front. The more versatile Bf 110E (DB 601N) and Bf 110F (DB 601F) appeared later that year, variants including the rocket-firing F-2 and the F-4 night fighter. By late 1942, when it became apparent that the Me 210 was not going to be a satisfactory replacement for its predecessor, Bf 110 production was stepped up again and the Bf 110G was introduced. This followed the pattern of earlier series, including the G-4 night fighter with 1,475 hp DB 605B engines, two or four 20 mm cannon and four 7·9 mm machine-guns. The four-seat Bf 110G-4/R3 was the first variant to incorporate Lichtenstein SN-2 airborne interception radar. The Bf 110H series, differing chiefly in carrying even heavier armament, was produced in parallel with the G series, and was the last production model. Total Bf 110 production, in all versions, was approximately six thousand one hundred and fifty, and ended early in 1945.

73 Siebel Si 204D

The Si 204D was developed in 1940–41 by Dipl-Ing Fecher from the pre-war Fh 104 *Hallore* and Si 204A

medium transports, from which its chief external difference was the replacement of the original 'stepped' solid nose by a bulbous, fully glazed section forming a continuous contour with the remainder of the front fuselage. The Si 204A was powered by two 360 hp Argus As 410A engines, and some served with the *Luftwaffe* in the light transport or liaison roles. The more powerful Si 204D, flown in prototype form in 1941, succeeded the Focke-Wulf Fw 58 as the standard *Luftwaffe* aircrew trainer and could be furnished to accommodate five trainees in addition to the 2-man crew. It remained in service until the end of World War 2, latterly for radar as well as navigation training. Most of its manufacture was undertaken in German-held factories in Czechoslovakia and France. The SNCA du Centre continued to build the Si 204D, in slightly modified form, as the NC 701 (military) and NC 702 Martinet (civil) after the war, and Aero in Czechoslovakia also built a substantial number of post-war examples as military and civil transports.

74 Fokker G.I

Before the G.I prototype had flown, it was exhibited at the 1936 *Salon de l'Aéronautique* in Paris, where its formidable armament – one arrangement offered eight machine-guns clustered in the nose and a ninth at the rear – quickly earned it the nickname *Le Faucheur* (the Grim Reaper). It was evolved by Fokker as a private venture 2-seat design for a bomber interceptor, and the prototype (X-2) first flew on 16 March 1937, powered by two 750 hp Hispano-Suiza 80-02 radial engines. In November 1937 thirty-six examples were ordered by the Dutch government of the G.IA, a slightly modified version with 830 hp Bristol Mercury VIII engines and provision in four aircraft for a third crew member. A slightly smaller 2-seat model, with 750 hp Twin Wasp Junior engines, was offered for export as the G.IB. For the latter, Denmark sought a manufacturing licence, and orders were received from Estonia (for nine), Finland (twenty-six), Sweden (eighteen, to be fitted with Swedish-built Bofors guns) and Spain. When Holland was invaded on 10 May 1940 twelve of the Finnish G.IB's were still at Schiphol, their delivery having been halted upon the outbreak of war. They were unarmed, but enough guns were taken from other nearby aircraft to fit three G.IB's with four guns each and fly them against the *Luftwaffe*. The remaining fourteen Finnish aircraft were completed after the German occupation and employed by the *Luftwaffe* as operational trainers. Meanwhile, delivery of the G.IA to the Dutch Air Force's 3rd and 4th Fighter Groups had started in July 1939, and twenty-three were operational when the invasion began. Several were destroyed on the ground before they could take part in the fighting, but those that survived gave a good account of themselves in the five days of bitter fighting that ensued. At the end of this, only one G.IA was left, but in this machine two senior Fokker pilots managed to escape later to Britain.

75 Lockheed P-38 Lightning

If one aeroplane were to be chosen from those taking part in World War 2 to epitomise the successful realisation of the long-range tactical fighter, few would dispute the claims of Lockheed's 'fork-tailed devil', the P-38 Lightning. Work on its design was started early in 1937, to meet an exacting USAAC requirement. The Lockheed Model 22 was a clear winner of the competition, and in June 1937 one prototype, designated XP-38, was ordered. This machine (37-457) first flew on 27 January 1939, followed on 16 September 1940 by the first of thirteen YP-38 evaluation aircraft with more powerful V-1710 engines and a nose armament of four machine-guns and a 37 mm cannon. Delivery of production P-38's began in the summer of 1941; thirty were built, one being modified to an XP-38A with a pressurised cabin. The next production model was the P-38D, thirty-six of which were manufactured with self-sealing fuel tanks and minor airframe modifications. The name Lightning was originally bestowed by the RAF, which had ordered the type in 1940, but initial deliveries were restricted to three Lightning I's (with non-supercharged engines) and a contract for five hundred and twenty-four Lightning II's was subsequently cancelled. The remaining one hundred and forty Mk I's were repossessed (as the P-322) by the USAAF, which acquired the Mk

II's built for Britain as well; many of these were later converted to P-38F or G standard. Meanwhile, the USAAF's own next choice, the P-38E, had entered production. Two hundred and ten were built, with double the D's ammunition for the nose guns and a 20 mm cannon replacing the heavier weapon. An increase in engine power was the major improvement in the F and G models, thus enabling the Lightning to carry a range of external weapons or supplementary fuel tanks for the first time. Production of five hundred and twenty-seven P-38F's and one thousand and eighty-two P-38G's, with deliveries beginning during 1942, heralded a marked expansion in the Lightning's deployment in the major theatres of the war in Europe, North Africa and the Pacific. A further increase in engine power appeared in 1943 with the P-38H, the first Lightning model to introduce the 'chin' air cooler intakes beneath the spinners. Six hundred and one P-38H's were delivered; the two thousand nine hundred and seventy P-38J's that followed were essentially similar, but an increased internal fuel load raised the endurance of the J model (when carrying drop-tanks as well) to a maximum of 12 hours. An even greater number were built of the rocket-carrying P-38L, with 1,600 hp V-1710-111/113 engines and a maximum speed of 414 mph (666 km/hr). Three thousand eight hundred and ten P-38L's were manufactured by Lockheed; a further two thousand were ordered from Vultee, who had completed only one hundred and thirteen before the remainder were cancelled at the end of the Pacific war. Lightnings converted for other duties included seventy-five P-38M night fighters (from P-38L), a small number of TP-38L conversion trainers, and the undesignated 'Droop Snoot' and 'Pathfinder' (former P-38J or L models). The Lightning was also the most widely used single photographic reconnaissance aircraft of World War 2, nearly fourteen hundred being converted from P-38E, F, G, H, J and L models and serving with F-4 or F-5 series designations.

76 Saab-21A

Considering that it was the first fighter design undertaken by the Swedish manufacturer, the Saab-21 was remarkable in many respects. It was the only single-engined, twin-boom, pusher-engined fighter to be produced during 1939–45, was the first fighter built in Sweden to have a liquid-cooled engine, and in later years became the only fighter in the world to be produced in both piston-engined and jet-engined forms. Yet the basic configuration was arrived at and presented to the Royal Swedish Air Board within *two weeks* of the Board's March 1941 specification. With the decision to adopt the German DB 605 engine in place of the American Twin Wasp radial originally planned, three prototypes were ordered, and the first of these was flown on 30 July 1943. Thanks to the tricycle landing gear, view from the cockpit for take-off and landing was excellent. The high operational speed of the J 21, as it was designated by the *Flygvapnet*, combined with the rear-mounted propeller, led to the Saab fighter being one of the first in the world to be equipped with an ejection seat for the pilot. Some minor development problems, almost inevitable in such an unorthodox design, delayed delivery of production J 21's until the latter part of 1945. The first machines entered service with F 9 Wing at Gothenburg, and after the first few production aircraft the locally built SFA version of the DB 605B engine was introduced in place of examples imported from Germany. Production of the J 21A continued until 1948, three hundred and one (including three prototypes) being built. Variants included the J 21A-1 (fifty-four built) and J 21A-2 (one hundred and twenty-four built), some of the latter being adapted subsequently as J 21A-2 attack aircraft. The J 21A-3 or A 21A-3 (one hundred and twenty built) had auxiliary wingtip fuel tanks, underwing points for bombs or rocket rails, and provision for a ventral pack of eight additional 13·2 mm machine-guns. The Saab-21B was a proposed development, with a pressurised cockpit and 2,000 hp Griffon engine, but this was discarded in favour of the jet-powered Saab-21R.

77 Bell P-59 Airacomet

The first aeroplane to be designed in the US to acquire experience of the Whittle-type gas turbine engine, the Airacomet project was initiated in the autumn of 1941, the first of three XP-59A prototypes being flown on 1 October 1942. These three machines, bearing for security reasons the designation originally allotted to an entirely different piston-engined Bell fighter project, were powered by two General Electric I-A turbojets, derived from the Whittle W.2B engine. A higher-rated engine, the 1,400 lb (635 kg) st I-16, was installed in the thirteen YP-59A service trials aircraft which followed. Two of these machines were evaluated by the US Navy, and a third was sent to the U.K. in exchange for one of the first Gloster Meteors. In addition to operating problems encountered with the early jet engines, the Airacomet's performance and stability were also below expectations; as a result, the original production order for one hundred aircraft was later reduced, and most of those built were employed for training, engine development and other non-operational duties. Although it took no active part in World War 2, the Airacomet served the primary purpose of establishing the jet fighter concept, paving the way for the P-80 Shooting Star and subsequent fighters with the new form of propulsion. Twenty P-59A's were built with J31-GE-3 engines, and thirty P-59B's with J31-GE-5's, additional internal fuel capacity and detail airframe modifications.

78 Gloster Meteor

Air Ministry Specification F.9/40 was the first official requirement to be promulgated in the UK for a single-seat interceptor powered by gas turbine engines. From it stemmed W. G. Carter's Gloster Meteor – the first British (and only Allied) jet fighter to achieve operational status during World War 2. The low thrust output of the engines then developed indicated the adoption of a twin-engined configuration, but apart from its radical form of propulsion the Meteor was of completely conventional design. Eight prototypes (of twelve originally ordered) were completed, and it was the fifth of these (DG 206/G) that was used for the first flight on 5 March 1943. Powerplant was two 1,500 lb (680 kg) st Halford H.1 turbojets. Production aircraft – which were to have been named Thunderbolt until that name was adopted for the Republic P-47 – began with twenty Meteor I's powered by 1,700 lb (771 kg) st Rolls-Royce Welland I engines. One of these aircraft was exchanged in 1944 for a Bell YP-59A Airacomet, three others were retained for further development trials, and the remaining sixteen delivered, from July 1944, to the RAF. The first recipient of the new fighters was No 616 Squadron, whose Meteors brought down two V1 flying bombs over southern England on 4 August 1944. One Meteor I was fitted with 2,700 lb (1,225 kg) st de Havilland Goblin I engines as the prototype Meteor II, but no production of this version was undertaken. The first model to be produced in any quantity was the Meteor III, of which two hundred and eighty were completed. The first fifteen of these had Welland engines, the remainder

Derwents, and the final fifteen had lengthened engine nacelles. Two RAF squadrons with the Meteor III were serving with the 2nd Allied Tactical Air Force in Europe during the final weeks of the war, but had no engagements with the Meteor's German counterpart, the Me 262, in aerial combat. One Meteor III, re-engined with 3,500 lb (1,588 kg) st Derwent V's, was flown in July 1945 as prototype for the post-war Mk IV, and all subsequent Meteor development and production also took place after the war had ended.

79 Messerschmitt Me 262
Design of the Me 262 jet fighter, under the Messerschmitt project number 1065, began a year before the outbreak of World War 2. Yet, due to delays in the development and delivery of satisfactory engines, the depredations caused by Allied air attacks, and Hitler's refusal to be advised regarding its most appropriate role, it was six years before the aircraft entered *Luftwaffe* squadron service. Even then, only a fraction of those manufactured before VE-day became operational. A mock-up of the design was completed during the latter half of 1939, examination of which prompted the RLM to order three prototypes in the spring of 1940. These were all completed long before the arrival of their engines and so, to test the basic attributes of the design, the Me 262V1 made its first flight on 4 April 1941 with dummy jet-engine nacelles and a single 700 hp Jumo 210 piston engine mounted in the nose. On 25 November 1941 it

attempted to fly with two underwing BMW 003 gas turbines, and still with the nose-mounted Jumo 210 in position. But the first all-jet flight was not made until 18 July 1942, when the third prototype took off under the power of two 1,852 lb (840 kg) st Jumo 004 turbojets. Several more prototypes were completed and used for trials with various armament and equipment installations, and from the fifth machine onward a tricycle landing gear was substituted for the original tailwheel type. A pre-series batch of Me 262A-o's was completed in the spring of 1944, but plans for priority mass-production were seriously affected by Allied air attacks upon Messerschmitt's Regensburg factory, and the planned introduction of the Me 262 into operational service in May 1944 did not take place until the following autumn. The two principal versions which did become operational were the Me 262A-1a Schwalbe (Swallow) interceptor and the Me 262A-2a Sturmvogel (Stormbird). The former was built in a number of sub-types with alternative armament installations; the latter, produced as a result of Hitler's insistence upon developing the aircraft as a bomber, was fitted with external bomb racks. Other variants built included the ground-attack Me 262A-3a and the photo-reconnaissance A-5a. A tandem 2-seat trainer version was designated Me 262B-1a, and one example was completed of a proposed 2-seat night fighter, the B-2a. The few Me 262C models completed before VE-day were fitted with rocket motors in

the fuselage to boost the fighter's climb to interception altitudes. Less than six hundred Me 262's had been produced by the end of 1944, but by VE-day the total had risen to one thousand four hundred and thirty-three. Probably less than a quarter of this total saw front-line combat service, and losses among these were quite heavy. In air-to-air combat, the Me 262 never engaged its British counterpart, the Meteor, but many were destroyed by Allied piston-engined Mustang, Thunderbolt, Spitfire and Tempest fighters.

80 Messerschmitt Me 163 Komet (Comet)
Probably the most ingenious and radical German combat aeroplane to serve during World War 2, the Me 163 achieved no small degree of success during the nine months or so that it was in active service, although it reached operational units too late and in numbers too small to affect the ultimate outcome. It was based on the experimental DFS 194, designed in 1938 by Prof Alexander Lippisch and transferred, together with its staff, to the Messerschmitt AG for further development. But for the subsequent clash of personalities between Lippisch and Prof Willy Messerschmitt, and the delay in delivery of its rocket engines in later years, it would almost certainly have been in service much earlier. The first two Me 163 prototypes were flown in the spring of 1941 as unpowered gliders, the Me 163V1 being transferred to Peenemünde later that year to receive its 1,653 lb (750 kg) st HWK R.II rocket motor.

The first rocket-powered flight was made in August 1941, and in trials the fighter soon exhibited speeds of more than 620 mph (1,000 km/hr). Ten unpowered Me 163A's were completed late in 1941 as conversion trainers, and development of the fighter was accelerated. The airframe of the third prototype (for the seventy Me 163B-0 and B-1 production machines ordered) was completed in May 1942, but over a year elapsed before its new engine, the HWK 509A, became available. By then more than half of the original production batch were also complete except for their power-plants. Additional Me 163 production was undertaken by Hans Klemm Flugzeugbau, the overall total being slightly more than three hundred and fifty. The first *Luftwaffe* unit to receive the Me 163B acquired its fighters in June/July 1944, making its operational debut in mid-August against US Eighth Air Force B-17's over Germany. The Komet's spectacular speed, and the element of surprise, resulted in many early successes against Allied bomber formations. However, the definitive version was nearly a ton heavier than its original design weight, necessitating the use of auxiliary booster rockets for take-off, while landings were hazardous in the extreme. All too often the Me 163, landing directly on its fuselage keel-skid and with some of the highly inflammable fuel still left in the tank, would come to a literally comet-like end, with fatal results for its pilot. When the war ended the pressurised and improved Me 163C (HWK 509C motor) had reached the pre-production stage, and a prototype had also been flown of a derivative known first as the Me 163D and later as the Me 263.

INDEX

The reference numbers refer to the illustrations and corresponding text.

Book II
BOMBERS
Patrol and Transport Aircraft
1939–45

Introduction to Book II

Most of the European nations involved in the war of 1939-45 had, during the latter half of the 1930s, embarked upon plans to expand and re-equip their air forces with more modern combat types. The natural process of evolution of new military aircraft was hastened by a belated recognition of the potential danger which existed in the form of the increasing might of the German *Luftwaffe*. However, by the outbreak of World War 2 Germany still possessed the strongest and most modern air force in Europe.

Germany had been categorically forbidden by the 1919 Treaty of Versailles to manufacture military aeroplanes, although the construction of light civil aircraft was allowed to continue on a modest scale. Most of the restrictions imposed by the Versailles Treaty were withdrawn in the 1926 Paris Air Agreement, and from then onward there began the re-establishment of a substantial aircraft industry, not only within Germany itself but in the form of new factories set up in Switzerland, the U.S.S.R. and elsewhere. The national airline, *Deutsche Lufthansa*, and the re-created *Luftsportverband*, ostensibly a private flying organisation, acted as a political cloak for new para-military activities whereby new bombers, fighters and transport aircraft were developed under the guise of fast 'air taxis', 'sporting' single-seaters and high-speed mailplanes. New military prototypes commonly appeared bearing civilian registration letters, but their quasi-civilian purpose was fairly apparent, and after Hitler came to power in 1933 little further attempt was made to preserve the pretence, although the practice of allocating civil registration marks to military prototypes continued. In 1935 the existence of the new *Luftwaffe* was confirmed officially when it was announced that *Reichsmarschall* Hermann Goering, the former Air Minister, had been appointed as its new Commander-in-Chief. After the German occupation of Austria in 1938 factories in that country were also utilised for the production of aeroplanes for the *Luftwaffe* and the output of combat aircraft for the German air force rose from some 300 a month at the end of 1935 to more than 1,000 a month by September 1939.

By comparison, the expansion programme embarked upon by the RAF before World War 2 was both modest and slow. Until 1936 the bomber force was composed principally of obsolescent biplanes or slow, ponderous monoplanes; but then, with the introduction of the 'shadow factory' programme, the extensive re-equipment of the RAF with more modern combat aircraft began, with the British motor-car industry geared to turn out aeroplanes to supplement those produced by the aircraft industry. In addition, substantial numbers of American types were ordered for the RAF by the British Purchasing Mission which visited the U.S.A. in 1938. Despite this augmented programme, however, on 3 September 1939 the RAF had no four-engined heavy bombers in service, and the total number of twin-engined medium bombers on charge at that time comprised only 226 Hampdens, 179 Wellingtons and 207 Whitleys. Of these, the Whitleys were already virtually obsolete, and only 169 Hampdens and 160 Wellingtons were with front-line squadrons. The light day bomber situation was slightly better, at least numerically, for there were 1,075 twin-engined Blenheims and 1,133 single-engined Battles on strength; but only half of these were with operational units, and the Battle was later to prove something of a disappointment. The Fleet Air Arm was in an even poorer state, its most modern fighter in September 1939 being the Sea Gladiator biplane. Seven new aircraft carriers had been ordered in 1938, but for the first three years or more of the war the best British torpedo-bomber-reconnaissance types that they had aboard them were also slow, vulnerable biplanes, and it is no small tribute to the quality of such aircraft as the Fairey Swordfish that it was capable of being flown with distinction and to good military effect for the major part of the war. Poland, France and the smaller European nations were, like Britain, still in the midst of their respective modernisation programmes when the war struck them. Each had excellent new types under development, but all too few were actually in service by the time they were needed.

The civil war which had broken out in Spain in 1936 had afforded an ideal opportunity for several European powers to send detachments of combat aircraft to that country, where they could gain valuable operational experience under genuine battle conditions. In the light of future events this was to prove something of a mixed blessing. In Spain, where they were generally opposed by aircraft older or technically inferior to those which they were flying themselves, the pilots of Germany's *Legion Condor* and Italy's *Aviazione Legionaria* were usually able to dispose of any aerial opposition with comparative ease. Bomber squadrons in particular were able to carry out raids with little or no fighter escort, since their opponents were either too few, too slow or too old to interrupt their progress seriously. The successful application of these tactics in Spain not unnaturally led the *Luftwaffe* to pursue similar tactics at the outset of World War 2, and in the initial advances across eastern and western Europe this policy continued to prove successful.

After the Dunkirk evacuation and the fall of France in 1940, the *Luftwaffe* began to increase its campaign of bombing raids against the United Kingdom as a preliminary softening-up process prior to the intended invasion of England. However, in the late summer of 1940 the *Luftwaffe* suffered its first serious defeat in the air when, in the Battle of Britain, operating without ground support and against superior fighter opposition, it failed to achieve the measure of air superiority required to allow the bomber force to achieve its objective. The success achieved by the RAF in the Battle of Britain gave the Allied air forces a valuable initial breathing space in which they were able to recover and remuster their strength before preparing first to withstand the continued German *blitzkrieg* and then to mount their own counter-bombing offensive.

Meanwhile, in June 1940 Italy had entered the war on the German side, and although the *Regia Aeronautica* possessed rather less modern warplanes than the *Luftwaffe*, it was still numerically a force to be reckoned with, having nearly 1,000 bombers and over 750 reconnaissance, transport and non-combatant types in its overall inventory. Germany did not immediately learn the lesson of the Battle of Britain, although one outcome was a marked increase in the defensive armament of her bomber fleet. The *Luftwaffe* continued daylight bombing attacks for quite some time afterwards; had it turned over immediately to a night bombing offensive while British night defences were still inadequate, the story might well have been a different one. As it was, Germany lost around 2,000 aircraft and 5,000 aircrew in continued daylight attacks before switching to a night offensive. For a short time during 1940-41 Italian bombers based in Belgium gave some support to the *Luftwaffe* during day and night raids on British targets, but they achieved little success in this quarter, and were soon required to return home for operations in the Mediterranean area or in North Africa. A serious blow was dealt to the Italian war machine in November 1940 by the Fleet Air Arm, which brought off a remarkably successful attack on the Italian Fleet at Taranto, inflicting losses and damage almost as serious in their effect as those incurred just over a year later by the U.S. Navy when its ships at Pearl Harbor were attacked by the Japanese Naval Air Force. With one or two exceptions, Italian bombers of the war period were not an outstandingly successful breed. The only four-engined Italian bomber, the Piaggio P.108B, served only in small numbers, and, coincidentally, none of the multi-engined strategic bombers developed by Germany and Japan were successful operationally.

One of the biggest single factors in the ultimate downfall of Naziism was undoubtedly Hitler's decision in 1941 to invade the U.S.S.R. The Soviet Air Force had been another participant in the Spanish Civil War of 1936-39, and in 1938-39 was also engaged against the air forces of Japan during the Siberian border disputes. A major expansion and re-equipment programme for the Soviet Air Force was put in hand as a result of these campaigns, but at the time of the German invasion few new aircraft had been developed and put into service, and the Soviet Air Force, although strong numerically, did not possess large numbers of modern combat aircraft. The gap was bridged to a considerable extent after March 1941, when the U.S. Congress gave approval to the Lend-Lease Act, which permitted the donation of American aircraft to the Allied powers. By the end of 1942 several of the new Soviet-designed types had become available in quantity. Most of these were fighters or ground-attack aircraft; the bomber force was made up largely of the Ilyushin DB-3F and Tupolev SB-2, supplemented by such U.S. medium bomber types as the Douglas A-20 and North American B-25.

The U.S.A. had always been overtly sympathetic to the Allied cause, and the substantial numbers of American aircraft ordered before the war by the British Purchasing Commission were now augmented still further by the diversion to Britain of unfulfilled

French orders and by further supplies made under the Lend-Lease Act. When the U.S.A. itself was forced in December 1941 to become an active participant in the war the already large work load placed upon the American aircraft industry was increased by many more huge orders for combat aircraft for its own services, and several newly developed types were also earmarked for production. By a coincidence, U.S. and British strategists had each pursued, according to their own convictions, the evolution of specialised warplanes for certain roles which they considered vital. Fortuitously, these types largely complemented rather than overlapped one another when it came to the matter of pooling British and American production resources in a common war effort. Thus, the major U.S. effort was concentrated upon the production of long-range heavy bombers, patrol aircraft and transports. Nevertheless, considerable numbers of medium and light bombers were among the early supplies of Lend-Lease aircraft supplied to Britain and the U.S.S.R. The U.S. industry undertook the mass production of virtually all the transport aircraft required by the Allied powers, and at the outset nearly one-third of the total U.S. productive effort was devoted to the manufacture of transport types. The subsequent intermixture of aircraft between Britain and the U.S.A. resulted in a more comprehensive array of combat types than either country could probably have achieved by itself.

Japan's action in precipitating the U.S. entry into the war proved to be the final undoing of the Axis powers. The aircraft in service with the Japanese Army and Naval Air Forces at this time, like those of the other combatants, were largely those that had begun to enter service in the middle and late 1930s. Japan, too, had tested her military equipment under operational conditions and against a technically inferior adversary during conflicts throughout the 1930s with China and, later, with Siberia. The Japanese entry into the war was heralded by bomber types of the Japanese Naval Air Force, which flew from their parent aircraft carriers to attack the U.S. Fleet in Pearl Harbor early on the morning of 7 December 1941. Japan's subsequent activity during the war can be divided broadly into that on the mainland of south-east Asia, carried out chiefly by the Army Air Force, and that among the numerous island groups in the south-west Pacific, which was largely the responsibility of the Naval Air Force. So long as it retained its aircraft carriers, the Japanese Fleet was a formidable adversary; but, as the war progressed and its carrier fleet was gradually diminished and ultimately demolished, its power in the Pacific was reduced to negligible proportions. The Japanese Army overran the southern mainland of Asia so quickly at the outset of its offensive that its air force became very thinly spread over the vast area which it now had to cover, and eventually home production was unable to keep pace with even the normal combat wastage of aircraft for each service. America's vast output of transport aircraft was of particular value in south-east Asia, although naturally they figured largely in every major campaign of the war. Especially noteworthy was the maintenance of the supply routes across the Himalayas between India and China, without which the Allied forces in that theatre would have been hard pressed to maintain or advance their position. In April 1942 General 'Jimmy' Doolittle's small force of Mitchell bombers, taking off from the aircraft carrier *Hornet* to carry out a bombing attack on Tokyo, made world headlines. This operation was noteworthy for the fact that it took place at all, even though it was more of a morale-booster than an operation of great military value; but two months later, in June 1942, Japan suffered a really serious defeat in the Battle of Midway Island, in the course of which she lost four aircraft carriers and over 250 aircraft. The Battle of Midway was as much a key turning-point of the war in the Pacific as the Battle of Britain had been in the war in Europe.

Within a year of Pearl Harbor the number of aircraft in service with the U.S. forces had trebled, and most of this strength was serving abroad, to such an extent that it became necessary for the USAAF to loan some of its aircraft to the U.S. Navy so that the latter could maintain adequate maritime patrols over American home waters. One of the first steps taken by the USAAF was the establishment of the U.S. Eighth Air Force at bases in the United Kingdom, from where its Fortress and Liberator four-engined bombers could join with the RAF's Stirling, Halifax and Lancaster 'heavies' in carrying out round-the-clock day and night bombing of German targets. In the autumn of 1942 part of the Eighth was detached to form the basis of the U.S. Twelfth Air Force in North Africa. In 1943, after the successful conclusion of the North African campaign. first Sicily and then Italy were invaded. The bombing offensive against Germany continued, now with frequent thousand-bomber raids; and smaller, faster types, such as the Mosquito, were making their presence felt, both in the precision bombing of specialised targets and as pathfinders for the bigger bombers. Mosquitos also performed a considerable amount of photographic reconnaissance work, bringing back valuable intelligence pictures of the damage inflicted by the bombers. By this time, the British Fleet Air Arm was at last beginning to receive more modern monoplane fighters and bombers of British design, to augment the American types received earlier under Lend-Lease arrangements. One effect of the sustained bombing of Germany was the wholesale recall of *Luftwaffe* fighter squadrons from other fronts, from which they could ill be spared, to defend the German homeland; moreover, defensive fighters were now outnumbering bombers in the overall *Luftwaffe* establishment. Nevertheless, by cutting its reserves to negligible proportions, the *Luftwaffe* was still able to claim a first-line strength in mid-1943 of around 4,000 aircraft.

On 8 September 1943 the Italian forces under the command of Marshal Badoglio surrendered to the Allies, and the aircraft based in Italy became divided into two opposing camps. Those in that half of Italy which had still not been reached by the Allied advance were formed into the *Aviazione della Repubblica Sociale Italiana* and continued to fight alongside the *Luftwaffe*, while those in southern Italy became known as the Italian Co-Belligerent Air Force, which continued to fight with mixed Italian, American and British types on behalf of the Allied cause. Towards the end of 1943 the forthcoming invasion of the Continent was fore-shadowed by the setting up in November of the Allied Second Tactical Air Force, and by the increase in ground-attack raids against enemy targets. By the time the invasion came on 6 June 1944, day and night raids upon German-held targets were being made with comparative impunity, and valuable diversionary raids were made to distract enemy defence resources away from the invasion area. The invasion of Normandy itself involved one of the largest single troop movements in history, in which even the prodigious numbers of American transport aircraft were augmented by the use of many older bomber types to act as tugs for the troop-carrying gliders.

The invasion did not bring any decrease in the mass bombing

of German industrial areas, and among the later weapons devised for attacking such specialised targets as railway centres and viaducts was the tremendous 22,000-lb 'Grand Slam' bomb, which could be carried only by specially modified Lancasters. Germany, too, produced some last-minute weapons in the form of the *Vergeltungswaffen* (Reprisal Weapons) V1 and V2. The V1 flying bombs constituted a slight setback for a time in the autumn of 1944, but their measure was soon taken by the RAF's piston-engined Tempest and jet-engined Meteor fighters. Repeated attacks on their factories and launching sites finally disposed of the menace both from the V1 and from the V2 rocket missiles, which were used against Britain for a time during 1944-45. The hard-hit German aviation industry achieved a partial respite by an extensive dispersal of its factories and by setting up new plants underground, almost exclusively by now for the production of defensive fighters; but even these new aircraft were prevented from entering service in appreciable numbers by the continued attentions of Allied bombers to their factories and airfields. Among the types whose careers were thus affected was the Arado Ar 234, the first jet bomber to go into service anywhere in the world. The *Luftwaffe* suffered a final indignity by having its surviving aircraft virtually grounded for lack of fuel during the closing weeks of the European war.

From the end of 1944, once the end of the war in Europe was in sight, South-East Asia Command underwent a considerable expansion preparatory to a final all-out offensive in the Pacific theatre. After the end of the European war some twenty bomber squadrons were nominated as part of a new 'Tiger Force' which was to be dispatched to the Far East to supplement the existing bomber force; but this formation was still working up to operational level when Japan surrendered.

The successful American campaigns to recapture the Philippines and Marianas island groups in 1944 had marked the beginning of the final stage of the Pacific war, for after these actions Japanese sea power in the area was virtually non-effective, and the fanatical suicide attacks engaged in by Japanese Army and Navy pilots in their explosive-laden aircraft provided only a temporary, if serious, setback. The recapture of the Marianas islands of Saipan, Tinian and Guam by the U.S. Naval and Marine forces had at last given the Army Air Force the forward bases that it needed for its new B-29 Superfortress bombers to mount a regular series of attacks against targets within Japan itself, and in November 1944 over 100 Superfortresses raided Tokyo. Apart from the tremendous damage inflicted by such raids, the waters around Japan were heavily laid with mines to cut off external supply routes by sea. The last significant gestures by *Kamikaze* suicide pilots were made at Iwo Jima and Okinawa; and finally, it fell to the Superfortress to become the instrument for delivering the two atomic bombs on Hiroshima and Nagasaki which brought World War 2 to its end in August 1945.

THE COLOUR PLATES

As an aid to identification, the eighty colour plates which follow have been arranged in an essentially visual order, within the broad sequence: biplanes, single-engined monoplanes and multi-engined monoplanes. The sole rocket-powered aircraft appears last of all. The reference number of each type corresponds to the appropriate text matter, and an index to all types illustrated appears on pp. 322-3.

The 'split' plan view, adopted to give both upper and lower surface markings within a single plan outline, depicts the colour scheme appearing above and below either the port half or starboard half of the aircraft, according to whichever aspect is shown in the side elevation. This should be borne in mind when studying, for example, the plan views of U.S. aircraft, on which, normally, the national insignia appear only on the port upper and starboard lower surfaces of the wings.

WALRUS (U.K.)

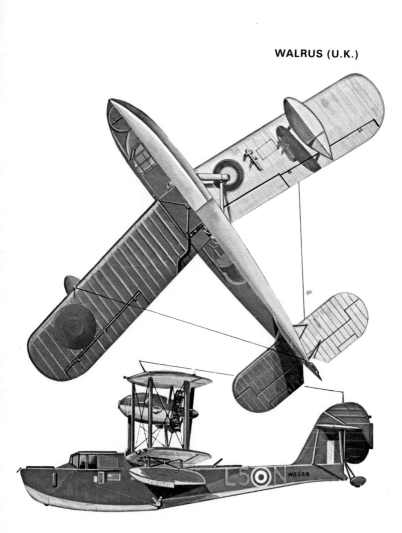

1

Saunders-Roe-built Walrus II of No. 711 Squadron Fleet Air Arm, *ca.* spring 1941. *Engine:* One 775 h.p. Bristol Pegasus VI radial. *Span:* 45 ft. 10 in. (13.97 m.). *Length:* 37 ft. 7 in. (11.46 m.). *Height:* 15 ft. 3 in. (4.65 m.). *Normal take-off weight:* 7,200 lb. (3,266 kg.). *Maximum speed:* 135 m.p.h. (217 km./hr.) at 4,750 ft. (1,448 m.). *Operational ceiling:* 18,500 ft. (5,639 m.). *Range:* 600 miles (966 km.). *Armament:* One 0.303 in. Vickers K gun on Scarff ring in each of bow and mid-upper positions; light load of small bombs or depth charges beneath lower wings.

ALBACORE (U.K.)

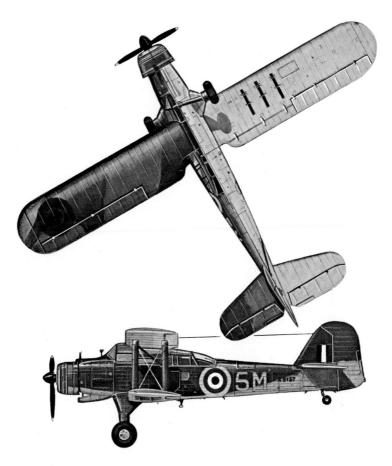

2

Fairey Albacore I of No. 826 Squadron, HMS *Formidable*, spring 1941. *Engine:* One 1,065 h.p. Bristol Taurus II radial. *Span:* 50 ft. 0 in. (15.24 m.). *Length:* 39 ft. 10 in. (12.14 m.). *Height:* 14 ft. 2¼ in. (4.32 m.). *Normal take-off weight:* 10,460 lb. (4,745 kg.). *Maximum speed:* 161 m.p.h. (259 km./hr.) at 4,000 ft. (1,219 m.). *Operational ceiling:* 20,700 ft. (6,310 m.). *Range with torpedo:* 930 miles (1,497 km.). *Armament:* One 0.303 in. machine-gun in starboard wing and two 0.303 in. Vickers K guns in rear cockpit; one 1,610 lb. (730 kg.) torpedo beneath fuselage or up to 2,000 lb. (907 kg.) or bombs beneath lower wings.

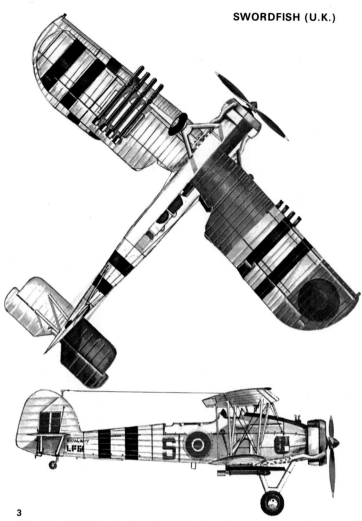

SWORDFISH (U.K.)

3

Fairey Swordfish II (unit unidentified) of the Fleet Air Arm, July 1944. *Engine:* One 690 h.p. Bristol Pegasus IIIM.3 radial. *Span:* 45 ft. 6 in. (13.87 m.). *Length:* 35 ft. 8 in. (10.87 m.). *Height:* 12 ft. 4 in. (3.76 m.). *Maximum take-off weight:* 7,510 lb. (3,406 kg.). *Maximum speed:* 138 m.p.h. (222 km./hr.) at 5,000 ft. (1,524 m.). *Operational ceiling:* 19,250 ft. (5,867 m.). *Typical range:* 546 miles (879 km.). *Armament:* One 0.303 in. Vickers machine-gun in upper engine cowling and one 0.303 in. Lewis or Vickers K gun in rear cockpit; eight 60 lb. (27 kg.). rocket projectiles beneath lower wings.

NORSEMAN (Canada)

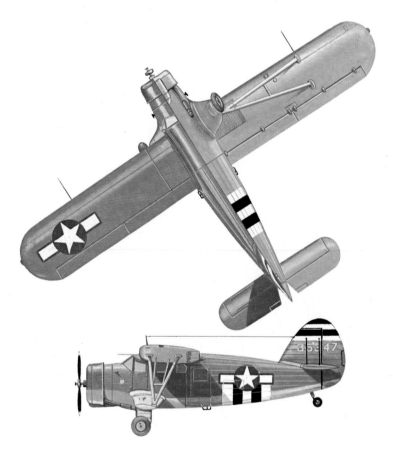

4
Noorduyn UC-64A Norseman of the USAAF, summer 1944. *Engine:* One 600 h.p. Pratt & Whitney R-1340-AN-1 Wasp radial. *Span:* 51 ft. 8 in. (15.75 m.). *Length:* 31 ft. 9 in. (9.68 m.). *Height:* 10 ft. 1 in. (3.07 m.). *Maximum take-off weight:* 7,400 lb. (3,357 kg.). *Maximum speed:* 165 m.p.h. (266 km./hr.) at 5,000 ft. (1,524 m.). *Operational ceiling:* 17,000 ft. (5,182 m.). *Typical range:* 600 miles (966 km.). *Armament:* None.

LYSANDER (U.K.)

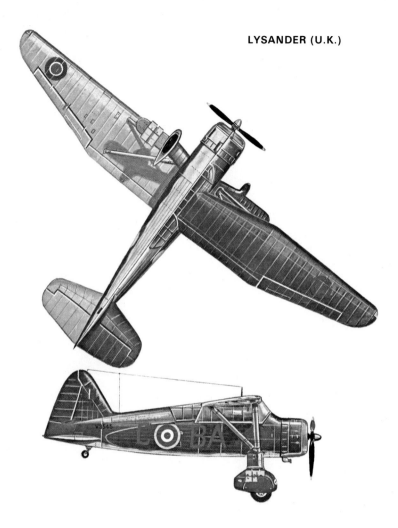

5

Westland Lysander ASR IIIA of No. 277 Squadron RAF, southern England, summer 1942. *Engine:* One 870 h.p. Bristol Mercury 30 radial. *Span:* 50 ft. 0 in. (15.24 m.). *Length:* 30 ft. 6 in. (9.30 m.). *Height:* 14 ft. 6 in. (4.42 m.). *Maximum take-off weight:* 6,318 lb. (2,866 kg.). *Maximum speed:* 212 m.p.h. (341 km./hr.) at 5,000 ft. (1,524 m.). *Operational ceiling:* 21,500 ft. (6,553 m.). *Typical range:* 500 miles (805 km.). *Armament:* One 0.303 in. Browning machine-gun in each wheel fairing; two more on movable mounting in rear of cabin.

FIESELER Fi 156 (Germany)

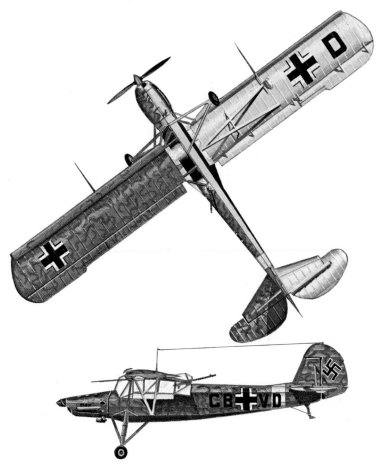

6

Fieseler Fi 156C-2 *Storch*, North Africa, *ca.* spring 1941. *Engine:* One 240 h.p.
Argus As 10C inverted-Vee type. *Span:* 46 ft. 9 in. (14.25 m.). *Length:* 32 ft.
5¾ in. (9.90 m.). *Height:* 10 ft. 0 in. (3.05 m.). *Normal take-off weight:* 2,923 lb.
(1,326 kg.). *Maximum speed:* 109 m.p.h. (175 km./hr.) at sea level. *Operational
ceiling:* 16,700 ft. (5,090 m.). *Maximum range with standard fuel:* 239 miles
(385 km.). *Armament:* One 7.9 mm. MG 15 machine-gun in rear of cabin.

BERIEV MBR-2 (U.S.S.R.)

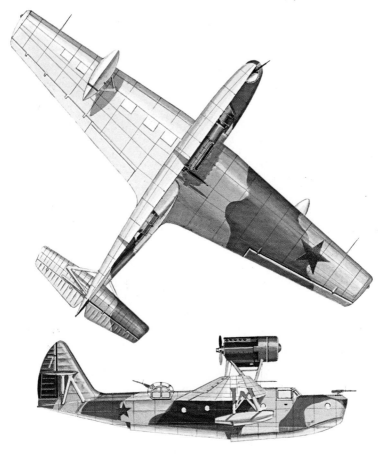

7

Beriev MBR-2 of the VVS-VMF (Soviet Naval Aviation), unit and date not determined. *Engine:* One 750 h.p. Mikulin AM-34N Vee type. *Span:* 62 ft. 4 in. (19.00 m.). *Length:* 44 ft. 3½ in. (13.50 m.). *Height:* approximately 14 ft. 9 in. (4.40 m.). *Maximum take-off weight:* 9,359 lb. (4,245 kg.). *Maximum speed:* 171 m.p.h. (275 km./hr.) at 6,560 ft. (2,000 m.). *Operatioñal ceiling:* 16,080 ft. (4,900 m.). *Maximum range:* 932 miles (1,500 km.). *Armament:* One 7.62 mm. PV-1 machine-gun in open bow position and one 7.62 mm. ShKAS machine-gun in dorsal turret; up to 661 lb. (300 kg.) of bombs, mines or depth charges beneath the wings.

AICHI D3A (Japan)

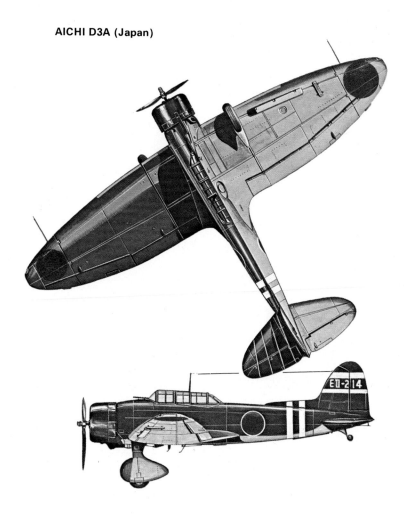

8

Aichi D3A1 Model 11 from the aircraft carrier *Zuikaku,* southern Pacific 1941–42. *Engine:* One 1,075 h.p. Mitsubishi Kinsei 44 radial. *Span:* 47 ft. 1½ in. (14.365 m.). *Length:* 33 ft. 5⅜ in. (10,195 m.). *Height:* 10 ft. 11⅞ in. (3.35 m.). *Normal take-off weight:* 8,047 lb. (3,650 kg.). *Maximum speed:* 242 m.p.h. (389 km./hr.) at 7,612 ft. (2,320 m.). *Operational ceiling:* 31,170 ft (9,500 m.). *Normal range:* 1,131 miles (1,820 km.). *Armament:* One 7.7 mm. machine-gun in each wing and one in rear cockpit; one 551 lb. (250 kg.) and two 130 lb. (60 kg.) bombs.

ARADO Ar 196 (Germany)

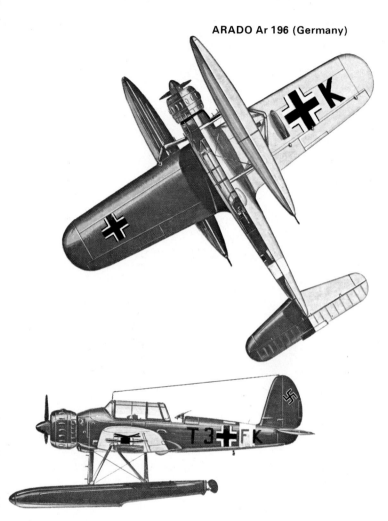

9

Arado Ar 196A-3 of 2/*Bordfl. Gruppe* 196, southern Italy, 1942. *Engine:* One 960 h.p. BMW 132K radial. *Span:* 40 ft. $8\frac{1}{8}$ in. (12.40 m.). *Length:* 36 ft. $1\frac{1}{8}$ in. (11.00 m.). *Height:* 14 ft. $4\frac{5}{8}$ in. (4.40 m.). *Normal take-off weight:* 8,223 lb. (3,730 kg.). *Maximum speed:* 193 m.p.h. (310 km./hr.) at 13,120 ft. (4,000 m.). *Operational ceiling:* 23,000 ft. (7,020 m.). *Range:* 665 miles (1,070 km.). *Armament:* One 20 mm. MG FF cannon in each wing, two 7.9 mm. MG 17 machine-guns in rear cockpit and one in front fuselage; one 110 lb. (50 kg.) bomb beneath each wing.

NAKAJIMA B5N (Japan)

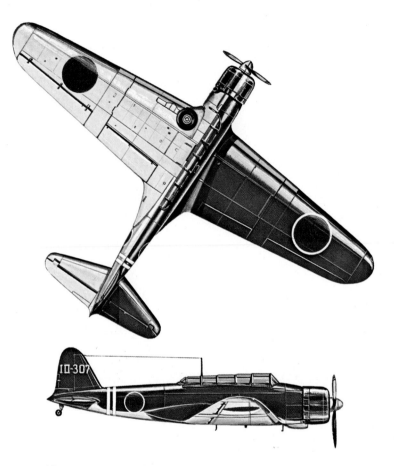

10

Nakajima B5N2 operating from the carrier *Zuikaku* during the Battle of the Coral Sea, May 1942. *Engine:* One 970 h.p. Nakajima Sakae 11 radial. *Span:* 50 ft. 11 in. (15.52 m.). *Length:* 33 ft. 9½ in. (10.30 m.). *Height:* 12 ft. 1⅝ in. (3.70 m.). *Maximum take-off weight:* 9,039 lb. (4,100 kg.). *Maximum speed:* 235 m.p.h. (378 km./hr.) at 11,810 ft. (3,600 m.). *Operational ceiling:* 27,100 ft. (8,260 m.). *Maximum range:* 1,075 miles (1,730 km.). *Armament:* Two 7.7 mm. machine-guns in upper engine cowling and one or two in rear cockpit; one 1,764 lb. (800 kg.) torpedo, or three 551 lb. (250 kg.) or 132 lb. (60 kg.) bombs, beneath the fuselage.

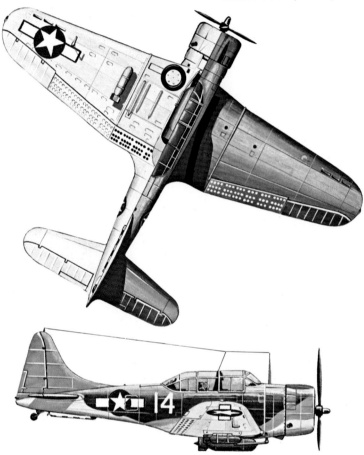

11

Douglas SBD-5 Dauntless of Squadron VB-5, USS *Yorktown,* August/
September 1943. *Engine:* One 1,200 h.p. Wright R-1820-60 Cyclone radial.
Span: 41 ft. 6 in. (12.65 m.). *Length:* 33 ft. 0 in. (10.06 m.). *Height:* 12 ft. 11 in.
(3.94 m.). *Maximum take-off weight:* 10,700 lb. (4,853 kg.). *Maximum speed:*
252 m.p.h. (406 km./hr.) at 13,800 ft. (4,200 m.). *Operational ceiling:* 24,300 ft.
(7,400 m.). *Range with 1,000 lb.* (*454 kg.) bomb load:* 1,115 miles (1,794 km.).
Armament: Two 0.50 in. machine-guns in front of fuselage, and two 0.30 in.
guns in rear cockpit; one 1,000 lb. (454 kg.) or 500 lb. (227 kg.) bomb beneath
fuselage, or two 100 lb. (45 kg.) bombs or two 250 lb. (113 kg.) depth charges
beneath the wings.

YOKOSUKA D4Y (Japan)

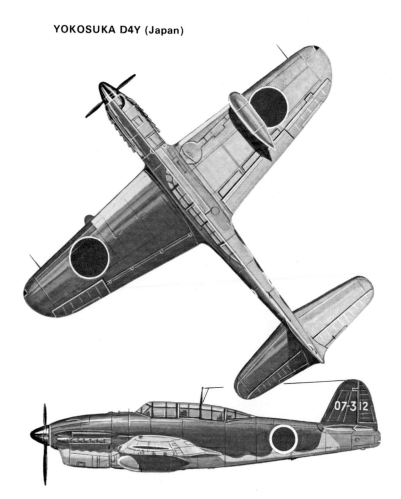

12

Yokosuka D4Y2 Model 12 *Suisei* of No. 107 Attack Squadron, No. 503 Air Corps, JNAF, 1944. *Engine:* One 1,400 h.p. Aichi Atsuta 32 inverted-Vee type. *Span:* 37 ft. $8\frac{1}{2}$ in. (11.49 m.). *Length:* 33 ft. $6\frac{3}{8}$ in. (10.22 m.). *Height:* 12 ft. $3\frac{1}{4}$ in. (3.74 m.). *Maximum take-off weight:* 9,597 lb. (4,353 kg.). *Maximum speed:* 366 m.p.h. (589 km./hr.) at 17,225 ft. (5,250 m.). *Operational ceiling:* 35,170 ft. (10,720 m.). *Normal range:* 749 miles (1,205 km.). *Armament:* Two 7.7 mm. machine-guns in upper engine cowling and one in rear cockpit; one 551 lb. (250 kg.) bomb internally and one 66 lb. (30 kg.) bomb beneath each wing.

AVENGER (U.S.A.)

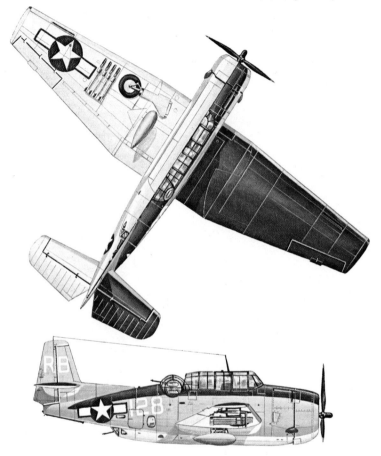

13
Eastern-built TBM-3 Avenger of Air Group 38, US Navy, August 1945. *Engine:* One 1,900 h.p. Wright R-2600-20 Cyclone radial. *Span:* 54 ft. 2 in. (16.51 m.). *Length:* 40 ft. 0⅛ in. (12.19 m.). *Height:* 16 ft. 5 in. (5.00 m.). *Maximum take-off weight:* 18,250 lb. (8,278 kg.). *Maximum speed:* 267 m.p.h. (430 km./hr.) at 15,000 ft. (4,572 m.). *Operational ceiling:* 23,400 ft. (7,132 m.). *Maximum range:* 2,530 miles (4,072 km.). *Armament:* One 0.50 in. machine-gun in each wing and one in dorsal turret; one 0.30 in. machine-gun in upper engine cowling and one in ventral position; one 22-in. torpedo or one 2,000 lb. (907 kg.) bomb internally. Provision for rocket projectiles beneath each wing.

SUKHOI Su-2 (U.S.S.R.)

14

Sukhoi Su-2 of an unidentified operational training unit of the Soviet Air Force, 1943. *Engine:* One 1,000 h.p. M-88B radial. *Span:* 46 ft. 11 in. (14.30 m.). *Length:* 33 ft. 7½ in. (10.25 m.). *Height:* approx. 12 ft. 3¾ in. (3.75 m.). *Maximum take-off weight:* 9,645 lb. (4,375 kg.). *Maximum speed:* 283 m.p.h. (455 km./hr.) at 14,435 ft. (4,400 m.). *Operational ceiling:* 28,870 ft. (8,800 m.). *Range with 882 lb. (400 kg.) bomb load:* 746 miles (1,200 km.). *Armament:* Four 7.62 mm. ShKAS machine-guns in wings and one in dorsal turret; up to 1,323 lb. (600 kg.) of bombs.

HELLDIVER (U.S.A.)

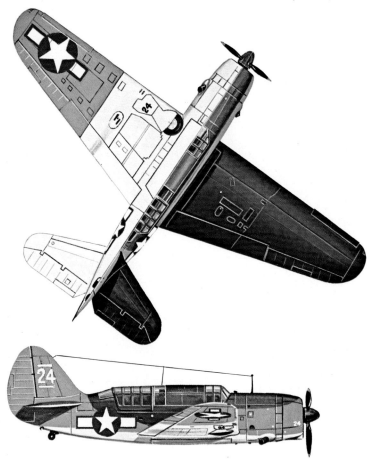

15

Curtiss SB2C-1C of Squadron VB-8, USS *Bunker Hill*, June 1944. *Engine:* One 1,700 h.p. Wright R-2600-8 Cyclone radial. *Span:* 49 ft. 8⅝ in. (15.15 m.). *Length:* 36 ft. 8 in. (11.18 m.). *Height:* 14 ft. 9 in. (4.50 m.). *Normal take-off weight:* 14,760 lb. (6,695 kg.). *Maximum speed:* 281 m.p.h. (452 km./hr.) at 12,400 ft. (3,780 m.). *Operational ceiling:* 24,700 ft. (7,529 m.). *Maximum range:* 1,895 miles (3,050 km.). *Armament:* One 20 mm. cannon in each wing and two 0.30 in. machine-guns in rear of cabin; one 1,000 lb. (454 kg.) bomb internally.

NAKAJÍMA B6N (Japan)

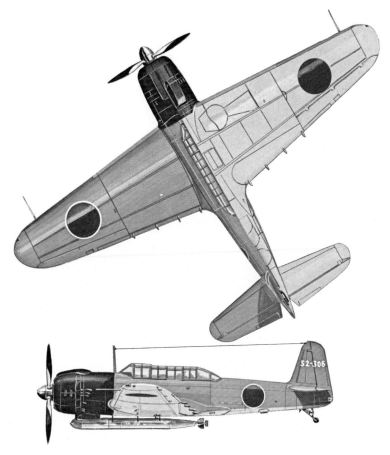

16

Nakajima B6N2 *Tenzan* of the 752nd Air Corps, JNAF, June 1944. *Engine:* One 1,850 h.p. Mitsubishi Kasei 25 radial. *Span:* 48 ft. 10⅝ in. (14.90 m.). *Length:* 35 ft. 7½ in. (10.86 m.). *Height:* 12 ft. 5⅜ in. (3.80 m.). *Maximum take-off weight:* 12,456 lb. (5,650 kg.). *Maximum speed:* 299 m.p.h. (482 km./hr.) at 16,080 ft. (4,900 m.). *Operational ceiling:* 29,660 ft. (9,040 m.). *Maximum range:* 1,644 miles (2,646 km.). *Armament:* One 7.7 mm. machine-gun in port wing, one in rear cockpit and one in ventral position; one 1,764 lb. (800 kg.) torpedo or six 220 lb. (100 kg.) bombs beneath the fuselage.

BARRACUDA (U.K.)

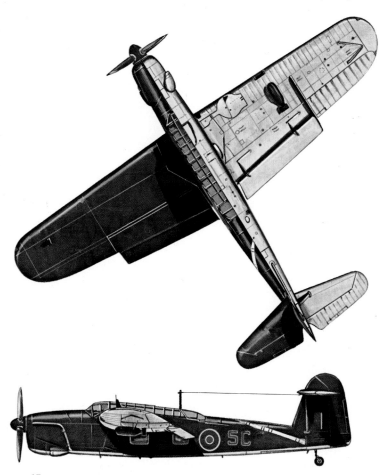

17

Fairey Barracuda II of No. 829 Squadron, HMS *Victorious* during attack on the *Tirpitz*, July 1944. *Engine:* One 1,600 h.p. Rolls-Royce Merlin 32 Vee type. *Span:* 49 ft. 2 in. (14.99 m.). *Length:* 39 ft. 9 in. (12.12 m.). *Height:* 15 ft. 1 in. (4.60 m.). *Maximum take-off weight:* 14,100 lb. (6,395 kg.). *Maximum speed:* 228 m.p.h. (367 km/hr.) at 1,750 ft. (533 m.). *Operational ceiling:* 16,600 ft. (5,060 m.). *Range with torpedo:* 686 miles (1,104 km.). *Armament:* Two 0.303 in. Vickers K guns in rear of cabin; one 1,620 lb. (735 kg.) torpedo or one 1,000 lb. (454 kg.) bomb beneath fuselage, or four 450 lb. (204 kg.) depth charges or six 250 lb. (113 kg.) bombs beneath the wings.

BATTLE (U.K.)

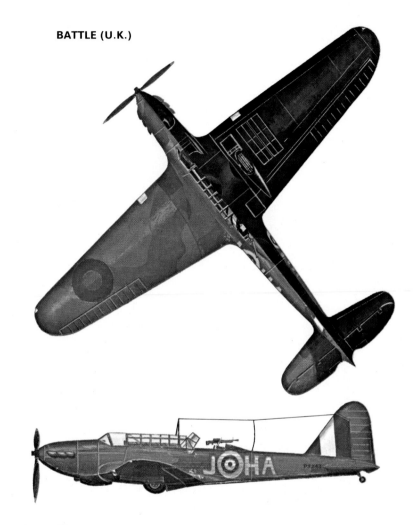

18

Fairey Battle II of No. 218 Squadron, after its re-formation in the UK ,in June 1940. *Engine:* One 1,030 h.p. Rolls-Royce Merlin II Vee type. *Span:* 54 ft. 0 in. (16.46 m.). *Length:* 42 ft. 1¾ in. (12.85 m.). *Height:* 15 ft. 6 in. (4.72 m.). *Normal take-off weight:* 10,792 lb. (4,895 kg.). *Maximum speed:* 257 m.p.h. (414 km./hr.) at 15,000 ft. (4,572 m.). *Operational ceiling:* 25,000 ft. (7,620 m.). *Maximum range:* 1,000 miles (1,609 km.). *Armament:* One 0.303 in. Browning machine-gun in starboard wing and one 0.303 in. Vickers K gun in rear of cabin; normal warload of four 250 lb. (113 kg.) bombs within the wings.

JUNKERS Ju 87 (Germany)

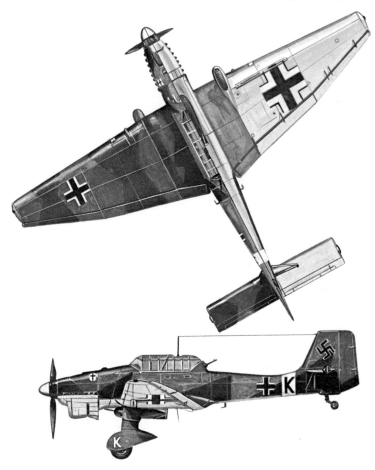

19

Junkers Ju 87B-1 of *Geschwader Stab/St. G. 2* "Immelmann", France, *ca.*
summer 1940. *Engine:* One 900 h.p. Junkers Jumo 211A-1 inverted-Vee type.
Span: 45 ft. 3¼ in. (13.80 m.). *Length:* 36 ft. 5 in. (11.10 m.). *Height:* 12 ft. 8½ in.
(3.87 m.). *Normal take-off weight:* 9,370 lb. (4,250 kg.). *Maximum speed:*
242 m.p.h. (390 km./hr.) at 13,410 ft. (4,400 m.). *Operational ceiling:* 26,250 ft.
(8,000 m.). *Range with 1,102 lb (500 kg.) bomb load:* 342 miles (550 km.).
Armament: One 7.9 mm. MG 17 machine-gun in each wing and one 7.9 mm.
MG 15 gun in rear of cabin; one 1,102 lb. (500 kg.) or 551 lb. (250 kg.) bomb
beneath fuselage and up to four 110 lb. (50 kg.) bombs beneath the wings.

NAKAJIMA C6N (Japan)

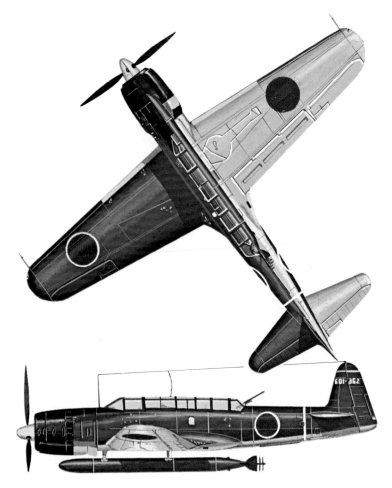

20

Nakajima C6N1-1B Model 21 *Saiun* from the carrier *Zuikaku*, 1944. *Engine:*
One 1,990 h.p. Nakajima Homare 21 radial. *Span:* 41 ft. $0\frac{1}{8}$ in. (12.50 m.).
Length: 36 ft. $5\frac{3}{4}$ in. (11.12 m.). *Height:* 12 ft. $11\frac{7}{8}$ in. (3.96 m.). *Maximum
take-off weight:* 11,596 lb. (5,260 kg.). *Maximum speed:* 395 m.p.h. (635 km./
hr.) at 19,685 ft. (6,000 m.). *Operational ceiling:* 37,070 ft. (11,300 m.).
Maximum range: 2,855 miles (4,595 km.). *Armament:* One 7.92 mm. machine-
gun in rear of cabin.

HEINKEL He 115 (Germany)

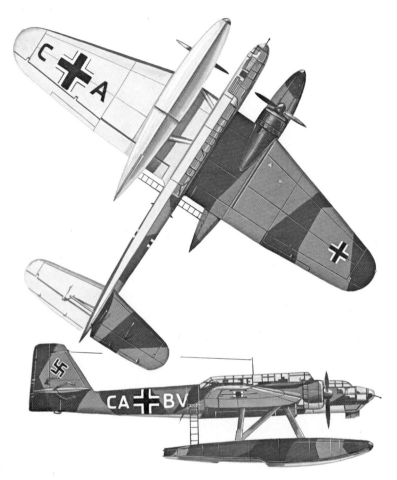

21

Heinkel He 115B-1, ex works with factory flight test codes, 1939-40. *Engines:*
Two 970 h.p. BMW 132K radials. *Span:* 73 ft. 1 in. (22.28 m.). *Length:* 56 ft.
9 in. (17.30 m.). *Height:* 21 ft. 7¾ in. (6.60 m.). *Maximum take-off weight:*
22,928 lb. (10,400 kg.). *Maximum speed:* 203 m.p.h. (327 km./hr.) at 11,155 ft.
(3,400 m.). *Operational ceiling:* 17,060 ft. (5,200 m.). *Maximum range:* 2,082
miles (3,350 km.). *Armament:* Single 7.9 mm. MG 15 machine-guns in nose
and dorsal positions; five 551 lb. (250 kg.) bombs, or two such bombs and one
1,764 lb. (800 kg.) torpedo or one 2,028 lb. (920 kg.) sea mine.

WELLINGTON (U.K.)

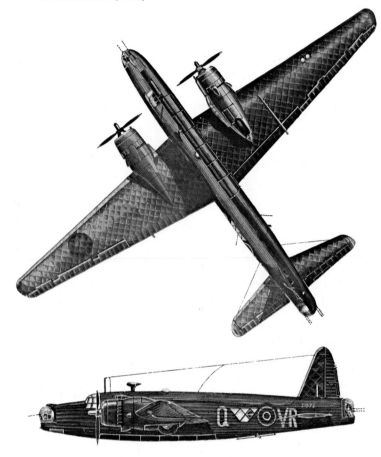

22

Vickers Wellington III of No. 419 Squadron RCAF, 1941-42. *Engines:* Two 1,500 h.p. Bristol Hercules XI radials. *Span:* 86 ft. 2 in. (26.26 m.). *Length:* 64 ft. 7 in. (19.68 m.). *Height:* 17 ft. 6 in. (5.33 m.). *Maximum take-off weight:* 29,500 lb. (13,381 kg.). *Maximum speed:* 255 m.p.h. (410 km./hr.) at 12,500 ft. (3,810 m.). *Operational ceiling:* 19,000 ft. (5,791 m.). *Range with 1,500 lb. (680 kg.) bomb load:* 2,200 miles (3,541 km.). *Armament:* Two 0.303 in. machine-guns in nose turret, four in tail turret and two in beam positions; up to 4,500 lb. (2,041 kg.) of bombs internally.

HEINKEL He 111 (Germany)

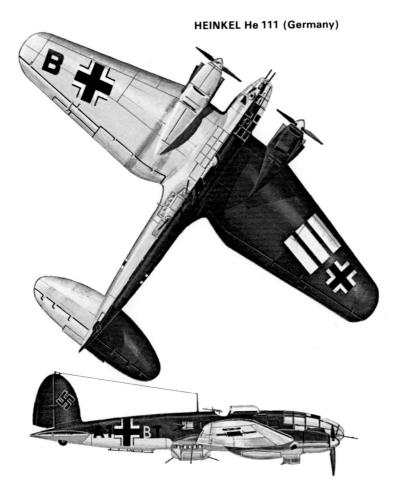

23

Heinkel He 111H-3 of III/KG.53 during the Battle of Britain, summer 1940.
Engines: Two 1,200 h.p. Junkers Jumo 211D-1 inverted-Vee type. *Span:* 74 ft.
1¾ in. (22.60 m.). *Length:* 53 ft. 9⅜ in. (16.40 m.). *Height:* 13 ft. 1½ in. (4.00 m.).
Normal take-off weight: 24,912 lb. (11,300 kg.). *Maximum speed:* 258 m.p.h.
(415 km./hr.) at 16,400 ft. (5,000 m.). *Operational ceiling:* 25,590 ft. (7,800 m.).
Range with maximum bomb load: 758 miles (1,220 km.). *Armament:* One 20
mm. MG FF cannon in ventral gondola, and five 7.9 mm. MG 15 machine-guns
in nose, dorsal, ventral and beam positions; up to 4,409 lb. (2,000 kg.) of bombs
internally.

ANSON (U.K.)

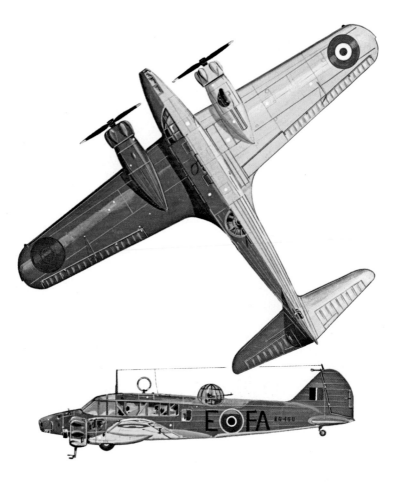

24

Avro Anson ASR I of No. 281 Squadron RAF, late 1943. *Engines:* Two 350 h.p. Armstrong Siddeley Cheetah IX radials. *Span:* 56 ft. 6 in. (17.22 m.). *Length:* 42 ft. 3 in. (12.88 m.). *Height:* 13 ft. 1 in. (3.99 m.). *Maximum take-off weight:* 8,000 lb. (3,629 kg.). *Maximum speed:* 188 m.p.h. (303 km./hr.) at 7,000 ft. (2,134 m.). *Operational ceiling:* 19,000 ft. (5,791 m.). *Range:* 790 miles (1,271 km.). *Armament:* One 0.303 in. machine-gun on port side of front fuselage and one in dorsal turret.

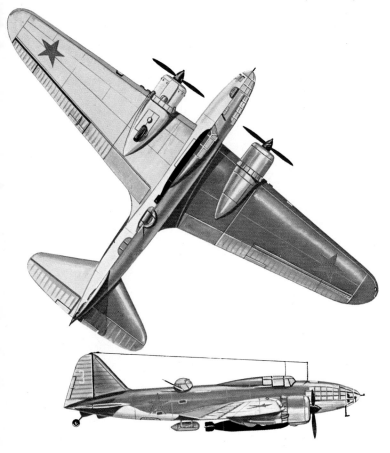

25

Ilyushin II-4 (DB-3F) of the VVS-VMF (Soviet Naval Aviation), Baltic Sea area, *ca.* 1941-42. *Engines:* Two 1,100 h.p. M-88B radials. *Span:* 70 ft. 4$\frac{1}{8}$ in. (21.44 m.). *Length:* 48 ft. 6$\frac{5}{8}$ in. (14.80 m.). *Height:* approximately 13 ft. 9 in. (4.20 m.). *Maximum take-off weight:* 22,046 lb. (10,000 kg.). *Maximum speed:* 255 m.p.h. (410 km./hr.) at 21,000 ft. (6,400 m.). *Operational ceiling:* 29,530 ft. (9,000 m.). *Maximum range with 2,205 lb.* (*1,000 kg.*) *bomb load:* 2,647 miles (4,260 km.). *Armament:* Three 7.62 mm. ShKAS or 12.7 mm. BS machine-guns, one each in nose, dorsal and ventral positions; 2,205 lb. (1,000 kg.) of bombs internally, plus one 2,072 lb. (940 kg.) 45-36-AN or -AV torpedo or up to 3,307 lb. (1,500 kg.) of bombs beneath the fuselage.

MARTIN 167 (U.S.A.)

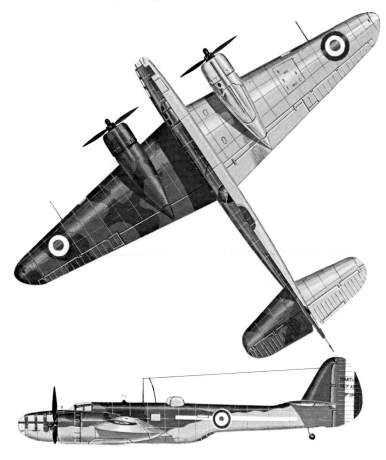

26

Martin 167A-3 (Model 167F) of the *Armée de l'Air* (unit unknown), France, *ca.*
March/April 1940. *Engines:* Two 1,050 h.p. Pratt & Whitney R-1830-S1C3-G
Twin Wasp radials. *Span:* 61 ft. 4 in. (18.69 m.). *Length:* 46 ft. 8 in. (14.22 m.).
Height: 10 ft. 1 in. (3.07 m.). *Normal take-off weight:* 15,297 lb. (6,939 kg.).
Maximum speed: 304 m.p.h. (489 km./hr.) at 14,000 ft. (4,267 m.). *Operational
ceiling:* 29,500 ft. (8,992 m.). *Maximum range:* 1,300 miles (2,092 km.).
Armament: Two 0.30 in. machine-guns in each wing and one each in dorsal
and ventral positions; up to 1,250 lb. (567 kg.) of bombs internally.

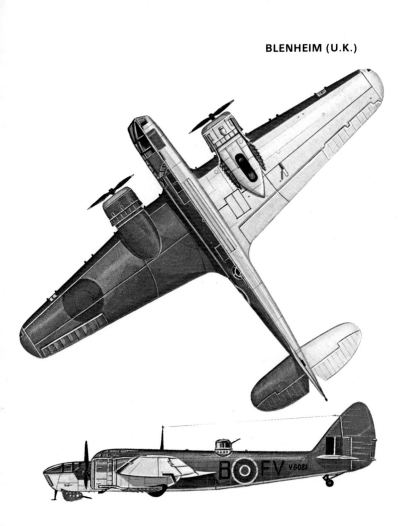

27

Rootes-built Blenheim IVL of No. 13 OTU, RAF, fitted with leading-edge balloon-cable cutters, *ca.* August 1942. *Engines:* Two 920 h.p. Bristol Mercury XV radials. *Span:* 56 ft. 4 in. (17.17 m.). *Length:* 42 ft. 9 in. (13.04 m.). *Height:* 12 ft. 10 in. (3.91 m.). *Maximum take-off weight:* 14,400 lb. (6,531 kg.). *Maximum speed:* 266 m.p.h. (428 km./hr.) at 11,800 ft. (3,597 m.). *Operational ceiling:* 27,000 ft. (8,230 m.). *Maximum range:* 1,950 miles (3,138 km.). *Armament:* One 0.303 in. Vickers K gun in nose, two 0.303 in. Browning machine-guns in dorsal turret and two in fairing beneath nose; up to 1,000 lb. (454 kg.) of bombs internally.

BEAUFIGHTER (U.K.)

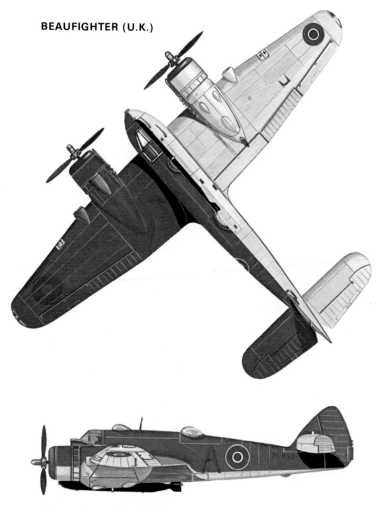

28

Bristol Beaufighter TF VIC of Coastal Command Development Unit, RAF *ca.* March/April 1943. *Engines:* Two 1,670 h.p. Bristol Hercules VI or XVI radials. *Span:* 57 ft. 10 in. (17.63 m.). *Length:* 41 ft. 4 in. (12.60 m.). *Height:* 15 ft. 10 in. (4.83 m.). *Maximum take-off weight:* 23,884 lb. (10,834 kg.). *Maximum speed:* 312 m.p.h. (502 km./hr.) at 14,000 ft. (4,267 m.). *Operational ceiling:* 26,000 ft. (7,925 m.). *Normal range:* 1,540 miles (2,478 km.). *Armament:* Four 20 mm. Hispano cannon in nose, three 0.303 in. Browning machine-guns in each wing, and one 0.303 in. Vickers K gun in dorsal position; one 1,605 lb. (728 kg.). torpedo beneath fuselage.

BEAUFORT (U.K.)

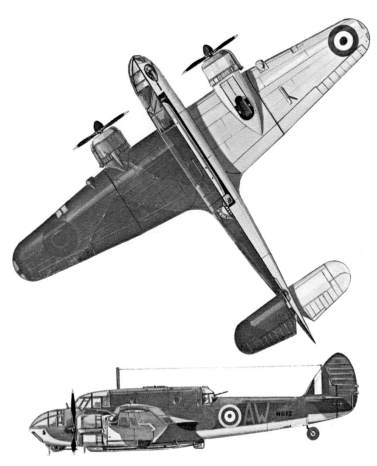

29

Bristol Beaufort I of No. 42 Squadron RAF, March 1941. *Engines:* Two 1,130 h.p. Bristol Taurus VI radials. *Span:* 57 ft. 10 in. (17.63 m.). *Length:* 44 ft. 2 in. (13.46 m.). *Height:* 14 ft. 3 in. (4.34 m.). *Maximum take-off weight:* 21,228 lb. (9,628 kg.). *Maximum speed (with torpedo):* 225 m.p.h. (362 km./hr.) at 5,000 ft. (1,524 m.). *Operational ceiling:* 16,500 ft. (5,029 m.). *Maximum range:* 1,600 miles (2,575 km.). *Armament:* Two 0.303 in. Vickers K guns in dorsal turret and one in port wing, plus one 0.303 in. rear-firing Browning machine-gun beneath nose; up to 1,000 lb. (454 kg.) of bombs internally and 500 lb. (227 kg.) externally, or one 1,605 lb. (728 kg.) torpedo semi-internally.

MOSQUITO (U.K.)

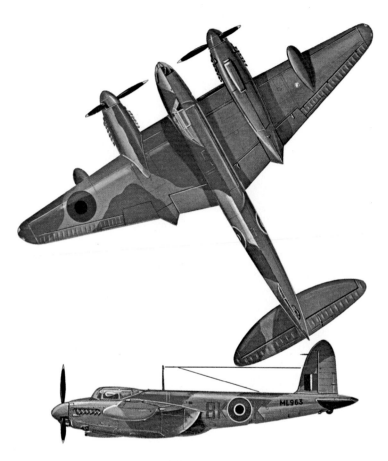

30

De Havilland Mosquito B XVI of No. 571 (Pathfinder) Squadron RAF, spring 1944. *Engines:* Two 1,680 h.p. Rolls-Royce Merlin 72 or 76 Vee type. *Span:* 54 ft. 2 in. (16.51 m.). *Length:* 40 ft. 6 in. (12.34 m.). *Height:* 15 ft. 3½ in. (4.66 m.). *Normal take-off weight:* 19,093 lb. (8,660 kg.). *Maximum speed:* 408 m.p.h. (656 km./hr.) at 26,000 ft. (7,925 m.). *Operational ceiling:* 37,000 ft. (11,278 m.). *Range with maximum bomb load:* 1,370 miles (2,205 km.). *Armament:* No guns; maximum bomb load of 4,000 lb. (1,814 kg.).

JUNKERS Ju 88 (Germany)

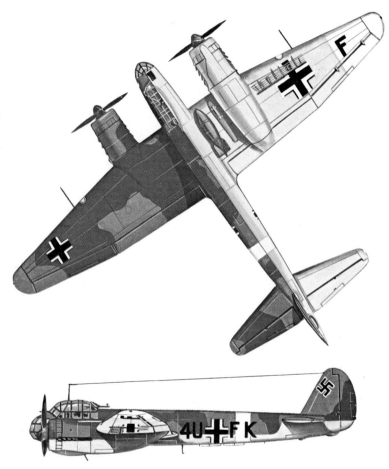

31

Junkers Ju 88A-4/Trop. of 2(F)/123, Western Desert, summer 1942. *Engines:* Two 1,340 h.p. Junkers Jumo 211J inverted-Vee type. *Span:* 65 ft. 7⅜ in. (20.00 m.). *Length:* 47 ft. 2⅞ in. (14.40 m.). *Height:* 15 ft. 11 in. (4.85 m.). *Maximum take-off weight:* 30,865 lb. (14,000 kg.). *Maximum speed:* 269 m.p.h. (433 km./hr.) at 14,765 ft. (4,500 m.). *Operational ceiling:* 26,900 ft. (8,200 m.). *Normal range:* 1,112 miles (1,790 km.). *Typical armament:* Nine 7.9 mm. MG 81 machine-guns, two in extreme nose, one in front of pilot, two in rear of cabin, and two forward and two aft in under-nose cupola; 1,102 lb. (500 kg.) of bombs internally and up to 2,205 lb. (1,000 kg.) externally.

BOSTON (U.S.A.)

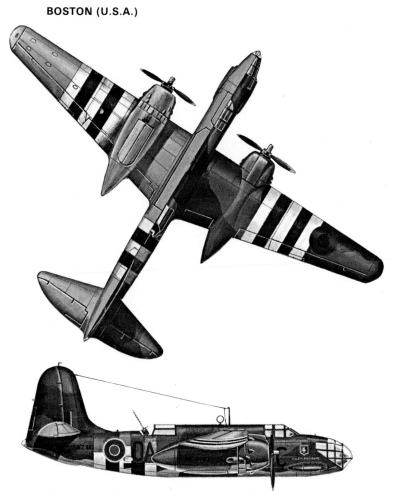

32

Douglas Boston IIIA of No. 342 (Lorraine) Squadron FAFL, summer 1944.
Engines: Two 1,600 h.p. Wright R-2600-23 Cyclone radials. *Span:* 61 ft. 4 in.
(18.69 m.). *Length:* 47 ft. 3 in. (14.40 m.). *Height:* 17 ft. 7 in. (5.36 m.).
Maximum take-off weight: 24,500 lb. (11,113 kg.). *Maximum speed:* 342 m.p.h.
(550 km./hr.) at 13,000 ft. (3,962 m.). *Operational ceiling:* 24,250 ft. (7,391 m.).
Range with maximum bomb load: 1,050 miles (1,690 km.). *Armament:* Two
0.303 in. Browning machine-guns on each side of nose, and two in dorsal
position, plus one 0.303 in. Vickers K gun in ventral position; up to 2,000 lb.
(907 kg.) of bombs internally.

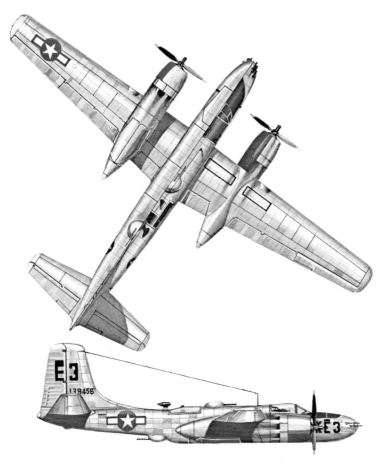

33

Douglas A-26B Invader of the US Ninth Air Force, ETO 1944-45. *Engines:* Two 2,000 h.p. Pratt & Whitney R-2800-27 or -71 Double Wasp radials. *Span:* 70 ft. 0 in. (21.34 m.). *Length:* 50 ft. 0 in. (15.24 m.). *Height:* 18 ft. 6 in. (5.64 m.). *Maximum take-off weight:* 35,000 lb. (15,876 kg.). *Maximum speed:* 355 m.p.h. (571 km./hr.) at 15,000 ft. (4,572 m.). *Operational ceiling:* 22,100 ft. (6,736 m.). *Range with maximum bomb load:* 1,400 miles (2,253 km.). *Armament:* Ten 0.50 in. machine-guns, six in nose and two each in dorsal and ventral turrets; up to 4,000 lb. (1,814 kg.) of bombs internally.

BALTIMORE (U.S.A.)

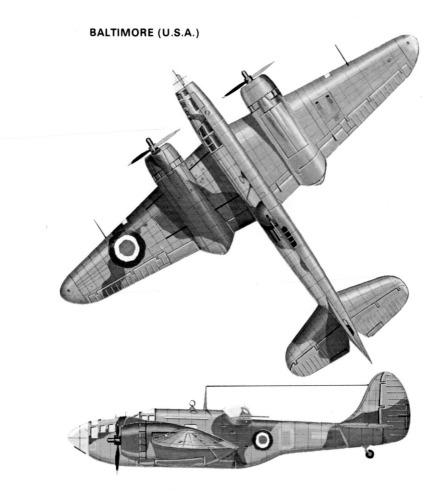

34

Martin Baltimore IV, ex-RAF machine seconded to the *Stormo Baltimore* of the Italian Co-Belligerent Air Force, *ca.* November 1944. *Engines:* Two 1.660 h.p. Wright R-2600-19 Double-Row Cyclone radials. *Span:* 61 ft. 4 in. (18.69 m.). *Length:* 48 ft. 6 in. (14.78 m.). *Height:* 17 ft. 9 in. (5.41 m.). *Maximum take-off weight:* 23,000 lb. (10,433 kg.). *Maximum speed:* 302 m.p.h. (486 km./hr.) at 11,000 ft. (3,353 m.). *Operational ceiling:* 24,000 ft. (7,315 m.). *Range with 1,000 lb.* (*454 kg.*) *bomb load:* 1,082 miles (1,741 km.). *Armament:* Two 0.50 in. machine-guns in dorsal turret, two 0.303 in. machine-guns in each wing and up to six 0.30 in. machine-guns in ventral positions; up to 2,000 lb. (907 kg.) of bombs internally.

MARAUDER (U.S.A.)

35

Martin B-26B-55 Marauder of the 598th Bomber Squadron, 397th Bomber Group, US Ninth Air Force, June 1944. Engines: Two 1,920 h.p. Pratt & Whitney R-2800-43 Double Wasp radials. *Span:* 71 ft. 0 in. (21.64 m.). *Length:* 58 ft. 3 in. (17.75 m.). *Height:* 21 ft. 6 in. (6.55 m.). *Maximum take-off weight:* 37,000 lb. (16,783 kg.). *Maximum speed:* 282 m.p.h. (454 km./hr.) at 15,000 ft. (4,572 m.). *Operational ceiling:* 21,700 ft. (6,614 m.). *Range with 3,000 lb. (1,361 kg.) bomb load:* 1,150 miles (1,851 km.). *Armament:* Eleven 0.50 in. machine-guns, in dorsal and tail turrets (two each), beam positions (one each), nose (one) and external nose blisters (two each side), plus one 0.30 in. gun in extreme nose; up to 5,200 lb. (2,359 kg.) of bombs.

211

PZL P.37 (Poland)

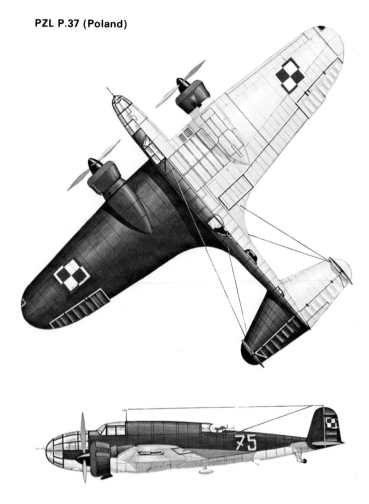

36

PZL P.37 Łoś B, possibly an aircraft of *Dyon* X/I, 1st Air Regiment, Warsaw 1939.
Engines: Two 918 h.p. PZL-built Bristol Pegasus XX radials. *Span:* 58 ft. 8¾ in.
(17.90 m.). *Length:* 42 ft. 3⅞ in. (12.90 m.). *Height:* 16 ft. 8 in. (5.08 m.).
Normal take-off weight: 18,739 lb. (8,500 kg.). *Maximum speed:* 273 m.p.h.
(440 km./hr.) at 12,140 ft. (3,700 m.). *Operational ceiling:* 19,685 ft. (6,000 m.).
Range with 3,880 lb. (1,760 kg.) bomb load: 1,616 miles (2,600 km.). *Armament:*
Single 7.7 mm. KM Wz.37 machine-guns in each of nose, dorsal and ventral
positions; normal warload of twenty 243 lb. (110 kg.) bombs in wing centre-
section; maximum permissible load of 5,688 lb. (2,580 kg.).

MITSUBISHI Ki-21 (Japan)

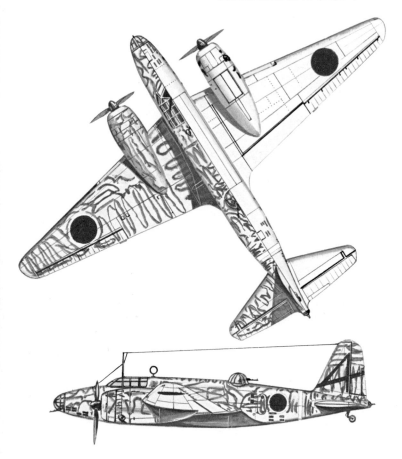

37

Mitsubishi Ki-21-IIb Model 2B of the 1st Squadron, 14th Group JAAF, Philippines, 1944. *Engines:* Two 1,500 h.p. Mitsubishi Ha-101 radials. *Span:* 73 ft. 9⅞ in. (22.50 m.). *Length:* 52 ft. 6 in. (16.00 m.). *Height:* 15 ft. 11 in. (4.85 m.). *Normal take-off weight:* 21,407 lb. (9,710 kg.). *Maximum speed:* 302 m.p.h. (486 km./hr.) at 15,485 ft. (4,720 m.). *Operational ceiling:* 32,810 ft. (10,000 m.). *Normal range:* 1,678 miles (2,700 km.). *Armament:* One 12.7 mm. Type 1 machine-gun in dorsal turret, five 7.7 mm. Type 89 machine-guns (one each in nose, tail, ventral and two beam positions); up to 2,205 lb. (1,000 kg.) of bombs internally.

MITSUBISHI G4M (Japan)

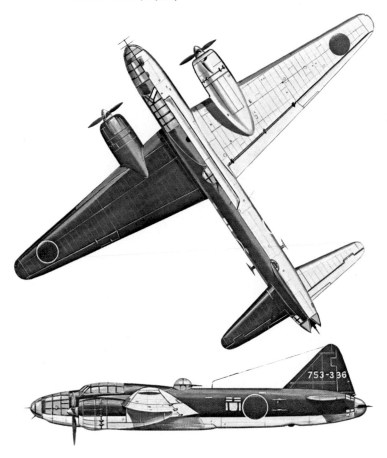

38

Mitsubishi G4M2a Model 24 of the 753rd Air Corps JNAF, Philippines, autumn 1944. *Engines:* Two 1,850 h.p. Mitsubishi Kasei 25 radials. *Span:* 81 ft. $7\frac{7}{8}$ in. (24.89 m.). *Length:* 64 ft. $4\frac{7}{8}$ in. (19.63 m.). *Height:* 13 ft. $5\frac{7}{8}$ in. (4.11 m.). *Maximum take-off weight:* 33,069 lb. (15,000 kg.). *Maximum speed:* 272 m.p.h. (437 km./hr.) at 15,090 ft. (4,600 m.). *Operational ceiling:* 29,365 ft. (8,950 m.). *Normal range:* 1,497 miles (2,410 km.). *Armament:* Four 20 mm. Type 99 cannon (one each in dorsal, tail and two beam positions), and one 7.7 mm. Type 97 machine-gun in nose; up to 2,205 lb. (1,000 kg.) of bombs internally or one 1,764 lb. (800 kg.) torpedo.

214

MITSUBISHI Ki-67 (Japan)

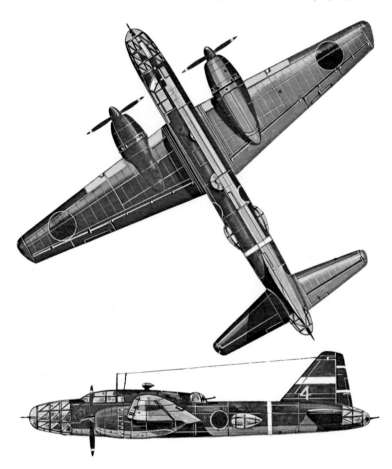

39

Mitsubishi Ki-67-Ib Model 1B *Hiryu* of the JAAF (unit unidentified), 1945. *Engines:* Two 1,900 h.p. Mitsubishi Ha-104 radials. *Span:* 73 ft. $9\frac{7}{8}$ in. (22.50 m.). *Length:* 61 ft. $4\frac{1}{4}$ in. (18.70 m.). *Height:* 18 ft. $4\frac{1}{2}$ in. (5.60 m.). *Normal take-off weight:* 30,346 lb. (13,765 kg.). *Maximum speed:* 334 m.p.h. (537 km./hr.) at 19,980 ft. (6,090 m.). *Operational ceiling:* 31,070 ft. (9,470 m.). *Normal range:* 1,740 miles (2,800 km.). *Armament:* One 20 mm. Ho-5 cannon in dorsal turret, four 12.7 mm. Type 1 machine-guns (one each in nose, tail and two beam positions); up to 1,764 lb. (800 kg.) of bombs internally.

NAKAJIMA Ki-49 (Japan)

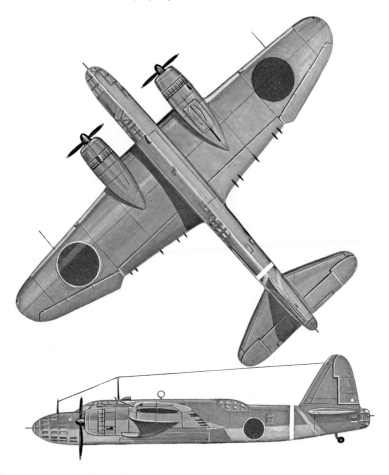

40

Nakajima Ki-49-IIa Model 2A *Donryu* of the 3rd Squadron, 95th Group JAAF, 1944-45. *Engines:* Two 1,450 h.p. Nakajima Ha-109-II radials. *Span:* 66 ft. 7¼ in. (20.30 m.). *Length:* 53 ft. 1¾ in. (16.20 m.). *Height:* 13 ft. 11⅜ in. (4.25 m.). *Normal take-off weight:* 23,545 lb. (10,680 kg.). *Maximum speed:* 304 m.p.h. (490 km./hr.) at 16,405 ft. (5,000 m.). *Operational ceiling:* 26,770 ft. (8,160 m.). *Normal range:* 1,491 miles (2,400 km.). *Armament:* One 20 mm. cannon in dorsal turret, and five 7.92 mm. machine-guns in nose, tail, ventral and beam positions; up to 2,205 lb. (1,000 kg.) of bombs internally.

MITSUBISHI Ki-46 (Japan)

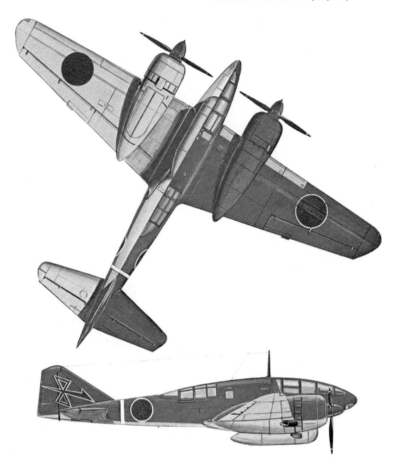

41

Mitsubishi Ki-46-III Model 3 of the 2nd Squadron, 81st Group JAAF, Burma 1944. *Engines:* Two 1,500 h.p. Mitsubishi Ha-112-II radials. *Span:* 48 ft. 2¾ in. (14.70 m.). *Length:* 36 ft. 1 in. (11.00 m.). *Height:* 12 ft. 8¾ in. (3.88 m.). *Maximum take-off weight:* 14,330 lb. (6,500 kg.). *Maximum speed:* 391 m.p.h. (630 km./hr.) at 19,685 ft. (6,000 m.). *Operational ceiling:* 34,450 ft. (10,500 m.). *Maximum range:* 2,485 miles (4,000 km.). *Armament:* None.

YOKOSUKA P1Y (Japan)

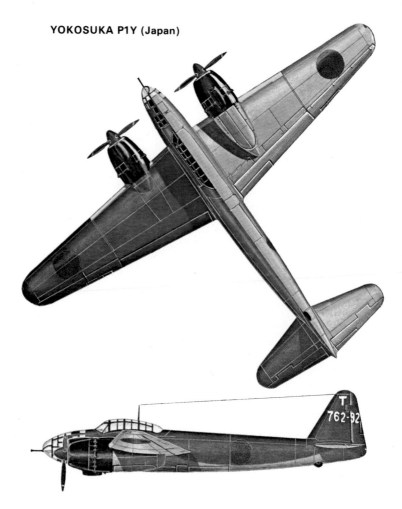

42

Yokosuka P1Y1 Model 11 *Ginga* of No. 262 Bomber Squadron, 762nd Air Corps JNAF, 1944-45. *Engines:* Two 1,820 h.p. Nakajima Homare 11 radials. *Span:* 65 ft. 7⅜ in. (20.00 m.). *Length:* 49 ft. 2½ in. (15.00 m.). *Height:* 14 ft. 1¼ in. (4.30 m.). *Maximum take-off weight:* 29,762 lb. (13,500 kg.). *Maximum speed:* 345 m.p.h. (556 km./hr.) at 19,360 ft. (5,900 m.). *Operational ceiling:* 33,530 ft. (10,220 m.). *Range:* 2,728 miles (4,390 km.). *Armament:* One 20 mm. cannon in nose, one 12.7 mm. machine-gun in dorsal position; up to 1,102 lb. (500 kg.). of bombs internally, and further small bombs, or one 1,874 lb. (850 kg.). or 1,764 lb. (800 kg.) torpedo, externally.

HEINKEL He 177 (Germany)

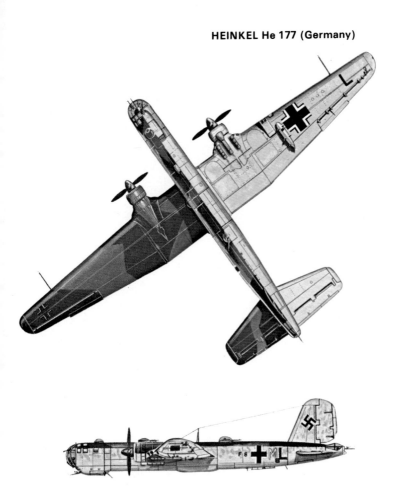

43

Heinkel He 177A-5/R7 *Greif* of *Staffel* 6, II/KG.40, Bordeaux-Mérignac, *ca.* November 1943. *Engines:* Two 2,950 h.p. Daimler-Benz DB 610 (coupled DB 605) radials. *Span:* 103 ft. 1¾ in. (31.44 m.). *Length:* 72 ft. 2⅛ in. (22.00 m.). *Height:* 21 ft. 0 in. (6.40 m.). *Normal take-off weight:* 59,966 lb. (27,200 kg.). *Maximum speed:* 303 m.p.h. (488 km./hr.) at 20,010 ft. (6,100 m.). *Operational ceiling:* 49,870 ft. (15,200 m.). *Maximum range with two Hs 293 missiles:* 3,107 miles (5,000 km.). *Armament:* One 20 mm. MG 151 cannon in front of under-nose cupola and one in tail; two 13 mm. MG 131 machine-guns in forward dorsal barbette and one in rear dorsal turret; and one 7.9 mm. MG 81 gun in nose and two in rear of under-nose cupola; up to 2,205 lb. (1,000 kg.) of bombs internally and two mines, torpedos or missiles externally.

CURTISS C-46 (U.S.A.)

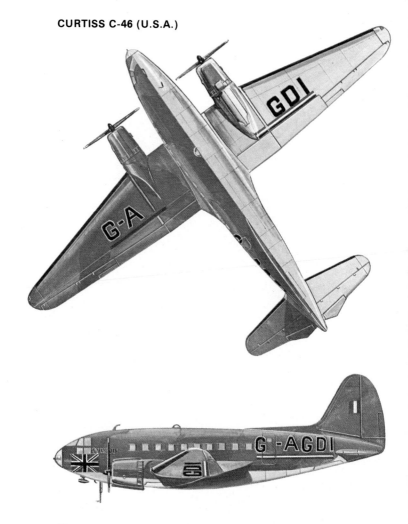

44

Curtiss CW-20 *St. Louis* (prototype for C-46 series), as delivered for operation by BOAC, December 1941. *Engines:* Two 1,700 h.p. Wright 586-C14-BA2 Double-Row Cyclone radials. *Span:* 108 ft. 1 in. (32.94 m.). *Length:* 76 ft. 4 in. (23.27 m.). *Height:* 21 ft. 9 in. (6.63 m.). *Maximum take-off weight:* 45,000 lb. (20,412 kg.). *Maximum speed:* 240 m.p.h. (386 km./hr.) at sea level. *Operational ceiling:* 26,900 ft. (8,199 m.). *Normal range with 4,621 lb. (2,096 kg.) payload:* 2,000 miles (3,219 km.). *Armament:* None.

SKYTRAIN/SKYTROOPER (U.S.A.)

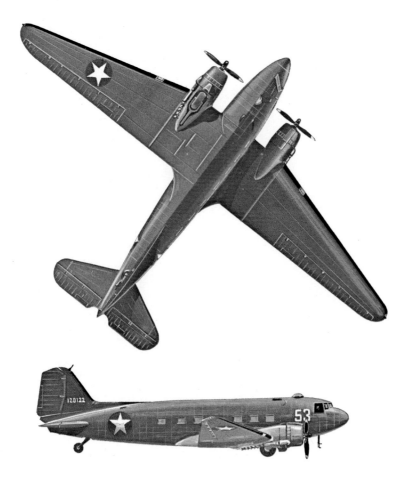

45

Douglas C-53C Skytrooper of the USAAF, El Kabrit, spring 1943. *Engines:* Two 1,200 h.p. Pratt & Whitney R-1830-92 Twin Wasp radials. *Span:* 95 ft. 0 in. (28.96 m.). *Length:* 64 ft. 5½ in. (19.65 m.). *Height:* 16 ft. 11 in. (5.16 m.). *Maximum take-off weight:* 29,300 lb. (13,290 kg.). *Maximum speed:* 210 m.p.h. (338 km./hr.) at 8,800 ft. (2,682 m.). *Operational ceiling:* 24,100 ft. (7,346 m.). *Normal range:* 1,350 miles (2,173 km.). *Armament:* None.

CATALINA (U.S.A.)

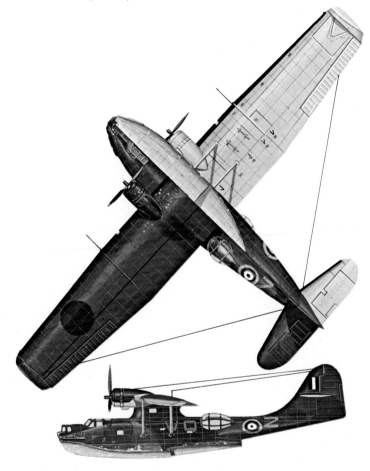

46

Consolidated Catalina I (PBY-5) of No. 209 Squadron RAF which spotted the *Bismarck* on 26 May 1941. *Engines:* Two 1,200 h.p. Pratt & Whitney R-1830-S1C3-G Twin Wasp radials. *Span:* 104 ft. 0 in. (31.70 m.). *Length:* 63 ft. 10½ in. (19.47 m.). *Height:* 18 ft 10⅝ in. (5.76 m.). *Normal take-off weight:* 27,080 lb. (12,283 kg.). *Maximum speed:* 190 m.p.h. (306 km./hr.) at 10,500 ft. (3,200 m.). *Operational ceiling:* 24,000 ft. (7,315 m.). *Maximum range:* 4,000 miles (6,437 km.). *Armament:* Six 0.303 in. Vickers guns, one in bow, two in each side blister and one in ventral tunnel aft of hull step; up to 2,000 lb. (907 kg.) of bombs.

SAAB-18 (Sweden)

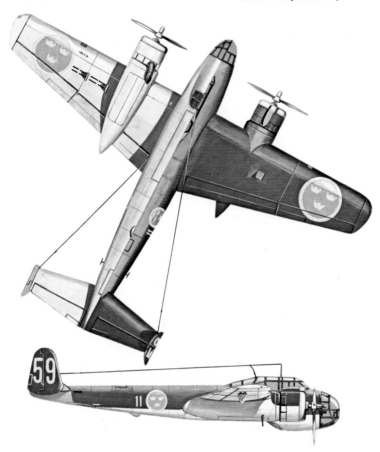

47

Saab-18A (B 18A) of F 11 Wing (3rd Division), *Kungl. Svenska Flygvapnet*, 1944-45. *Engines:* Two 1,065 h.p. SFA-built Pratt & Whitney R-1830-S1C3-G Twin Wasp radials. *Span:* 55 ft. 9¼ in. (17.00 m.). *Length:* 43 ft. 4⅞ in. (13.23 m.). *Height:* 14 ft. 3¼ in. (4.35 m.). *Normal take-off weight:* 17,946 lb. (8,140 kg.). *Maximum speed:* 289 m.p.h. (465 km./hr.) at 19,685 ft. (6,000 m.). *Operational ceiling:* 26,250 ft. (8,000 m.). *Maximum range:* 1,367 miles (2,200 km.). *Armament:* One 13.2 mm. machine-gun in rear of crew cabin and one in rear of under-nose fairing, and one 7.9 mm. gun in starboard side of nose; up to 3,307 lb. (1,500 kg.) of bombs.

DORNIER Do 217 (Germany)

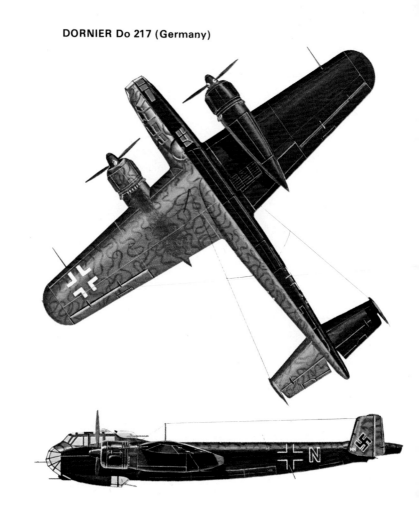

48

Dornier Do 217E-2 of 5/KG.6, France, early 1943. *Engines:* Two 1,580 h.p. BMW 801 M radials. *Span:* 62 ft. 4 in. (19.00 m.). *Length:* 56 ft 9⅛ in. (17.30 m.). *Height:* 16 ft. 4⅞ in. (5.00 m.). *Normal take-off weight:* 33,069 lb. (15,000 kg.). *Maximum speed:* 320 *m.p.h.* (515 km./hr.) at 17,060 ft. (5,200 m.). *Operational ceiling:* 24,610 ft. (7,500 m.). *Maximum range:* 1,429 miles (2,300 km.). *Armament:* One 15 mm. MG 151 cannon in nose, one 13 mm. MG 131 machine-gun in dorsal turret and one in rear of under-nose cupola, one 7.9 mm. MG 15 gun in nose and one each side in rear of cabin; up to 5,512 lb. (2,500 kg.) of bombs internally and 3,307 lb. (1,500 kg.) externally.

DORNIER Do 17 (Germany)

49

Dornier Do 17Z-2 of 15/KG.53 (*Kroaten*), Eastern Front, September 1942. *Engines:* Two 1,000 h.p. Bramo Fafnir 323P radials. *Span:* 59 ft. 0⅜ in. (18.00 m.). *Length:* 51 ft. 9⅜ in. (15.79 m.). *Height:* 14 ft. 11½ in. (4.56 m.). *Normal take-off weight:* 18,872 lb. (8,560 kg.). *Maximum speed:* 224 m.p.h. (360 km./hr.) at 13,120 ft. (4,000 m.). *Operational ceiling:* 22,965 ft. (7,000 m.). *Maximum range with 1,102 lb. (500 kg.) bomb load and auxiliary fuel:* 721 miles (1,160 km.). *Armament:* Six 7.9 mm. MG 15 machine-guns: one in nose, one in front of cabin, one each side in rear of cabin, one aft of cabin and one in ventral position; up to 2,205 lb. (1,000 kg.) of bombs internally.

WHITLEY (U.K.)

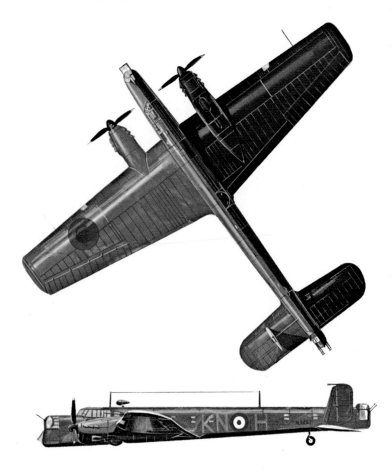

50

Armstrong Whitworth Whitley V of No. 77 Squadron RAF, April 1940. *Engines:* Two 1,075 h.p. Rolls-Royce Merlin X Vee type. *Span:* 84 ft. 0 in. (25.60 m.). *Length:* 70 ft. 6 in. (21.49 m.). *Height:* 15 ft. 0 in. (4.57 m.). *Normal take-off weight:* 33,500 lb. (15,196 kg.). *Maximum speed:* 230 m.p.h. (370 km./hr.) at 16,400 ft. (5,000 m.). *Operational ceiling:* 26,000 ft. (7,925 m.). *Maximum range:* 2,400 miles (3,862 km.). *Armament:* One 0.303 in. Vickers gun in nose turret and four 0.303 in. Browning machine-guns in tail turret; up to 7,000 lb. (3,175 kg.) of bombs internally.

HAMPDEN (U.K.)

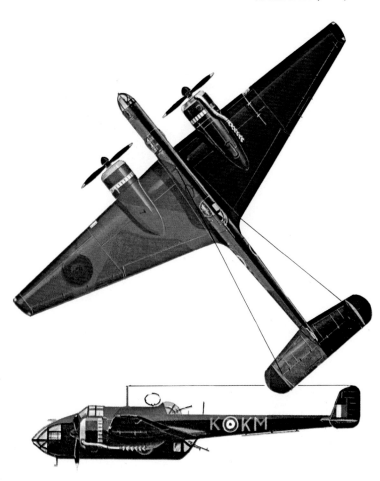

51

Handley Page Hampden I of No. 44 (Rhodesia) Squadron RAF, summer 1941.
Engines: Two 980 h.p. Bristol Pegasus XVIII radials. *Span:* 69 ft. 2 in. (21.08 m.).
Length: 53 ft. 7 in. (16.33 m.). *Height:* 14 ft. 4 in. (4.37 m.). *Normal take-off
weight:* 18,756 lb. (8,508 kg.). *Maximum speed:* 265 m.p.h. (426 km./hr.) at
15,500 ft. (4,724 m.). *Operational ceiling:* 22,700 ft. (6,919 m.). *Range with
maximum bomb load:* 1,095 miles (1,762 km.). *Armament:* Six 0.303 in.
Vickers K guns (two in nose and two each in dorsal and ventral positions); up
to 4,000 lb. (1,814 kg.) of bombs internally.

FIAT B.R.20 (Italy)

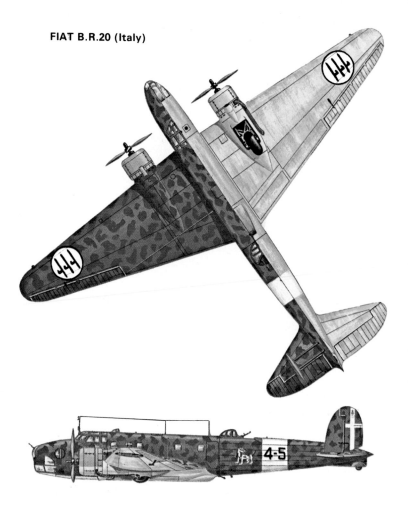

52

Fiat B.R.20M *Cicogna* of the 4° *Squadriglia*, 11° *Gruppo*, 13° *Stormo B.T.*, northern Italy, autumn 1940. *Engines:* Two 1,000 h.p. Fiat A.80 RC 41 radials. *Span:* 70 ft. 8⅞ in. (21.56 m.). *Length:* 55 ft. 0¾ in. (16.78 m.). *Height:* 15 ft. 7 in. (4.75 m.). *Normal take-off weight:* 23,038 lb. (10,450 kg.). *Maximum speed:* 267 m.p.h. (430 km./hr.) at 13,120 ft. (4,000 m.). *Operational ceiling:* 22,145 ft. (6,750 m.). *Range:* 1,243 miles (2,000 km.). *Armament:* One 12.7 mm. Breda-SAFAT machine-gun in dorsal turret and three 7.7 mm. Breda-SAFAT guns (one each in nose, tail and ventral positions); up to 3,527 lb. (1,600 kg.) of bombs internally.

MITCHELL (U.S.A.)

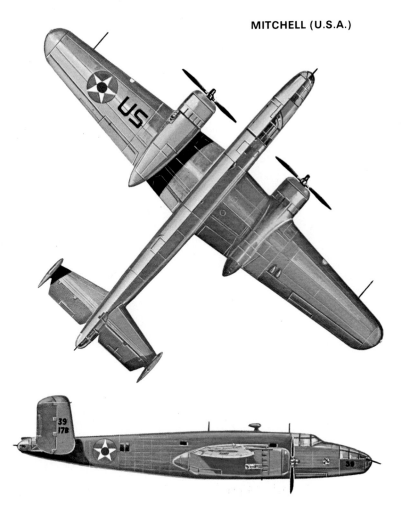

53
North American B-25A of the 34th Bomber Squadron, 17th Bombardment
Group USAAC, summer 1941. *Engines:* Two 1,700 h.p. Wright R-2600-9
Cyclone radials. *Span:* 67 ft. 7 in. (20.60 m.). *Length:* 54 ft. 1 in. (16.48 m.).
Height: 15 ft. 9 in. (4.80 m.). *Maximum take-off weight:* 27,100 lb. (12,292 kg.).
Maximum speed: 315 m.p.h. (507 km./hr.) at 15,000 ft. (4,572 m.). *Operational
ceiling:* 27,000 ft. (8,230 m.). *Range with maximum bomb load:* 1,350 miles
(2,173 km.). *Armament:* One 0.50 in. machine-gun in tail, and three 0.30 in.
guns (one in nose and one in each beam position); up to 3,000 lb. (1,361 kg.)
of bombs internally.

HUDSON (U.S.A.)

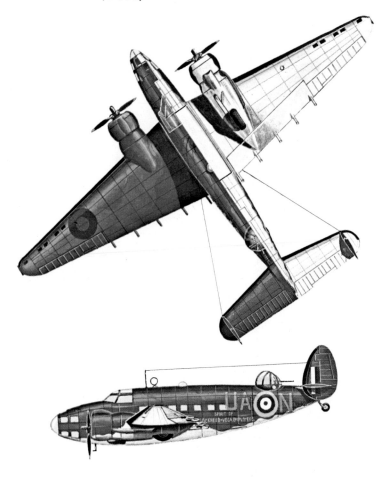

54

Lockheed Hudson III of No. 269 Squadron RAF, winter 1941-42. *Engines:* Two 1,200 h.p. Wright GR-1820-G205A Cyclone radials. *Span:* 65 ft. 6 in. (19.96 m.). *Length:* 44 ft. 4 in. (13.51 m.). *Height:* 11 ft. 10½ in. (3.62 m.). *Maximum take-off weight:* 20,000 lb. (9,072 kg.). *Maximum speed:* 255 m.p.h. (410 km./hr.) at 5,000 ft. (1,524 m.). *Operational ceiling:* 24,500 ft. (7,468 m.). *Maximum range:* 2,160 miles (3,476 km.). *Armament:* Seven 0.303 in. machine-guns (two each in nose and dorsal turret, one in each beam position, and one in ventral position); up to 750 lb. (340 kg.) of bombs.

VENTURA (U.S.A.)

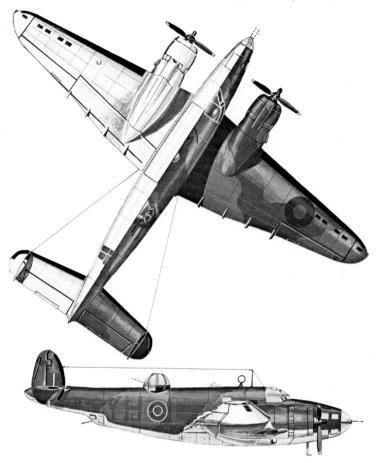

55

Lockheed Ventura I of No. 21 Squadron RAF, summer/autumn 1942. *Engines:* Two 2,000 h.p. Pratt & Whitney GR-2800-S1A4-G Double Wasp radials. *Span:* 65 ft. 6 in. (19.96 m.). *Length:* 51 ft. 5 in. (15.67 m.). *Height:* 11 ft. 10½ in. (3.62 m.). *Maximum take-off weight:* 26,000 lb. (11,793 kg.). *Maximum speed:* 312 m.p.h. (502 km./hr.) at 6,800 ft. (2,073 m.). *Operational ceiling:* 25,200 ft. (7,681 m.). *Range with maximum bomb load:* 1,000 miles (1,609 km.). *Armament:* Two 0.50 in. machine-guns in nose, six 0.303 in. machine-guns (two each in nose, dorsal turret and ventral position); up to 2,500 lb. (1,134 kg.) of bombs internally.

LODESTAR (U.S.A.)

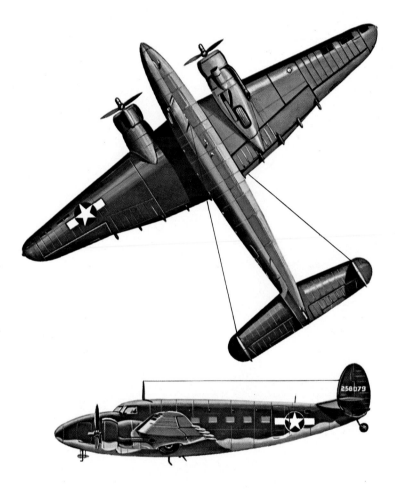

56

Lockheed C-60A Lodestar of the USAAF, 1943-44. *Engines:* Two 1,200 h.p. Wright R-1820-87 Cyclone radials. *Span:* 65 ft. 6 in. (19.96 m.). *Length:* 49 ft. $9\frac{7}{8}$ in. (15.19 m.). *Height:* 11 ft. $10\frac{1}{2}$ in. (3.62 m.). *Normal take-off weight:* 18,500 lb. (8,392 kg.). *Maximum speed:* 266 m.p.h. (428 km./hr.) at 17,000 ft. (5,182 m.). *Operational ceiling:* 27,000 ft. (8,230 m.). *Maximum range with full load:* 1,660 miles (2,672 km.). *Armament:* None.

ALBEMARLE (U.K.)

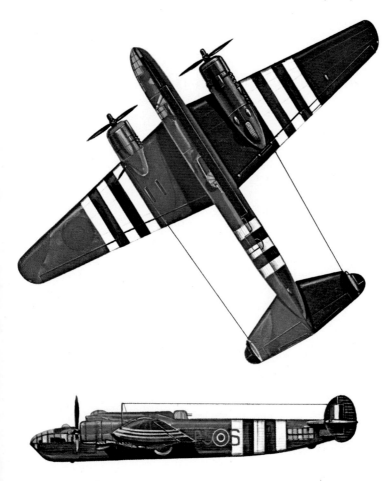

57

Armstrong Whitworth Albemarle ST I of No. 297 Squadron RAF, June 1944.
Engines: Two 1,590 h.p. Bristol Hercules XI radials. *Span:* 77 ft. 0 in. (23.47 m.).
Length: 59 ft. 11 in. (18.26 m.). *Height:* 15 ft. 7 in. (4.75 m.). *Maximum take-off
weight:* 36,500 lb. (16,556 kg.). *Maximum speed:* 265 m.p.h. (426 km./hr.) at
10,500 ft. (3,200 m.). *Operational ceiling:* 18,000 ft. (5,486 m.). *Normal range:*
1,300 miles (2,092 km.). *Armament:* Four 0.303 in. machine-guns in dorsal
turret.

EXPEDITER (U.S.A.)

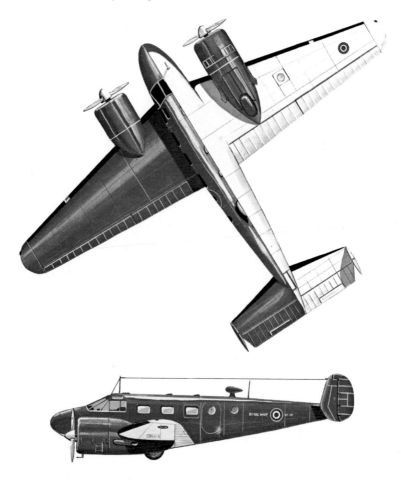

58

Beech Expediter II (UC-45F) of the Royal Navy, personal transport of Vice-Admiral Sir Dennis Boyd, 1945. *Engines:* Two 450 h.p. Pratt & Whitney R-985-AN-1 Wasp Junior radials. *Span:* 47 ft. 7¾ in. (14.52 m.). *Length:* 34 ft. 2¾ in (10.43 m.). *Height:* 9 ft. 4 in. (2.84 m.). *Normal take-off weight:* 7,500 lb. (3,402 kg.). *Maximum speed:* 223 m.p.h. (359 km./hr.) at sea level. *Operational ceiling:* 27,000 ft. (8,230 m.). *Maximum range:* 1,200 miles (1,931 km.). *Armament:* None.

FOCKE-WULF Fw 189 (Germany)

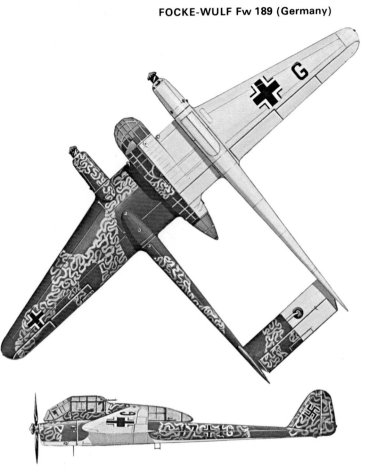

59

Focke-Wulf .Fw 189A-2 of 1(H)/32 serving with *Luftflotte* 5, Eastern Front (White Sea area) October 1942. *Engines:* Two 465 h.p. Argus As 410A-1 inverted-Vee type. *Span:* 60 ft. 4⅜ in. (18.40 m.). *Length:* 39 ft. 4½ in. (12.00 m.). *Height:* 10 ft. 2 in. (3.10 m.). *Normal take-off weight:* 8,708 lb. (3,950 kg.). *Maximum speed:* 217 m.p.h. (350 km./hr.) at 7,870 ft. (2,400 m.). *Operational ceiling:* 23,950 ft. (7,300 m.). *Normal range:* 416 miles (670 km.). *Armament:* Four 7.9 mm. MG 81 machine-guns (two in dorsal position and two in rear of nacelle), and one 7.9 mm. MG 17 gun in each wing root; four 110 lb. (50 kg.) bombs beneath the wings.

BLOHM und VOSS Bv 138 (Germany)

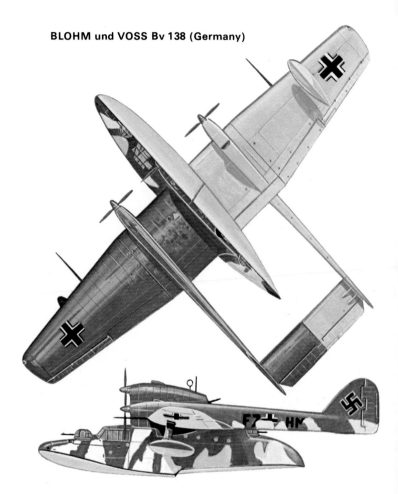

60

Blohm und Voss Bv 138C-1 of an unidentified *Aufklärungsgruppe* (Reconnaissance Group), possibly in the Baltic Sea area, *ca.* 1942-43. *Engines:* Three 880 h.p. Junkers Jumo 205D vertically-opposed diesel type. *Span:* 88 ft. 7 in. (27.00 m.). *Length:* 65 ft. $1\frac{1}{2}$ in. (19.85 m.). *Height:* 19 ft. $4\frac{1}{4}$ in. (5.90 m.). *Normal take-off weight:* 31,967 lb. (14,500 kg.). *Maximum speed:* 171 m.p.h. (275 km./hr.) at 6,560 ft. (2,000 m.). *Operational ceiling:* 16,400 ft. (5,000 m.). *Maximum range:* 2,760 miles (4,355 km.). *Armament:* Two 20 mm. MG 151 cannon (one each in bow and rear turrets), one 13 mm. MG 131 machine-gun aft of central engine, and provision for one 7.9 mm. MG 15 gun in starboard side of hull; three or six 110 lb. (50 kg.) bombs or four 331 lb. (150 kg.) depth charges beneath starboard centre-section.

CANT. Z.506B (Italy)

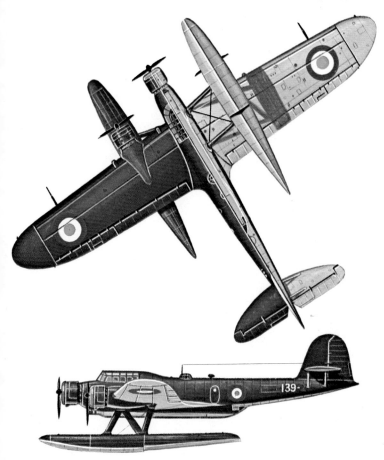

61

C.R.D.A. Cant. Z.506B *Airone* Serie XII, formerly of the 139° *Squadriglia da Ricognizione Marittima,* in the insignia of the Italian Co-Belligerent Air Force, 1943–44. *Engines:* Three 750 h.p. Alfa Romeo 126 RC 34 radials. *Span:* 86 ft. 11¼ in. (26.50 m.). *Length:* 63 ft. 1⅞ in. (19.25 m.). *Height:* 24 ft. 5⅜ in. (7.45 m.). *Maximum take-off weight:* 28,008 lb. (12,705 kg.). *Maximum speed:* 217 m.p.h. (350 km./hr.) at 13,120 ft. (4,000 m.). *Operational ceiling:* 24,000 ft. (7,320 m.). *Range with 2,094 lb. (950 kg.) bomb load:* 1,243 miles (2,000 km.). *Armament:* One 12.7 mm. Scotti machine-gun in dorsal turret, one 7.7 mm. Breda-SAFAT machine-gun in ventral position and one in each beam position; up to 2,645 lb. (1,200 kg.) of bombs.

237

JUNKERS Ju 52/3m (Germany)

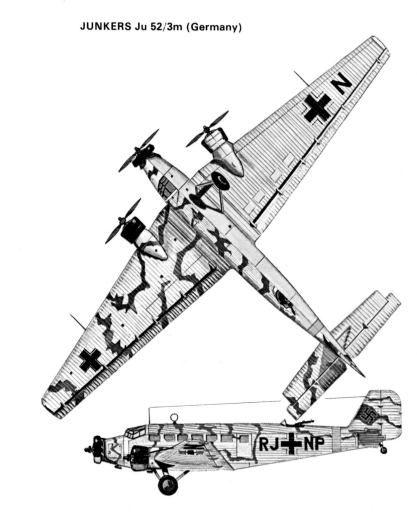

62

Junkers Ju 52/3m of *Kampffliegerschüle* Thorn, winter 1942–43. *Engines:* Three 830 h.p. BMW 132T radials. *Span:* 95 ft. 11½ in. (29.25 m.). *Length:* 62 ft. 0 in. (18.90 m.). *Height:* 14 ft. 9⅛ in. (4.50 m.). *Maximum take-off weight:* 24,317 lb. (11,030 kg.). *Maximum speed:* 190 m.p.h. (305 km./hr.) at 8,200 ft. (2,500 m.). *Operational ceiling:* 18,045 ft. (5,500 m.). *Range with 2,205 lb. (1,000 kg.) payload:* 808 miles (1,300 km.). *Armament:* One 13 mm. MG 131 machine-gun in dorsal position and two 7.9 mm. MG 15 guns firing through passengers' windows.

CANT. Z.1007 (Italy)

63

C.R.D.A. Cant. Z.1007*bis Alcione* of the 211° *Squadriglia B.T.,* Mediterranean
area 1941–42. *Engines:* Three 1,000 h.p. Piaggio P.XI*bis* RC 40 radials. *Span:*
81 ft. $4\frac{3}{8}$ in. (24.80 m.). *Length:* 60 ft. $2\frac{3}{8}$ in. (18.35 m.). *Height:* 17 ft. $1\frac{1}{2}$ in.
(5.22 m.). *Maximum take-off weight:* 30,029 lb. (13,621 kg.). *Maximum speed:*
283 m.p.h. (455 km./hr.) at 17,220 ft. (5,250 m.). *Operational ceiling:* 24,610 ft.
(7,500 m.). *Range with maximum bomb load:* 1,367 miles (2,200 km.).
Armament: One 12.7 mm. Breda-SAFAT machine-gun in dorsal turret, one in
ventral position and one 7.7 mm. gun in each beam position; up to 4,409 lb.
(2,000 kg.) of bombs internally.

239

SAVOIA-MARCHETTI S.M.79 (Italy)

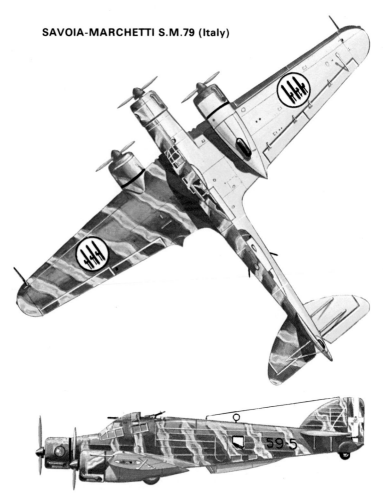

64

Savoia-Marchetti S.M.79-II *Sparviero* of the 59° *Squadriglia*, 33° *Gruppo*, 11° *Stormo B.T.*, Cyrenaica November 1940. *Engines:* Three 1,000 h.p. Piaggio P.XI RC 40 radials. *Span:* 69 ft. 6⅝ in. (21.20 m.). *Length:* 53 ft. 1¾ in. (16.20 m.). *Height:* 15 ft. 11 in. (4.60 m.). *Normal take-off weight:* 25,133 lb. (11,400 kg.). *Maximum speed:* 295 m.p.h. (475 km./hr.) at 13,120 ft. (4,000 m.). *Operational ceiling:* 27,890 ft. (8,500 m.). *Range with maximum bomb load:* 1,243 miles 2,000 km.). *Armament:* Three 12.7 mm. Breda-SAFAT machine-guns (one above pilot's cabin, one in dorsal position, one in ventral gondola), and one 7.7 mm. Lewis gun amidships to fire to port or starboard; up to 2,756 lb. (1,250 kg.) of bombs internally.

PETLYAKOV Pe-8 (U.S.S.R.)

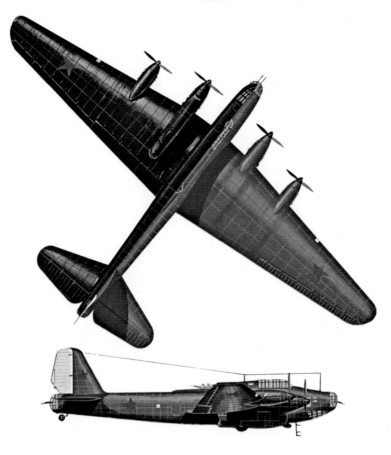

65

Petlyakov Pe-8 of the Soviet Air Force, used for communications between Moscow and the UK, 1942. *Engines:* Four 1,350 h.p. Mikulin AM-35A Vee type. *Span:* 131 ft. 0⅜ in. (39.94 m.). *Length:* 73 ft. 8⅜ in. (22.47 m.). *Height:* 20 ft. 0⅛ in. (6.10 m.). *Maximum take-off weight:* 73,469 lb. (33,325 kg.). *Maximum speed:* 272 m.p.h. (438 km./hr.) at 24,935 ft. (7,600 m.). *Operational ceiling:* 31,988 ft. (9,750 m.). *Maximum range with 4,409 lb. (2,000 kg.) bomb load:* 3,383 miles (5,445 km.). *Armament:* One 20 mm. ShVAK cannon in each of the dorsal and tail turrets, one 12.7 mm. Beresin machine-gun in the rear of each inboard engine nacelle, and two 7.62 mm. ShKAS guns in nose turret; up to 8,818 lb. (4,000 kg.) of bombs internally.

STIRLING (U.K.)

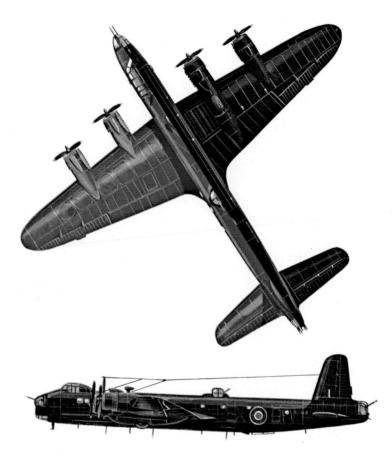

66

Short Stirling B III of No. 199 Bomber Support Squadron RAF, autumn 1944. *Engines:* Four 1,650 h.p. Bristol Hercules XVI radials. *Span:* 99 ft. 1 in. (30.20 m.). *Length:* 87 ft. 3 in. (26.59 m.). *Height:* 22 ft. 9 in. (6.93 m.). *Maximum take-off weight:* 70,000 lb. (31,751 kg.). *Maximum speed:* 270 m.p.h. (435 km./hr.) at 14,500 ft. (4,420 m.). *Operational ceiling:* 17,000 ft. (5,182 m.). *Range with 3,500 lb. (1,588 kg.) bomb load:* 2,010 miles (3,235 km.). *Armament:* Two 0.303 in Browning machine-guns in each of nose and dorsal turrets, and four more in tail turret; up to 14,000 lb. (6,350 kg.) of bombs internally.

FOCKE-WULF Fw 200 (Germany)

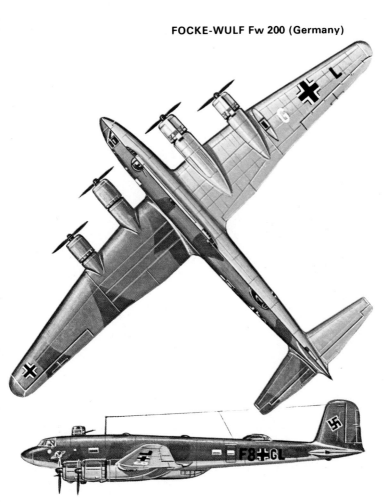

67

Focke-Wulf Fw 200C-3/U1 *Condor* of I/KG.40 operating with *Fliegerführer Atlantik*, summer 1941. *Engines:* Four 1,200 h.p. Bramo 323R-2 Fafnir radials. *Span:* 107 ft. 9½ in. (30.855 m.). *Length:* 76 ft. 11½ in. (23.46 m.). *Height:* 20 ft. 8 in. (6.30 m.). *Maximum take-off weight:* 50,045 lb. (22,700 kg.). *Maximum speed:* 207 m.p.h. (333 km./hr.) at 15,750 ft. (4,800 m.). *Operational ceiling:* 19,030 ft. (5,800 m.). *Range (standard fuel):* 2,206 miles (3,550 km.). *Armament:* One 20 mm. MG 151/20 cannon in the front of the ventral gondola, one 15 mm. MG 151 machine-gun in forward dorsal turret, and three 7.9 mm. MG 15 guns (one in the rear of the ventral gondola and one in each beam position); up to 4,630 lb. (2,100 kg.) of bombs internally and externally.

243

FORTRESS (U.S.A.)

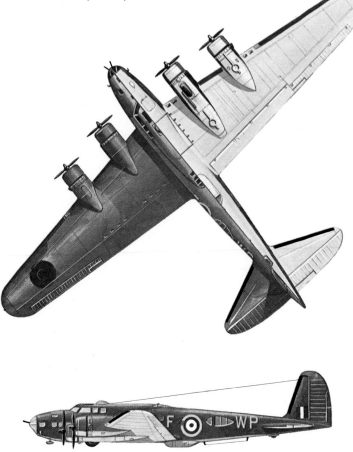

68

Boeing Fortress I (B-17C) of No. 90 Squadron RAF Bomber Command, summer 1941. *Engines:* Four 1,200 h.p. Wright R-1820-666C Cyclone radials. *Span:* 103 ft. 9⅜ in. (31.63 m.). *Length:* 67 ft. 10½ in. (20.69 m.). *Height:* 15 ft. 4½ in. (4.68 m.). *Normal take-off weight:* 47,500 lb. (21,546 kg.). *Maximum speed:* 325 m.p.h. (523 km./hr.) at 25,000 ft. (7,620 m.). *Operational ceiling:* 36,700 ft. (11,186 m.). *Maximum range:* 3,500 miles (5,633 km.). *Armament:* Six 0.50 in. Browning machine-guns (two each in dorsal and ventral positions, one in each beam position) and one 0.30 in. gun in nose; up to 4,000 lb. (1,814 kg.) of bombs internally.

244

FORTRESS (U.S.A.)

69

Douglas-built Boeing B-17F-60-DL of the 390th Bombing Group, US Eighth Air Force, UK 1943–45. *Engines:* Four 1,200 h.p. Wright R-1820-97 Cyclone radials. *Span:* 103 ft. 9⅜ in. (31.63 m.). *Length:* 74 ft. 8⅞ in. (22.78 m.). *Height:* 19 ft. 2½ in. (5.85 m.). *Normal take-off weight:* 55,000 lb. (24,948 kg.). *Maximum speed:* 299 m.p.h. (481 km./hr.) at 25,000 ft. (7,620 m.). *Operational ceiling:* 37,500 ft. (11,431 m.). *Range with 6,000 lb. (2,722 kg.) bomb load:* 1,300 miles (2,092 km.). *Armament:* Eight or nine 0.50 in. Browning machine-guns (two in forward dorsal turret, one in rear dorsal position (optional), two in ventral turret, two in tail turret and one in each beam position), and one 0.30 in. gun in nose; maximum permitted short-range load of 12,800 lb. (5,806 kg.) of bombs internally and 8,000 lb. (3,629 kg.) externally.

SUPERFORTRESS (U.S.A.)

70

Boeing B-29 Superfortress of the 795th Bomber Squadron, 468th Bomber Group, US 20th Air Force, CBI theatre early autumn 1944. *Engines:* Four 2,200 h.p. Wright R-3350-23 Cyclone radials. *Span:* 141 ft. 3 in. (43.05 m.). *Length:* 99 ft. 0 in. (30.18 m.). *Height:* 27 ft. 9 in. (8.46 m.). *Maximum take-off weight:* 135,000 lb. (61,235 kg.). *Maximum speed:* 357 m.p.h. (575 km./hr.) at 30,000 ft. (9,144 m.). *Operational ceiling:* 33,600 ft. (10,241 m.). *Range with 10,000 lb. (4,536 kg.) bomb load:* 3,250 miles (5,230 km.). *Armament:* One 20 mm. M2 cannon and two 0.50 in. machine-guns in tail turret; eight other 0.50 in. guns, two each in fore and aft dorsal and ventral turrets; up to 20,000 lb. (9,072 kg.) of bombs internally.

LANCASTER (U.K.)

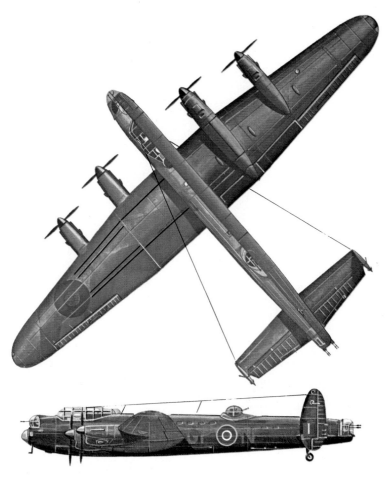

71

Avro Lancaster B I of No. 1661 Conversion Unit RAF, February 1944. *Engines:*
Four 1,280 h.p. Rolls-Royce Merlin XX or 22 Vee type. *Span:* 102 ft. 0 in.
(31.09 m.). *Length:* 69 ft. 4 in. (21.13 m.). *Height:* 19 ft. 7 in. (5.97 m.).
Maximum take-off weight: 68,000 lb. (30,844 kg.). *Maximum speed:* 287 m.p.h.
(462 km./hr.) at 11,500 ft. (3,505 m.). *Operational ceiling:* 24,500 ft. (7,467 m.).
Range with 12,000 lb. (5,443 kg.) bomb load: 1,730 miles (2,784 km.).
Armament: Eight 0.303 in. Browning machine-guns (two each in nose and
dorsal turrets, four in tail turret); up to 18,000 lb. (8,165 kg.) of bombs internally.

247

HALIFAX I (U.K.)

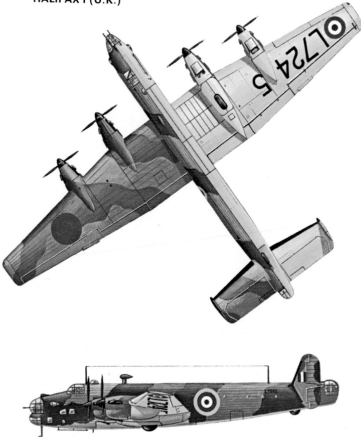

72

Handley Page Halifax second prototype (representative of Mk I configuration), ca. September 1940. Data apply to production Mk I Series I. Engines: Four 1,075 h.p. Rolls-Royce Merlin X Vee type. Span: 98 ft. 10 in. (30.12 m.). Length: 70 ft. 1 in. (21.36 m.). Height: 20 ft. 9 in. (6.32 m.). Maximum take-off weight: 55,000 lb. (24,948 kg.). Maximum speed: 265 m.p.h. (426 km./hr.) at 17,500 ft. (5,334 m.). Operational ceiling: 22,800 ft. (6,949 m.). Range with 5,800 lb. (2,631 kg.) bomb load: 1,860 miles (2,993 km.). Armament: Two 0.303 in. Browning machine-guns in nose turret, four others in tail turret and (on some aircraft) two in beam positions; up to 13,000 lb. (5,897 kg.) of bombs internally.

248

HALIFAX III (U.K.)

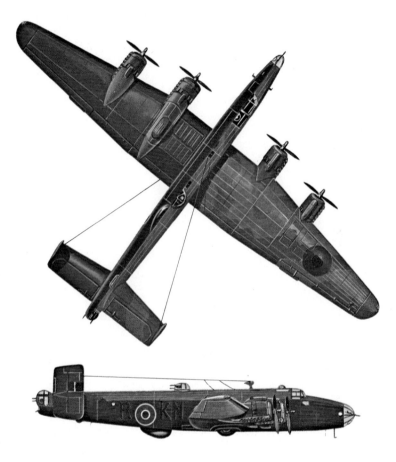

73

Handley Page Halifax B III of No. 77 Squadron RAF Bomber Command, 1944.
Engines: Four 1,615 h.p. Bristol Hercules XVI radials. *Span:* 104 ft. 2 in.
(31.75 m.). *Length:* 71 ft. 7 in. (21.82 m.). *Height:* 20 ft. 9 in. (6.32 m.).
Normal take-off weight: 54,400 lb. (24,675 kg.). *Maximum speed:* 282 m.p.h.
(454 km./hr.) at 13,500 ft. (4,115 m.). *Operational ceiling:* 24,000 ft. (7,315 m.).
Range with maximum bomb load: 1,030 miles (1,658 km.). *Armament:* Eight
0.303 in. Browning machine-guns (four each in dorsal and tail turrets) and one
0.303 in. Vickers K gun in nose; up to 13,000 lb. (5,897 kg.) of bombs internally.

LIBERATOR (U.S.A.)

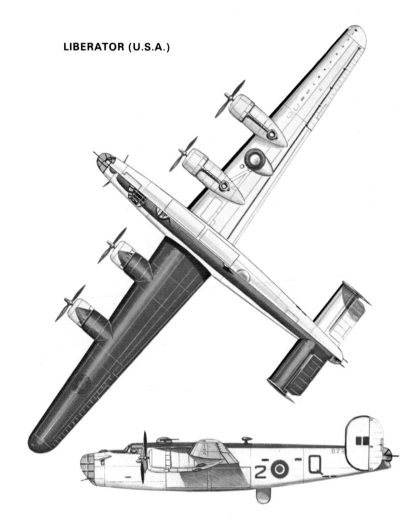

74

Consolidated Liberator GR III (B-24D) of RAF Coastal Command, late 1943. *Engines:* Four 1,200 h.p. Pratt & Whitney R-1830-43 Twin Wasp radials. *Span:* 110 ft. 0 in. (33.53 m.). *Length:* 66 ft. 4 in. (20.22 m.). *Height:* 17 ft. 11 in. (5.46 m.). *Maximum take-off weight:* 64,000 lb. (29,030 kg.). *Maximum speed:* 303 m.p.h. (488 km./hr.) at 25,000 ft. (7,620 m.). *Operational ceiling:* 32,000 ft. (9,754 m.). *Maximum range:* 4,600 miles (7,403 km.). *Armament:* Two 0.50 in. Browning machine-guns in dorsal turret, and seven 0.303 in. Browning guns (one in nose, four in tail turret and one in each beam position); up to 8,000 lb. (3,629 kg.) of bombs internally.

LIBERATOR (U.S.A.)

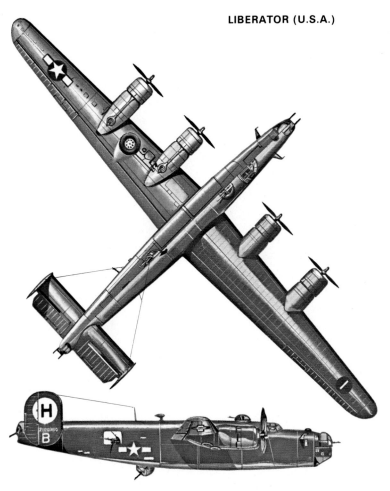

75

Convair B-24J-95-CO of the 448th Bombardment Group, US Eighth Air Force,
UK *ca.* spring 1944. *Engines:* Four 1,200 h.p. Pratt & Whitney R-1830-65
Twin Wasp radials. *Span:* 110 ft. 0 in. (33.53 m.). *Length:* 67 ft. 2 in. (20.47 m.).
Height: 17 ft. 7½ in. (5.37 m.). *Normal take-off weight:* 56,000 lb. (25,401 kg.).
Maximum speed: 290 m.p.h. (467 km./hr.) at 25,000 ft. (7,620 m.). *Operational
ceiling:* 28,000 ft. (8,534 m.). *Range at maximum overload weight of 64,500 lb.
(29,257 kg.), including 5,000 lb. (2,268 kg.) bomb load:* 2,100 miles (3,380 km.).
Armament: Ten 0.50 in. Browning machine-guns (two each in nose, tail,
dorsal and ventral turrets and one in each beam position); normally up to
5,000 lb. (2,268 kg.) of bombs internally.

SUNDERLAND (U.K.)

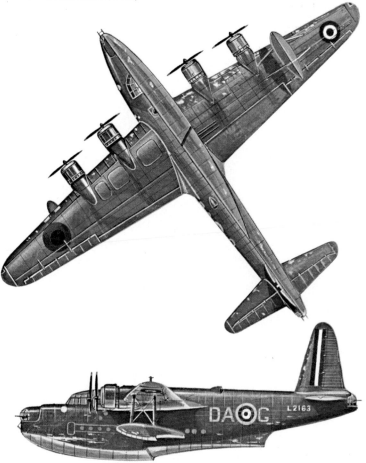

76

Short Sunderland I of No. 210 (GR) Squadron RAF Coastal Command, 1940. *Engines:* Four 1,010 h.p. Bristol Pegasus XXII radials. *Span:* 112 ft. 8 in. (34.34 m.). *Length:* 85 ft. 8 in. (26.11 m.). *Height:* 32 ft. 10½ in. (10.02 m.). *Normal take-off weight:* 44,600 lb. (20,230 kg.). *Maximum speed:* 210 m.p.h. (338 km./hr.) at 6,500 ft. (1,981 m.). *Range with maximum load:* 1,780 miles (2,865 km.). *Armament:* Four 0.303 in. Browning machine-guns in tail turret, one 0.303 in. Vickers K or Lewis gun in nose turret, and two Vickers K guns amidships; up to 2,000 lb. (907 kg.) of bombs internally.

KAWANISHI H8K (Japan)

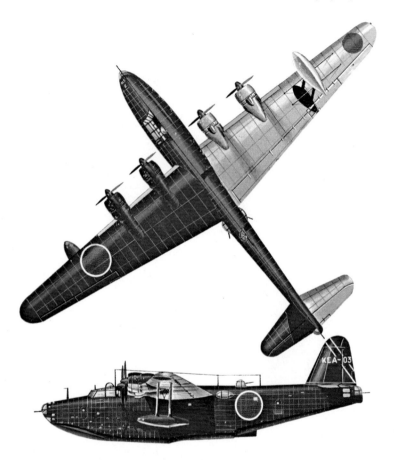

77

Kawanishi H8K2 Model 12 of the JNAF Combined Maritime Escort Force, *ca.*
1944-45. *Engines:* Four 1,850 h.p. Mitsubishi Kasei 22 radials. *Span:* 124 ft.
8 in. (38.00 m.). *Length:* 92 ft. 3½ in. (28.13 m.). *Height:* 30 ft. 0¼ in. (9.15 m.).
Maximum take-off weight: 71,650 lb. (32,500 kg.). *Maximum speed:* 290 m.p.h.
(467 km./hr.) at 16,400 ft. (5,000 m.). *Operational ceiling:* 28,770 ft. (8,770 m.).
Maximum range: 4,474 miles (7,200 km.). *Armament:* Two 20 mm. cannon in
each of nose and tail turrets, one 20 mm. cannon in dorsal turret, and four
7.7 mm. machine-guns in beam blisters and on flight deck; up to eight 551 lb.
(250 kg.) bombs or two 1,764 lb. (800 kg.) torpedos.

253

KAWANISHI H6K (Japan)

78

Kawanishi H6K4-L transport of No. 801 Air Corps JAAF, 1942. *Engines:* Four 1,070 h.p. Mitsubishi Kinsei 46 radials. *Span:* 131 ft. 2¾ in. (40.00 m.). *Length:* 84 ft. 1 in. (25.63 m.). *Height:* 20 ft. 6⅞ in. (6.27 m.). *Normal take-off weight:* 37,479 lb. (17,000 kg.). *Maximum speed:* 211 m.p.h. (340 km./hr.) at 13,120 ft. (4,000 m.). *Operational ceiling:* 31,530 ft. (9,610 m.). *Maximum range:* 2,535 miles (6,080 km.). *Armament (H6K4 patrol version only):* One 20 mm. cannon in tail turret, four 7.7 mm. machine-guns (one each in bow, dorsal and two beam positions); up to 3,527 lb. (1,600 kg.) of bombs internally or two 1,764 lb. (800 kg.) torpedos externally.

MESSERSCHMITT Me 323 (Germany)

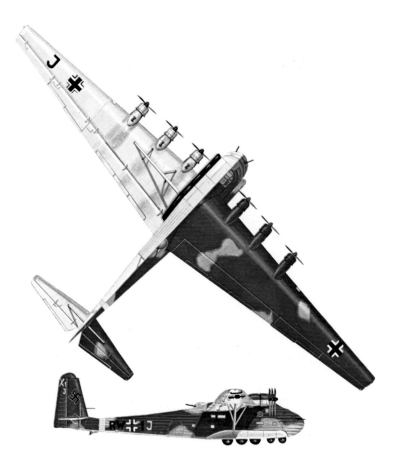

79

Messerschmitt Me 323D-1 (unit unknown), Eastern Front 1942–43. *Engines:* Six 990 h.p. Gnome-Rhône 14N 48/49 radials. *Data apply to Me 323D-6. Span:* 181 ft. 1¼ in. (55.20 m.). *Length:* 93 ft. 4½ in. (28.46 m.). *Height:* approximately 27 ft. 6 in. (8.38 m.). *Normal take-off weight:* 95,901 lb. (43,500 kg.). *Maximum speed:* 137 m.p.h. (220 km./hr.) at sea level. *Maximum payload:* 24,251 lb. (11,000 kg.). *Typical range:* 696 miles (1,120 km.). *Armament:* Five 13 mm. MG 131 machine-guns firing through apertures in nose-loading doors and from dorsal positions.

OHKA (Japan)

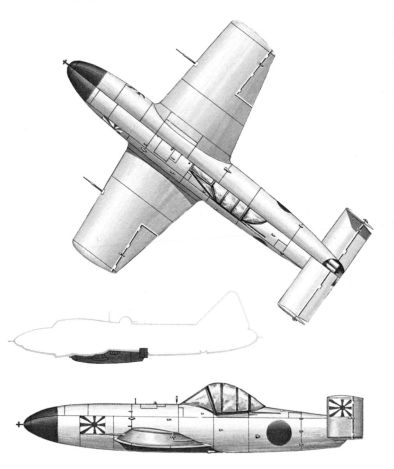

80

Yokosuka MXY-7 *Ohka* Model 11 piloted bomb, exhibited in the Indian Air Force Museum, New Delhi. *Engine:* One 1,764 lb. (800 kg.) st Type 4 Model 20 solid-propellant rocket motor. *Span:* 16 ft. 4⅞ in. (5.00 m.). *Length:* 19 ft. 10⅞ in. (6.07 m.). *Height:* approximately 3 ft. 11¼ in. (1.20 m.). *Maximum weight:* 4,718 lb. (2,140 kg.). *Maximum level speed:* 534 m.p.h. (860 km./hr.). *Maximum diving speed:* 621 m.p.h. (1,000 km./hr.). *Range:* 55 miles (88 km.).

1 Supermarine Walrus

Originally in the Fleet reconnaissance role, and later as an air/sea rescue aeroplane, the Walrus amphibious flying boat was one of the best known sights in the wartime skies, especially those over British home waters. The Walrus could trace its lineage back to the Seagull amphibians of the 1920s, and when the prototype (K 4797) first appeared it was known as the Seagull V. It first flew on 21 June 1933, powered by a 635 hp Bristol Pegasus IIM.2 radial engine driving a pusher propeller. Twenty-four Seagull V's were ordered by the Australian Government, and a further twelve, to Specification 2/35, by the Fleet Air Arm, to whom it was known as the Walrus. In the following year Specification 37/36 was issued to cover another two hundred and four Walrus I's, and additional contracts followed later. Three from FAA orders were diverted to the Irish Army Air Corps in 1939. The metal-hulled Walrus I was delivered to FAA units from July 1936, initial allocations being made to battleships, cruisers and other warships equipped with catapults. These units were combined in January 1940 as No 700 Squadron, whose total aircraft strength included forty-two Walruses. Other Fleet-spotter squadrons to employ the Walrus included Nos 711, 712 and 714. From 1941 onward the Walrus was also employed increasingly by the Royal Air Force as an air/sea rescue amphibian, a task which it performed with distinction until the end of the war.

Seven RAF squadrons in Britain and four in the Middle East operated the Walrus in this role. From the two hundred and eighty-eighth machine onward production was undertaken by Saunders-Roe at Cowes with the designation Walrus II. The Saro-built aircraft had wooden hulls and Pegasus VI engines, and most of the ASR squadrons were equipped with this version. Despite its archaic appearance, the Walrus was a more rugged aeroplane than it seemed, and operated with utter reliability in sharply contrasted climates. Some operating in the Argentine were retired as recently as 1966.

2 Fairey Albacore

Two prototypes of the Albacore were built, to the requirements of Specification S.41/36 for a three-seat torpedo/spotter/reconnaissance aircraft for the FAA. The first of these (L 7074) flew on 12 December 1938, and production began in 1939 of the initial order for ninety-eight, placed in May 1937. When production ended in 1943 this total had increased to eight hundred and one. Early production Albacores, like the prototypes, were powered by Bristol Taurus II engines, but the 1,130 hp Taurus XII was installed in later batches; otherwise the 'Applecore' underwent comparatively little modification during its wartime career. This began with the formation of No 826 Squadron of the FAA specially to operate the Albacore, and the first dozen were officially accepted in mid-March 1940. The first operational sorties were made some ten weeks later, and in 1941 Albacores began to equip carrier-based FAA squadrons as well as those at shore stations. They subsequently gave extensive service in home waters and in the Mediterranean and Middle East theatres of war, until the arrival of Barracuda monoplane torpedo-bombers during 1943. At the peak of their career they equipped fifteen FAA squadrons, and figured in such major campaigns as the Battles of Cape Matapan and El Alamein, and the Allied landings in Sicily and at Salerno. When the last FAA squadron to fly Albacores (No 841) disbanded late in 1943 its aircraft were taken over by the Royal Canadian Air Force, in whose service they helped to keep the sea lanes open during the Allied invasion of Normandy in June 1944. Thus the Albacore, originally brought into being to replace the Fairey Swordfish, served alongside its sister aeroplane throughout its career and was actually retired from British service before the Swordfish.

3 Fairey Swordfish

Fortunately for the wartime Royal Navy, the loss of the Fairey T.S.R.I prototype in an accident in September 1933 was not sufficient to deter the Fairey Aviation Co from following it with a second, slightly larger development, the T.S.R.II. Designed, as its initials indicated, for the torpedo/spotter/reconnaissance role, the T.S.R.II (K 4190) was the true prototype of the later Swordfish and made its first flight on 17 April 1934. Delivery of production Swordfish to the FAA began

in July 1936, the first recipient being No 825 Squadron. These were built to Specification S.38/34 and had the Pegasus IIIM.3 as powerplant. As an alternative to the 1,610 lb (730 kg) torpedo which it was designed to carry beneath the fuselage, the Swordfish I could carry a 1,500 lb (680 kg) mine in the same position or a similar total weight of bombs distributed under the fuselage and lower wings. Thirteen FAA squadrons were equipped with Swordfish at the outbreak of World War 2, a figure which was later almost doubled. At first they were employed largely on convoy or fleet escort duties, but in April 1940 the first major torpedo attack was made by Swordfish from HMS *Furious* during the Norwegian campaign, and their duties were soon extended to include minelaying. Their most notable achievement was the destruction of three battleships, two destroyers, a cruiser and other warships of the Italian Fleet at Taranto on 10-11 November 1940, for the loss of only two Swordfish. The next variant was the Mk II, which appeared in 1943 and was built with metal-covered lower wings, enabling it to carry rocket projectiles. Later Mk II's were fitted with Pegasus XXX engines of 820 hp, and these also powered the Mk III, identifiable by its ASV radar housing beneath the front fuselage. Swordfish from all three Marks underwent conversion to Mk IV for service with the Royal Canadian Air Force; these were provided with enclosed cockpits. A substantial number of Mk I's were converted as twin-float seaplanes for service aboard catapult-equipped warships. The Swordfish was in action until less than four hours before the German surrender was signed, but after the war in Europe ended it was swiftly retired, the last FAA squadron disbanding on 21 May 1945. Total Swordfish production (including the prototype T.S.R.II) amounted to six hundred and ninety-two by Fairey and one thousand six hundred and ninety-nine by Blackburn. The Swordfish was universally known as the 'Stringbag' to all associated with it. Its lengthy and successful career, outlasting that of the Albacore which was meant to replace it, was a tribute to its excellent flying qualities, robust construction and uncomplaining adaptability.

4 Noorduyn Norseman

The first example of this Canadian 'bush' transport was completed in January 1935, and was then operated by Dominion Skyways, which later became a part of Canadian Pacific Air Lines. During the next five years Noorduyn sold only seventeen more of these aircraft, to commercial operators and to the Royal Canadian Mounted Police. Following the outbreak of World War 2, however, demand for military versions of this 9-seat utility transport increased spectacularly, both the RCAF and the USAAF placing orders. The former ordered thirty-eight Norseman Mk IV for radio and navigational training under the Empire Air Training Scheme. The USAAF, after evaluating seven

YC-64 Norsemen delivered in mid-1942, placed orders early in the following year for seven hundred and forty-six C-64A (later UC-64A) production aircraft; under Lend-Lease, thirty-four of these went to the RCAF as the Norseman VI, and forty-three others to various other Allied air forces; three others were diverted to the U.S. Navy with the designation JA-1. Plans for Aeronca also to build the C-64A were cancelled, but six C-64B floatplanes were ordered for the Engineering Corps, these all being delivered in 1943. Interchangeable wheel, ski or twin-float landing gear was available for all Norseman aircraft; the type was used by the U.S. forces mainly as a passenger or freight transport, but other duties included those of communications or casualty evacuation. Production of the Norseman by Noorduyn continued until 1946, when it was taken over by the Canadian Car and Foundry Company. The last of nine hundred and eighteen Norsemen was completed in January 1960. The post-war commercial version, the Norseman V continues to be used in substantial numbers, alongside many de-militarised C-64A's.

5 Westland Lysander

Evolved to Specification A.39/34 for a 2-seat Army co-operation aeroplane, the Lysander was destined to play a far from passive role in the forthcoming war, and drew attention to its capabilities as early as

November 1939, when a Lysander shot down an He 111 bomber over France. The first of two Lysander prototypes (K 6127) flew on 15 June 1936, and in the following September one hundred and forty-four were ordered for the RAF under Specification 36/36. Deliveries, to No 16 Squadron, began in June 1938, and on 3 September 1939 the RAF had on charge sixty-eight Lysander Mk I and one hundred and ninety-five Mk II. Ultimately, one hundred and sixty-nine Mk I and four hundred and forty-two Mk II were completed. These differed principally in powerplant, the Mk I having an 890 hp Bristol Mercury XII and the Mk II a 905 hp Perseus XII. During wartime production of the Mks III (two hundred and sixty-seven) and IIIA (four hundred and forty-seven) many of these were built, and many earlier Lysanders converted, for service as target tugs. But the Lysander was to serve with distinction in roles of more direct value than these, notably those of air/sea rescue and agent-dropping. Here the low flying speeds and remarkable STOL characteristics of the Lysander provided a unique performance, especially for landing in and taking off from small fields or roads in Occupied Europe while fulfilling its 'cloak and dagger' role. Up to six bombs could be carried attached to the wheel fairings. All except the Mk IIIA carried only a single 0·303 in Lewis or Browning gun in the rear cockpit, but experimental versions with two 20-mm cannon or a four-gun Boulton Paul turret were evolved in 1939. Other experimental Lysanders included the Steiger-wing P 9105, a converted Mk II, and the short-fuselage, tandem-wing project produced in 1941 by modifying the original prototype. Lysander production at Yeovil ended in January 1942, but an additional seventy-five Mk II and two hundred and fifty Mk III were built in Canada by the National Steel Car Corporation. Lysanders were supplied to Egypt (twenty), Eire (six), Finland (nine) and Turkey (thirty-six), and also served with the Free French and various Commonwealth air forces.

6   **Fieseler Fi 156 Storch (Stork)**
Germany's counterpart to the Westland Lysander, the Fieseler Storch was also of pre-war design, three of the five prototypes being flown during 1936. A small pre-series batch of Fi 156A-0's was followed by the initial production model, the A-1, in 1938. No examples were completed of the Fi 156B, a projected civil version, and production continued with the Fi 156C series. The Fi 156C-0, which appeared early in 1939, introduced a defensive MG 15 machine-gun, mounted in a raised section at the rear of the 3-seat cabin, and was followed by C-1 staff transport and C-2 observation versions. All models thus far had been powered by Argus As 10C engines, but most of the multi-purpose C-3's built were fitted with the As 10P version of this engine. Detail improvements introduced during the production life of the C-3 were incorporated in

its successor, the C-5, which was able to carry such optional items as three 110-lb (50-kg) bombs, a 298-lb (135-kg) mine, a pod-mounted reconnaissance camera or an auxiliary drop-tank with which its range was increased to 628 miles (1,010 km). Final models were the Fi 156D-0 (As 10C) and Fi 156D-1 (As 10P), with increased cabin space and enlarged doors to permit the loading of a stretcher. From 1942 until the end of the war the C-5 and D-1 were the principal models in production. The Fi 156E-0 was a successful but experimental-only version with caterpillar-track landing gear for operation on rough or soft terrain. The Storch's remarkable STOL qualities enabled it to take off and land in extremely short distances, due to the full-span Handley Page wing leading-edge slats, and the slotted flaps and ailerons extending over the entire trailing edge. The wings could be folded back alongside the fuselage. Wartime production of the Storch, which amounted to two thousand five hundred and forty-nine aircraft, was transferred during 1944 to the Mraz factory in Czechoslovakia (which built sixty-four) and to the Morane-Saulnier works at Puteaux. The Storch served with the *Luftwaffe*, the *Regia Aeronautica* and in small numbers with the air forces of Bulgaria, Croatia, Finland, Hungary, Rumania, Slovakia and Switzerland. Both companies continued to build the type after the war, the Mraz version being known as the K-65 Cap (Stork) and the French version as the Criquet

(Locust). The Fi 256 was a wartime Puteaux-built prototype for an enlarged 5-seat development.

7 Beriev MBR-2

In many ways the MBR-2 was to the Soviet Navy what the Supermarine Walrus was to the RAF and Fleet Air Arm, both types enjoying long production lives and service careers. The MBR-2 was designed by Georgi M. Beriev and flown in 1931, the functional letters in its designation indicating *Morskoi Blizhnii Razvedchik*, or Naval Short Range Reconnaissance. The prototype was powered by an imported BMW VI.Z engine of 500 hp, and it was a licence-built development of this, the 680 hp M-17B, which powered the initial production version of the flying boat in 1934. This version carried a crew of four or five, with the two pilots seated side by side in an open cockpit; had open gun positions in the bow and midway along the top of the fuselage, each with a PV-1 machine-gun on a movable mounting; and was characterised by a square-topped fin and rudder. The flying boat, which became a standard Soviet Naval Aviation type during 1935, could also be fitted with a fixed wheel or ski landing gear, to enable it to operate from land or ice-covered waters. In 1934 an 8-passenger commercial version, designated MP-1, was put into service on internal routes by Aeroflot, and an MP-1T freighter counterpart appeared two years later. In 1935, however, an extensive redesign had been carried out by Beriev, based upon the installation of the more powerful Mikulin AM-34N engine. Other major changes included the provision of a manually operated dorsal turret, an enclosed crew cabin and larger, redesigned vertical tail surfaces. This version, sometimes referred to as the MBR-2*bis*, remained in production until 1941, and saw extensive service throughout World War 2. Many were still in service for fishery patrol and similar duties ten years later, and a few may still be flying today. The AM-34N-powered civil version was designated MP-1*bis* and entered Aeroflot service in 1937, after the prototype had been used to establish several distance and load-to-altitude records for women pilots.

8 Aichi D3A

Aichi was one of three companies to compete, in 1936, for the Imperial Japanese Navy's 11-Shi requirement for a new carrier-borne dive bomber, and its design showed strongly the influence of current German products by Heinkel, with whom the Japanese Navy had a clandestine agreement. Aichi's design was awarded a development contract, and entered production in 1937 as the D3A1 Model 11, or Type 99 carrier-based dive bomber. The Model 11 remained in production until August 1942; it was a standard JNAF type at the time of the attack on Pearl Harbor (in which it took part), and in April 1942 the British carrier *Hermes* and the cruisers *Cornwall* and *Dorsetshire* were sunk in the Indian Ocean by D3A1's. A single 250 kg bomb could be carried on a ventral cradle which was swung forward and downward to clear the propeller during delivery, and a 60 kg bomb could be attached to each outer wing section. After delivering its bombs the D3A1 was sufficiently well armed and manoeuvrable to put up a creditable fight against the Allied fighters then in service. Four hundred and seventy-eight D3A1's were built, production then continuing with the D3A2 Model 22 until January 1944, when eight hundred and sixteen D3A2's had been completed. The D3A2 introduced cockpit and minor airframe improvements, but differed chiefly in having a 1,300 hp Kinsei 54 engine which raised the maximum speed to 266 mph (428 kmh) at 18,540 ft (5,650 m). Normal and maximum take-off weights of this model were 8,378 lb (3,800 kg) and 9,088 lb (4,122 kg) respectively, and the maximum range 1,572 miles (2,530 km). Both the D3A1 and the D3A2 (which were code named 'Val' by the Allies) figured prominently in the major Pacific battles, including those of Santa Cruz, Midway and the Solomon Islands; but increasing losses, both of aircraft and of experienced pilots, progressively reduced their contribution to the Japanese war effort, and during the second half of the Pacific War they were encountered much less often. Some were converted as single-seat suicide attack aircraft, and a number of D3A2's were adapted for the training role with the designation D3A2-K.

9 Arado Ar 196

Possessing a general appearance similar to many of the Arado biplanes of the immediate pre-war years, the Arado Ar 196 monoplane entered service in the month preceding the outbreak of World War 2. Its design had been started some years earlier, as a replacement for the obsolescent Heinkel He 60 catapult biplanes then carried by German capital ships, and during 1938 two twin-float prototypes (the Ar 196V1 and V2), and two others (the V3 and V4) with one centrally mounted main float, were flown. Towards the end of 1938 production was started at Warnemünde of the Ar 196A-1. Apart from replacement of the 880 hp BMW 132Dc radial (which had powered all four prototypes) by the more powerful BMW 132K, the Ar 196A-1 basically resembled the V2 prototype, the smaller fin and horn-balanced rudder of the V1 having been discarded in favour of a more typical Arado empennage. The Ar 196A-1 was armed with single forward- and rearward-firing 7·9 mm MG 17 machine-guns, one fixed in the front fuselage and the other on a flexible mount in the aft cockpit. The Ar 196A-1's, twenty-six of which were completed during 1939, were deployed chiefly aboard such major warships as the *Bismarck*, *Gneisenau*, *Graf Spee*, *Lützow*, *Scharnhorst* and *Scheer*, and at shore-based training establishments. In 1940 the initial version began to be joined by the principal production version, the Arado Ar 196A-3. This had improved internal equipment, but was notable chiefly for its augmented armament. When they first entered service the Ar 196A-3's operated from newly acquired bases in France, and were frequently used against Allied anti-submarine patrols in the Biscay area until countered by the appearance of the Beaufighter. Thereafter they themselves were used for anti-submarine patrols, and for convoy escort and reconnaissance, from seaplane shore bases in the Mediterranean theatre (notably Crete). The only other known operational version was the Ar 196A-5, which differed from the A-3 simply in internal equipment. Sixty-nine examples of this model were completed by Fokker in the Netherlands during 1943-44. Production by Arado, which ceased in 1943, amounted to four hundred and one aircraft, the great majority of which were the A-3 model. A further twenty-three A-3's were completed in 1942-43 by the Sud-Ouest factory at St Nazaire in Vichy France. *Luftwaffe* units employing the Ar 196 included *Seeaufklärungsgruppen* 125 and 126 and *Bordfliegergruppe* 196. Small numbers of Ar 196A-3's were also in service in the Adriatic during the war, with the air forces of Rumania and Bulgaria. The Ar 196V3, with its central main float and outer stabilising floats, was intended to serve as prototype for a proposed Ar 196B production model following this configuration, but which proved to be unnecessary. The V4 was used for armament trials.

10 Nakajima B5N

The B5N was designed by Nakajima to a 10-Shi (1935) requirement by the JNAF for a carrier-based attack bomber. It exhibited several advanced features for its time, and its design was influenced in no small part by the Northrop 5A, an example of which had arrived in Japan in 1935. The prototype B5N1 flew for the first time in January 1937, and was a clean-looking 2/3-seat monoplane with mechanically folding wings, Fowler-type landing flaps and a fully retractable main undercarriage. Its 770 hp Hikari 3 radial engine was installed beneath a neat NACA cowling, and on test the prototype aircraft exceeded the performance specification in many respects. The B5N1 Model 11 entered production late in 1937, and saw combat service in the Sino-Japanese conflict that preceded Japan's entry into World War 2. The B5N1 was armed with a single defensive machine-gun at the rear. Production of the B5N1 was simplified by adopting manual instead of mechanical wing-folding, and by substituting slotted flaps for the Fowler type. Late production aircraft (designated Model 12) were fitted with 985 hp Sakae 11 engines. A prototype appeared in December 1939 of the B5N2 Model 23, a torpedo bomber version powered by a 1,115 hp Sakae 21 engine. This was armed with two forward-firing guns and one or two guns in the rear cockpit; and it could carry an 18 in torpedo or bombs under the fuselage. The B5N2 entered JNAF service in 1940, and both variants were con-cerned in the attack on Pearl Harbor in December 1941. Subsequently they were responsible for the destruction of several other major U.S. carriers during the early part of the war. The B5N, known by the Allied code name 'Kate', was encountered operationally as late as June 1944, when a number were engaged in the Marianas Islands campaign. For a year or more, however, the B5N had been obsolescent, and indeed several B5N1's were withdrawn from operations and converted to B5N1-K trainers soon after the B5N2 began to enter service. More than one thousand two hundred 'Kates' were completed, some of them by Aichi, before the B5N began to be superseded by its newer and faster stablemate, the B6N Tenzan. A number of B5N's were, however, employed as suicide aircraft in the final stages of the war.

11 Douglas SBD Dauntless

Evolution of the Dauntless began in 1934, when a Northrop team under Ed Heinemann based a new Navy dive-bomber design on the company's Army A-17A. Designated XBT-1, it flew in July 1935, and in February 1936 fifty-four BT-1's with 825 hp R-1535-94 engines were ordered. The last of these was completed as the XBT-2, with a 1,000 hp R-1820-32 engine. With further modifications, notably to the landing gear and vertical tail contours, this was redesignated XSBD-1 when Northrop was absorbed by Douglas on 31 August 1937. At about this time the perforated dive flaps, a distinctive Dauntless feature, were introduced. Delivery of fifty-seven SBD-1's to the Marine Corps began in mid-1940. Simultaneously, the U.S. Navy ordered eighty-seven SBD-2's with additional fuel, protective armour and autopilots. Both versions were armed with two 0·30 in machine-guns in the upper engine cowling and a single 0·30 in gun in the rear cockpit. Bombs up to 1,000 lb (454 kg) in size could be carried on an under-fuselage cradle; maximum bomb load was 1,200 lb (544 kg). Delivery of SBD-2's, from November 1940, was followed from March 1941 by one hundred and seventy-four SBD-3's, with R-1820-52 engines and 0·50 in front guns. The two models were standard U.S. Navy carrier-borne dive-bombers at the time of Pearl Harbor; subsequently, the Navy received a further four hundred and ten SBD-3's. In May 1942 SBD pilots from the USS *Lexington* and *York-town* were credited with forty of the ninety-one enemy aircraft lost during the Battle of the Coral Sea; a month later, at Midway, SBD's from the *Enterprise, Hornet* and *Yorktown* sank the Japanese carriers *Akagi, Kaga* and *Soryu* and put the *Hiryu* out of action. Their own attrition rate was the lowest of any U.S. carrier aircraft in the Pacific, due largely to an outstanding ability to absorb battle damage, and the Dauntless at this time did more than any other type to turn the tide of the war in the Pacific. Later, Dauntlesses continued the war from the decks of escort carriers, flying anti-submarine or close-support missions with depth charges or rocket projectiles. In October 1942 delivery began of seven hundred and eighty SBD-4's fitted with radar and radio-navigation equipment. They were followed by the major production model, the SBD-5, with increased engine power. To the two thousand nine hundred and sixty-five SBD-5's for the U.S. Navy were added sixty SBD-5A's, built to an Army contract but delivered instead to the Marine Corps. One SBD-5, with a 1,350 hp R-1820-66 engine, acted as a prototype for the four hundred and fifty SBD-6's which completed Dauntless production in July 1944. Overall production amounted to five thousand nine hundred and thirty-six, the balance consisting of one hundred and sixty-eight A-24's and six hundred and fifteen A-24B's for the USAAF, delivered from June 1941. These corresponded to the SBD-3 and -3A, SBD-4 and SBD-5 respectively, but had new tailwheels, internal equipment changes and no arrester gear. The Army machines were not flown with a great degree of combat success, and were used chiefly for training or communications. The Royal New Zealand Air Force received eighteen SBD-3's, twenty-seven SBD-4's and twenty-three SBD-5's. Thirty-two SBD-5's were supplied to the French Navy, and between forty and fifty A-24B's to the *Armée de l'Air*; but the latter, like their U.S. Army counterparts, were employed mainly on second-line duties. Nine SBD-5's were delivered to the British Fleet Air Arm, but were not used operationally.

12 Yokosuka D4Y Suisei (Comet)

When the prototype D4Y1 made its first flight in November 1940 it became the first Japanese Navy aircraft since 1932 to fly with an in-line engine. The Navy's 1937 specification, to which it was designed, had called for a 2-seat, carrier-based dive bomber with a range of 920-1,380 miles (1,480-2,220 km) and a speed as fast as the A6M2 Zero fighter. Yokosuka's design proposed an aeroplane with a comparatively small airframe, in which the minimal frontal area of an in-line engine was an important factor. The prototype was powered by an imported Daimler-Benz DB 600G of 960 hp; production D4Y1's by the 1,200 hp Aichi Atsuta 21. Apart from five hundred completed by the Hiro Naval Air Arsenal, Aichi also built all of the two thousand three hundred and nineteen D4Y's that were produced. The D4Y1 Model 11 entered production early in 1941, but when various structural weaknesses became apparent during service this was supplanted by the strengthened D4Y2 with the Atsuta 32 engine. Delivery of Atsuta engines, however, fell behind the airframe production date, and gave rise to the D4Y3 Model 33, in which a change was made to the 1,560 hp Mitsubishi Kinsei 62 radial engine. Some loss of performance with this engine was accepted as the price for virtual elimination, in the D4Y3, of undercarriage retraction difficulties and other problems encountered in earlier models. The Suisei first appeared operationally in a reconnaissance role, designated D4Y1-C, when aircraft from the carrier *Soryu* took part in the Battle of Midway Island. The D4Y2 was used initially as a dive bomber, but by the time of the Marianas campaign in September 1944 – its first major action – this also (as the D4Y2-C) had become used for reconnaissance. By the time the radial-engined D4Y3 appeared, Japanese carrier losses were such that the 'Judy' (as the D4Y was coded by the Allies) operated almost equally from shore bases. During the final year of the war there appeared the D4Y4 Model 43, a single-seat conversion of the D4Y3 adapted for suicide attacks with 1,764 lb (800 kg) of high explosive on board; and a number of Model 12's were converted to D4Y2-S emergency night fighters for home defence in 1945. These had one or two 20 mm cannon placed behind the rear cockpit to fire obliquely forward and upward.

13 Grumman TBF Avenger

The Avenger was a pre-war design, two XTBF-1 prototypes of which were ordered by the U.S. Navy in April 1940. The first of these made its maiden flight on 1 August 1941, by which time a substantial first order had been placed. The first production TBF-1's were delivered to Squadron VT-8 late in January 1942, and the Avenger made its combat debut early in the following June at the Battle of Midway. The aircraft had typical Grumman lines, the most noticeable feature being the very deep fuselage, which enabled the torpedo or bomb load to be totally enclosed. The TBF-1C had two wing-mounted 0·50 in machine-guns in addition to the nose, dorsal and ventral guns of the original TBF-1, and could carry auxiliary drop-tanks. Both models were 3-seaters and were powered by the 1,700 hp R-2600-8 engine. Up to December 1943 Grumman built two thousand two hundred and ninety-three TBF-1/-1C Avengers, including the two original proto-types, one XTBF-2 and one XTBF-3. Four hundred and two of them were supplied to the Royal Navy as Avenger Mk I's (=TBF-1B) and sixty-three to the RNZAF. The British aircraft were briefly known as Tarpons, but the U.S. name was later standardised. Meanwhile, in the U.S.A. production had also begun in September 1942 by the Eastern Aircraft Division of General Motors, which built two thousand eight hundred and eighty-two as the TBM-1 and -1C. Three hundred and thirty-four of these went to the Royal Navy as Avenger II's. The 'dash two' variant was not built by either company, but Eastern completed a prototype and four thousand six hundred and sixty-four TBM-3's with uprated Cyclone engines and their wings strengthened to carry rocket projectiles or a radar pod. Two hundred and twenty-two of these became the British Avenger III. Further strengthening of the airframe produced the XTBM-4, but production of this model was cancelled when the war ended. This did not, however, end the Avenger's long and productive career: those

of the U.S. Navy were not finally retired until 1954, and post-war variants served with some foreign naval air forces for several years after this. During the major part of World War 2 the Avenger was the standard U.S. Navy torpedo-bomber, operating alike from car-riers or shore bases, mostly in the Pacific theatre.

14 Sukhoi Su-2

While a member of the Tupolev design collective, Pavel Sukhoi designed a low-wing, single-engined bomber designated ANT-51. Test flights of this aeroplane, which began in August 1937, were dis-appointing, but Sukhoi continued to develop the basic concept after establishing his own design bureau early in 1939. Three prototypes were completed and flown, with 950 hp M-87A, M-87B and M-88 engines respectively, and the third version was accepted for production in 1940 with the functional designation BB-1. The production BB-1 had a well-armoured cockpit and crew of two, and the internal weapons bay could, if necessary, contain the entire 1,323 lb (600 kg) bomb load. More usually, however, the internal load was restricted to 882 lb (400 kg), the remaining weapons (bombs or rocket projectiles) being distributed under the wings. Early in 1941 the uprated M-88B engine began to be installed, and with the revision of the Soviet designation system the BB-1 became known as the Su-2. During the early period of the Nazi attack on the U.S.S.R. the Su-2 was in fairly widespread use, but it was no match for the *Luftwaffe's* superior fighters, and after about a hundred Su-2's had been completed (some with twin dorsal guns) an attempt was made to improve its performance to bridge the gap until the Ilyushin Il-2 became available in quantity. Protective crew armour was increased, but the major alteration was the introduction of the 1,400 hp Shvetsov M-82 engine, which became the standard powerplant until production ceased during the latter half of 1942. Despite the numbers produced, the installation of the M-82 engine proved a retrograde step, for, while it improved the Su-2's performance on paper, its higher installed weight upset the aircraft's handling characteristics. Combat losses continued to be high, and the Su-2 was withdrawn from operational units from 1942 onward. An Su-2 re-engined with a 2,100 hp M-90 radial was test-flown in 1941 with the designation Su-4. A much superior development was the ground-attack Su-6, but as a contemporary of the already-established Il-2, this did not go into large-scale production.

15 Curtiss SB2C Helldiver

The XSB2C-1 Helldiver prototype, following its first flight on 18 December 1940, was lost in a crash early in the following year – an inauspicious beginning to the career of perhaps the most successful dive bomber ever to enter U.S. Navy service. The initial Navy order, placed in November 1940, was later increased until nine hundred and seventy-eight SB2C-1's had been completed, the first of which was delivered in June 1942. They were succeeded by one thousand one hundred and twelve SB2C-3's, two thousand and forty-five SB2C-4's and nine hundred and seventy SB2C-5's. The SB2C-3 had the 1,900 hp R-2600-20 model of the Cyclone engine, while the SB2C-4 introduced search radar in an under-wing fairing and provision for an external warload of 1,000 lb (454 kg) of bombs or eight 5 in rocket projectiles. The SB2C-5 was essentially a longer-range variant of the -4. Nine hundred Helldivers purchased by the USAAF, and built by Curtiss and Douglas with the Army title A-25A Shrike, were mostly transferred to the Marine Corps as SB2C-1A's. Starting in the summer of 1943 the Canadian Car and Foundry Co built eight hundred and ninety-four SBW-1, -3, -4 and -5 Helldivers, including twenty-six supplied to the British Fleet Air Arm. Fairchild in Canada contributed three hundred SBF-1, -3 and -4 versions to bring the overall Helldiver production total to seven thousand two hundred aircraft. The British machines were not used on active service, but the American Helldivers, perpetuating the name given to Curtiss's earlier SBC biplane dive bomber, played a prominent part in the Pacific war, operating from the USS *Bunker Hill*, *Enterprise*, *Essex*, *Independence* and other carriers. Their first major action was the Rabaul campaign in November 1943, and they took part in virtually every major naval/air action during the rest of the war. One SB2C-1 was fitted experimentally with twin floats as the XSB2C-2, and an SB2C-5 with 2,100 hp R-2600-22 engine became the sole XSB2C-6, but neither version went into production.

16 Nakajima B6N Tenzan

Just as Nakajima's earlier B5N attack bomber had exhibited superiority over most of its Allied contemporaries, so did its successor, the B6N, despite the engine troubles encountered early in its career. Only the lack of a carrier fleet and sufficient experienced pilots by the JNAF prevented the B6N from being a more serious threat to Allied shipping during the later part of the war. The powerplant chosen for the B6N1, which flew in prototype form in March 1942, was the 1,870 hp Nakajima Mamori II. Despite the bulk of this powerful two-row radial engine, it was installed in a close-fitting cowling that did little to mar the outstandingly clean lines of the B6N design. However, the engine was prone to overheating and vibration, which eventually caused the B6N1 Model 11 to be withdrawn from production, though not from service. It was superseded by the B6N2 Model 12, powered by the more reliable Mitsubishi Kasei 25, which offered a lighter installed weight and more straightforward maintenance for only a slight reduction in output. The B6N was named Tenzan by the Japanese, after a Chinese mountain, and in the Allied code naming system was known as 'Jill'. The B6N1 carried dorsal and ventral machine-guns,

the latter gun being extended into the airstream after the torpedo had been releasedt, to discourage anti-aircraft fire from the ship just attacked. In the B6N2 an additional forward-firing gun was provided in one wing. To avoid fouling the bombs or torpedo, the oil cooler was offset to port on the lower portion of the engine cowling. First combat appearance of the Tenzan was in December 1943, when a group of B6N1's attacked a U.S. task force off the Marshall Islands, but most of the one thousand two hundred and sixty-eight Tenzans built at Nakajima's Handa and Koizumi factories were B6N2's. This version made its first operational appearance in the Marianas campaign in June 1944, and was encountered again in engagements in the Caroline and Solomon Islands groups and at Iwo Jima. Tenzans carrying ASV radar attacked Allied naval concentrations off Kyushu in March 1945, and from April to June 1945 the JNAF mounted a considerable torpedo and suicide attack campaign with Tenzans against Allied ships in the vicinity of Okinawa.

17 Fairey Barracuda

The ungainly form of the Barracuda, and its 'Christmas-tree' appearance when bedecked with torpedos, bombs, lifeboats, radar arrays and the like, were the direct outcome of the exacting Specification S.24/37 to which it was designed. It was the first British carrier-based monoplane torpedo bomber of all-metal construction, yet its high, strut-braced tailplane and large, Fairey-Youngman trailing-edge flaps might have suggested to the uninitiated a less sophisticated design than was actually the case. Abandonment of the intended Rolls-Royce Exe engine delayed the trials of the first prototype (P 1767), which eventually flew on 7 December 1940 with a 1,260 hp Merlin 30. Priority afforded to other types of aircraft then delayed production, the first Barracuda I not being flown until 18 May 1942. Thirty of this model were completed (including five by Westland), and they were followed by one thousand six hundred and eighty-eight Barracuda II's with the uprated Merlin 32, which permitted higher operating weights but slightly reduced the overall performance. The Barracuda I's were used chiefly for trials or conversion training, the first operational unit being No 827 Squadron, which received the Mk II in January 1943. First combat action was with No 810 Squadron during the Salerno landings eight months later. In service, the Barracuda was more often employed as a dive bomber than with a torpedo, and it was in this role that forty-two Barracudas, from four Squadrons aboard the carriers *Victorious* and *Furious*, carried out the attack on the *Tirpitz* in *Kaafioord* in northern Norway in April 1944, scoring fifteen direct hits on the German battleship with armour-piercing 500 lb and 1,000 lb bombs for the loss of only three Barracudas. Later that month Barracudas from *Illustrious* carried out the type's first combat action in the Pacific theatre. Final wartime version was the Mk III, with a ventral ASV radome for anti-submarine patrols but otherwise generally similar to the Mk II. Fairey built six hundred and seventy-five Mk II's, Blackburn seven hundred, Boulton Paul three hundred and Westland thirteen. Four hundred and sixty Mk III's were built by Fairey, and three hundred and ninety-two by Boulton Paul. One Mk II was re-engined with a 1,850 hp Griffon VII as prototype for the unarmed Mk V (the Mk IV was not built), and this aircraft (P 9976) flew on 16 November 1944. Thirty production Mk V's, with tail surfaces and other features extensively redesigned, were built by Fairey, with 2,020 hp Griffon 37's, but were not completed until after the war and served mainly as trainers.

18 Fairey Battle

Often, when a particular aeroplane type is utilised as a flying test-bed for a variety of experimental engines, such employment is an indication that its general handling qualities are rather above the average. Such was the case with the Battle, several examples of which were employed in this fashion to air-test various engines of up to 2,000 hp. This was a considerable increase over the 1,030 hp of the Merlin I that powered the prototype (K 4303) when it made its first flight on 10 March 1936. The Battle was designed by Marcel Lobelle to Specification P.27/32 for a 2-seat day bomber to replace the Hawker Hart biplane, and an initial order for one hundred and fifty-five Battles, to Specification P.23/35, was placed before the prototype had flown. The first production Battle was completed in June 1937, and the bomber – now a 3-seater – was one of the types chosen for large-scale priority production as part of the RAF expansion programme. Under the 'shadow factory' scheme Austin Motors shared the production with Fairey, and on 3 September 1939 the RAF had well over a thousand Battle Mks I-III on charge. (Production Battles were powered successively by Merlin Mk I, II, III or V engines, and took their own Mark numbers from that of the engine. This famous engine series first entered production as the powerplant for the Battle.) Ultimately, Fairey built one thousand one hundred and fifty-six Battles, and Austin one thousand and twenty-nine; an additional eighteen were completed before the war by Avions Fairey in Belgium. First RAF deliveries were made to No 63 Squadron in May 1937, and on 2 September 1939 ten Battle squadrons flew to France as part of the Advanced Air Striking Force. Normal bomb load was stowed in four cells in the wings, but this could be increased to a maximum of 1,500 lb (680 kg) by carrying extra bombs on under-wing racks. Many brave actions were fought by Battle crews, but the bomber was already outdated by the time the war started and was no match for the *Luftwaffe* fighters ranged against it. Consequently, it was soon withdrawn to non-combatant duties, such as operational training and

target towing. In the former role it flew also with the air forces of Australia, Canada and South Africa, and pre-war exports also included twenty-nine for the Turkish Air Force. The type was finally withdrawn from RAF service in 1949.

19 **Junkers Ju 87**
The United States and Germany, in particular, were enthusiastic proponents of the dive bomber during the later 1930s and the early part of World War 2. This particular species of warplane seemed to be typified in the Ju 87, whose ugly lines and wailing engine struck an especial note of terror in the skies above Poland, France and the Low Countries in 1939–40. Design of the Ju 87, by Dipl-Ing Pohlmann, started in 1933, and the first prototype flew early in 1935. This was powered by a Rolls-Royce Kestrel engine and had rectangular twin fins and rudders, but the Ju 87V2, flown in the following autumn, had a single tail and a 610 hp Junkers Jumo 210A engine, and was more representative of the production aircraft to follow. A pre-series batch of Ju 87A-0's was started in 1936, and in the spring of 1937 delivery began of the Ju-87A-1 initial production model, followed by the generally similar A-2. About two hundred A series were built before, in the autumn of 1938, there appeared the much-modified Ju 87B. Powered by the Jumo 211, this had an enlarged vertical tail, redesigned crew canopy and new-style cantilever fairings over the main legs of

the landing gear. Both the A and B models were sent for service with the Condor Legion in Spain in 1938, but by the outbreak of World War 2 the A series had been relegated to the training role, and the three hundred and thirty-six aircraft in front-line service were all Ju 87B-1's. The fighter superiority of the *Luftwaffe* ensured the Ju 87 a comparatively uninterrupted passage in 1939–40, but opposition during the Battle of Britain was much sterner, and losses of the Ju 87 were considerably heavier. Nevertheless, production of the B series continued into 1941, and substantial numbers were supplied to the *Regia Aeronautica*, and to the air forces of Bulgaria, Hungary and Rumania. In production alongside the B series was the long-range Ju 87R, which from 1940 was used for anti-shipping and other missions. Before the war small numbers were also completed of the Ju 87C, a version of the B with arrester hook, folding wings and other 'navalised' attributes. This was planned for service aboard the carrier *Graf Zeppelin*, but the ship was never completed, and the few Ju 87C-0's built served with a land-based unit. Others laid down as C-1's were completed as B-2's. After the setbacks in the Battle of Britain the Ju 87B continued to serve in the Mediterranean and North Africa. Its subsequent development and employment was mainly in the close-support role or as a trainer; these versions are described in Book I *Fighters, Attack and Training Aircraft 1939–45.*

20 Nakajima C6N Saiun (Colourful Cloud)

The Saiun was designed by Yasuo Fukuda to a 17-Shi (1942) requirement for a carrier-based reconnaissance aircraft. Originally, Fukuda contemplated the use of two 1,000 hp radial engines mounted in tandem, but a single, small-diameter Homare engine, which promised to develop around 2,000 hp, was chosen instead. To shorten the Saiun's development period, no less than twenty-three prototypes were ordered, and many of these were completed by the end of 1943. Several of the prototypes were assigned to active units as part of the test programme, and it was they that made the aircraft's operational debut. The Saiun, to which the Allies gave the code name 'Myrt', was first encountered in June 1944, when a number of these aircraft made a reconnaissance of the U.S. task force assembling for the attack on the Marianas Islands. Later the Saiun also reconnoitred the force being assembled to attack Saipan. Series production of the Saiun, as the C6N1 Model 11, began in 1944, the first deliveries to JNAF units being made in August. By the end of the war Nakajima's Handa and Koizumi factories had built four hundred and ninety-eight Saiuns, but their service career was delayed and interrupted by continual troubles with the problematical Homare engine, and they were not met in large numbers. The light armament of the reconnaissance version reflected the aircraft's ability to outpace and outclimb most of the late-war Allied fighters, but those converted for other roles were more comprehensively equipped. The C6N1-S was a home defence night fighter, with a crew of two and twin 20 mm cannon fixed in the rear fuselage to fire obliquely forward and upward. The C6N1-B was a 3-seat torpedo bomber conversion. Two prototypes were also completed of an improved reconnaissance variant, the C6N2 Model 22, powered by the 2,000 hp Homare 24 engine. The final development, designated C6N3 Saiun-Kai, was to have been powered by a Hitachi 92 engine, but this had only reached the project stage when the war ended.

21   **Heinkel He 115**

It was to be expected that Ernst Heinkel, designer of several fine marine aircraft during World War 1, should produce one of the leading seaplanes of the 1939-45 conflict. The first He 115 prototype (D-AEHF) flew in 1936, being modified later for attempts on the prevailing world seaplane speed records, eight of which it captured on 20 March 1938. The definitive production aircraft was fore-shadowed by the third and fourth prototypes, with an extensively glazed nose and long 'greenhouse' canopy, and, in the latter case, no wire bracing for the twin floats. Ten pre-production He 115A-0's and thirty-four He 115A-1's were completed in 1937 and 1938 respectively, the latter having an MG 15 gun in the nose as well as the observer's dorsal gun. The A-2 was the export

equivalent of the *Luftwaffe's* A-1, and was sold to Norway (six) and Sweden (ten). The first large-scale domestic version, the He 115A-3, was soon followed by the He 115B series, comprising ten B-0's and fifty-two B-1/B-2's. These had increased fuel capacity and could carry one of Hitler's much-vaunted 'secret weapons', the magnetic mine, in addition to their internal bomb load. With these they caused considerable havoc to Allied shipping during the early years of the war. In 1940-41 there appeared the He 115C series, of which the C-0, C-1 and C-2 sub-types had an extra forward-firing 20 mm MG 151 cannon in a fairing under the nose. On some aircraft, a 7·9 mm MG 17 gun was installed in each wing root as well. The C series concluded with eighteen C-3 minelayers and thirty C-4 torpedo bombers, the latter having the dorsal MG 15 as its only defensive gun. One He 115A-1 was re-engined with 1,600 hp BMW 801C radials and equipped with five machine-guns and a cannon to become the He 115D; but although this was used operationally, no production of the D series was undertaken. In fact, all production was halted for a time, but was resumed in 1943-44 to build one hundred and forty-one examples of the E-0 and E-1 variants, bringing the overall total to about four hundred aircraft. These were similar to earlier models except for variations in armament. Two of the Norwegian A-2's, which escaped to Britain after the invasion of Norway in 1940, were later employed in RAF colours to transport Allied agents between Malta and North Africa.

22 Vickers Wellington

On 3 September 1939 the RAF had one hundred and seventy-nine Wellingtons on strength, rather less than the number of Hampdens or Whitleys, but these three types bore the brunt of Bomber Command's operations during the early part of the war until the arrival of the four-engined heavy bombers from 1941. The Wellington went on to outstrip both of its contemporaries, an ultimate total of eleven thousand four hundred and sixty-one being built before production ceased in October 1945. After being withdrawn from Bomber Command in 1943, Wellingtons began a second career with Coastal Command as maritime reconnaissance aircraft, at home and in the Middle and Far East; others were employed briefly as transports and (after the war) as aircrew trainers. The 'Wimpey' was designed to Specification B.9/32, the prototype (K 4049) flying on 15 June 1936. Considerable redesign of the fuselage and vertical tail was evident in the production aircraft, ordered to Specification 29/36. The first of these was flown on 23 December 1937, and the first Wellington squadron was No 9, which received its aircraft in October 1938. Those in service when war broke out were Pegasus-engined Mks I or IA, but the most numerous early model was the Mk IC, of which two thousand six hundred and eighty-five were built. Prototypes had also flown before the war

of the Merlin-engined Mk II and the Mk III with Bristol Hercules radials. Wellingtons of Nos 9 and 149 Squadrons, in company with Blenheims, carried out the RAF's first bombing attack of the war when they bombed German shipping at Brunsbüttel. From mid-December 1939 they were switched to night bombing only, joining in the first raid on Berlin late in August 1940. In the following month they made their Middle East debut, and appeared in the Far East from early 1942. By this time the Mk III (one thousand five hundred and nineteen built) was the principal service version, although two squadrons operated the Twin Wasp-engined Mk IV. The first general reconnaissance version for Coastal Command, the Mk VIII, appeared in the spring of 1942. Three hundred and ninety-four, with similar engines to the Mk IC, were built. They were followed by substantial batches of the Mks XI, XII, XIII and XIV, with differing versions of the Hercules and variations in operational equipment. Overseas, the Wellington maintained its combat role, the Mk X in particular (three thousand eight hundred and four built) serving with the Middle East Air Forces as well as with Bomber Command. Wellingtons of No 40 Squadron made a bombing attack on Treviso, Italy, as late as March 1945. Other Wellingtons were converted as torpedo bombers, mine-layers and transports, and a special variant designated D.W.1 was fitted with a large electro-magnetic 'degaussing' ring to trigger off enemy mines. The light but extremely strong geodetic method of the Wellington's construction not only enabled it to carry a creditable bomb load but was capable of withstanding a considerable amount of battle damage without failure.

23 Heinkel He 111

In one form or another, the He 111's service career extended over more than thirty years, an outstanding tribute to the design, evolved by the Günter brothers early in 1934. Of the original four prototypes, the first was flown on 24 February 1935, and the second and fourth were completed ostensibly as civilian transports. Bomber production was heralded in the summer of 1935 by the He 111V4 and a pre-series batch of He 111A-0's, but their BMW engines provided insufficient power, and the first major type was the He 111B, with DB 600-series engines. This was one of the most successful types to serve with the Condor Legion in Spain, where it was fast enough to fly unescorted. To preserve supplies of DB 600's for fighter production, the He 111D did not enter large-scale production, the next major versions being the Jumo-powered He 111E and F. The latter employed the revised, straight-tapered wings originally evolved for the proposed commercial G model. Both E and F models also served in Spain, and after the Civil War the surviving He 111's became a part of the Spanish Air Force. Production of the variants so far mentioned had reached nearly a thousand by the outbreak of World War 2, but a new

model had also made its appearance. This was the He 111P, whose extensively glazed, restyled front section, with its offset ball turret in the extreme nose, became characteristic of all subsequent variants. It was built in comparatively small numbers, again because of the use of Daimler-Benz engines, but its Jumo-powered counterpart, the He 111H, became the most widely used series of all, well over five thousand being built before production ended in 1944. Reflecting their rough reception during the Battle of Britain, successive H and subsequent types appeared with progressive increases in defensive armament, the number of crew members being increased to five or six according to the number of guns. Although most extensively used in its intended role as a medium bomber, the He 111H carried a variety of operational loads during its service. The H-6 was particularly effective as a torpedo bomber, carrying two of these weapons usually, while other H sub-types became carriers for the Hs 293 glider bomb and the FZG-76 (V1) flying bomb. More bizarre variants included the H-8 fitted with balloon-cable cutters, and the He 111Z *Zwilling* (Twin) glider tug, a union of two H-6 airframes linked by a new centre-section supporting a fifth Jumo engine. The H-23 was an 8-seat paratroop transport. German production, of all versions, was well in excess of seven thousand. Licence-built He 111H-16's, designated C.2111, were built in Spain by CASA, and served with the

Spanish Air Force until well into the 1960s.

24 Avro Anson

Design of the Anson twin-engined coastal reconnaissance monoplane was based upon that of the Avro 652 commercial 6-seater, and was known as the Avro 652A. The military prototype (K 4771) was flown on 24 March 1935, and in the following summer Specification 18/35 was issued to cover the initial contract for one hundred and seventy-four Anson Mk I's for Coastal Command. The first Ansons were delivered to No 48 Squadron in March 1936. By the outbreak of war the RAF had seven hundred and sixty serviceable Anson I's, equipping ten squadrons of Coastal Command and sixteen of Bomber Command, and production was still continuing. Strictly, by then they were obsolescent, and from 1940 began to be replaced by Whitleys and imported American Hudsons, but some continued to serve in the general reconnaissance role until 1942, while others carried out air/sea rescue duty with Coastal Command squadrons over an even longer period. Almost from the outset, the Anson had also been envisaged as an aircrew trainer, and it was essentially the impetus given by the gigantic Empire Air Training Scheme of 1939 that led ultimately to the manufacture of eight thousand one hundred and thirty-eight Ansons in Britain by 1952 (including six thousand seven hundred and four Mk I's), and a further two thousand eight hundred and eighty-two under the super-

vision of Federal Aircraft Ltd in Canada. Canadian-built Ansons, differing principally in powerplant, comprised the Mk II (330 hp Jacobs L-6BM), and the Mks V and VI (both with 450 hp Pratt & Whitney R-985-AN 14B). As an interim measure, two hundred and twenty-three British-built Mks III (Jacobs) and IV (Wright Whirlwind) were supplied to Canada. Anson trainers subsequently served with all major Commonwealth air forces, as well as those of Egypt, Finland, Greece, Ireland and the U.S. Army. Anson I's later converted for ambulance or light transport duty included one hundred and four as Mk X's, ninety as Mk XI's and twenty as Mk XII's. An additional two hundred and twenty-one aircraft were built as Mk XII's from the outset. The Mks XI and XII both featured the taller cabin that also characterised the post-war Avro XIX civil transport version.

25 Ilyushin Il-4

The most widely used Soviet bomber of the war years, the Il-4 began its career under the design bureau designation TsKB-26 in 1935; its military or functional designation was DB-3, the letters indicating *Dalnii Bombardirovchtchik* or Long-Range Bomber. It was chosen for development, in preference to the contemporary DB-2 designed by Pavel Sukhoi, in its slightly modified TsKB-30 form, and delivery of production DB-3's began in 1937. The initial production DB-3, a manoeuvrable aeroplane despite its size and weight, was characterised by its squarish, blunt nose, and was powered by two 765 hp M-85 radial engines; 960 hp M-86 engines replaced these in later production batches. Armament consisted of single hand-operated 7·62 mm ShKAS machine-guns in nose and dorsal turrets, with a third gun firing down through a trap in the rear fuselage floor. Some aircraft of the original type saw service during World War 2, although by then the current version was the DB-3F (for *Forsirovanni* = boosted), design of which had started in 1938. This was at first powered by 950 hp M-87A engines and later by the more powerful M-88B, but the chief structural difference lay in the complete redesign of the nose section. This was now longer, more streamlined, well provided with windows, and instead of the DB-3's angular turret its gun was provided with a universal joint mounting. The DB-3F entered production after completing its acceptance trials in June 1939, and during the following year (when it was redesignated Il-4) large numbers were built. As a result of the war, strategic materials became in short supply, and deliveries of M-87A engines could not be maintained at an adequate rate. Further redesign therefore took place, in which several of the fuselage components, and later the outer wing panels, were manufactured from wood instead of metal; and by mid-1942 the M-88B engine was introduced as the standard powerplant. Output then increased steadily until 1944, when Il-4 production ceased. The bomber

served extensively throughout the war with both the Soviet Air Force and Soviet Navy, and it was a force of Il-4's from the latter service which carried out the first long-range attack by Soviet aircraft on Berlin on the night of 8 August 1941. Subsidiary duties included reconnaissance and glider training.

26   Martin 167 Maryland

The slim, twin-engined monoplane that the British services came to know as the Maryland was evolved in 1938 to enter a USAAC design competition ultimately won by the Douglas DB-7. One prototype of the Martin 167W was ordered by the U.S. Army as the XA-22, and this aircraft (NX 22076) made its first flight on 14 March 1939. No U.S. orders were forthcoming, but in 1939 the French Government placed total orders for two hundred and fifteen for the *Armée de l'Air*. These had the Martin export designation 167F and the French military designation 167A-3. The first 167F flew in August 1939, and deliveries began in October. Probably no more than one-third of those ordered were delivered to France, where they were in action against the German advance in the spring of 1940. After the fall of France several of the survivors were operated by the Vichy Air Force during 1940-41. At least five are known to have escaped to serve with the Royal Air Force, and delivery of a further seventy-six from the original French orders was also diverted to the RAF. These received the name Maryland Mk I, and almost all of them were employed by bomber and reconnaissance squadrons in the Middle East. A further one hundred and fifty, with British equipment and a different mark of Twin Wasp engine, were ordered by the British Purchasing Mission as the Maryland Mk II. The clean but unusually slender lines of the Martin 167 led *The Aeroplane* to remark, in September 1940, that it 'is nice as an aeroplane but a little cramped as a fighting machine'. Nevertheless, the Maryland was comparatively fast for a twin-engined machine, especially when relieved of the necessity to carry a bomb load, and made a useful reconnaissance type during the middle years of the war. A reconnaissance by RAF Marylands preceded the Fleet Air Arm's November 1940 assault on the Italian Fleet at Taranto, and in May 1941 a Maryland of the Fleet Air Arm (which received a few of the RAF machines) first brought the news of the movement of the *Bismarck* which led to the action in which the German warship was sunk. Seventy-two of the final batch of Maryland II's were re-allocated to serve with four squadrons of the South African Air Force.

27 Bristol Blenheim

Developed from the Bristol 142 *Britain First*, the Blenheim twin-engined medium bomber first appeared in production form as the short-nosed Blenheim Mk I, whose prototype (K 7033) first flew on 25 June 1936. By that time an initial contract had already been placed, and the first Blenheim I's were delivered in March 1937 to No 114 Squadron. One thousand two hundred and eighty Mk I's were built, and at the outbreak of World War 2 one thousand and seven of these were on RAF charge, including one hundred and forty-seven completed as Mk IF fighters with a ventral pack of four Browning guns. Most of the bombers were serving in the Middle and Far East, home squadrons of the RAF having already begun to re-equip with the long-nosed Mk IV bomber, one hundred and ninety-seven of which were on strength at 3 September 1939. From the eighty-first machine onward these were designated Blenheim IVL, the suffix indicating a longer range by virtue of additional wing fuel tanks. With Mercury XV engines replacing the 840 hp Mercury VIII's of the Blenheim I, the Mk IV was better armed and had a slightly improved performance over its predecessor. One thousand nine hundred and thirty Mk IV's were completed. By contrast, the performance of the final British variant, the Mk V, was disappointing. This version was redesigned to meet Specification B.6/40, and in 1941 one Mk VA day bomber prototype and one close-support Mk VB were built by Bristol. Rootes Securities Ltd built nine hundred and forty-two examples, mostly as the Mk VD (a 'tropical' version of the VA), but including a proportion of Mk VC dual-control trainers. Combat losses of the Mk VD were heavy, and it was quickly replaced by US Baltimores and

Venturas. During their career Blenheims served with every operational command of the RAF and in every theatre of the war. Pre-war exports included Blenheim I's for Finland, Rumania, Turkey and Yugoslavia. The Mk I was built under licence in Yugoslavia, and both the Mks I and IV in Finland. In Canada, Fairchild built six hundred and seventy-six Blenheims for the Royal Canadian Air Force, by whom they were designated Bolingbroke Mks I to IV.

28 Bristol Beaufighter

The Beaufighter was originally designed as a fighter, and the principal variants to serve in this capacity are described in the opening section *Fighters, Attack and Training Aircraft 1939–45*. Its design was, however, based to a large extent upon the Beaufort torpedo bomber, and although the torpedo-carrying models were officially designated TF (Torpedo Fighter), it was considered more appropriate to include them in this volume for purposes of comparison with other types performing a similar function. The first torpedo-dropping experiments were made in 1942 with X 8065, a standard Beaufighter VIC (the Coastal Command version) adapted to carry a standard British or U.S. torpedo beneath the fuselage. Thereafter an experimental squadron was formed, which achieved its first combat success off Norway in April 1943. The so-called 'Torbeau' proved an effective torpedo bomber while retaining enough of its former performance to carry out its other coastal duties of escort fighter and reconnaissance. Sixty Mk VI's on the production line were completed as ITF (Interim Torpedo Fighters), but two new variants soon began to appear. These were the TF Mk X torpedo bomber and the non-torpedo-carrying Mk XIC, both with 1,770 hp Hercules XVII engines. The TF Mk X, two thousand two hundred and five of which were built, had AI radar installed in a characteristic nose 'thimble' fairing, and a dorsal fin extension was introduced on later production batches. It could carry a heavier torpedo than the Mk VI (ITF), or could, alternatively, be equipped with two 250 lb (113 kg) bombs and eight rocket projectiles beneath the wings. The Mk VI (ITF) aircraft were later re-engined and brought up to Mk X standard. Three hundred and sixty-four Beaufighter Mk 21's were built for the RAAF by the Government Aircraft Factories at Fishermen's Bend and Mascot, NSW. Except for Hercules XVIII engines and four 0·50 in wing guns in place of the six Brownings, these were generally similar to the RAF's Mk X. It was they upon whom their Japanese opponents bestowed the respectful nickname of 'Whispering Death'. In spite of its later designation, the Mk XIC was only an interim model pending large-scale delivery of the Mk X, and only one hundred and sixty-three were built.

29 Bristol Beaufort

The Type 152 proposals submitted in April 1936 were designed to meet two Air Ministry Specifications: M.15/35 for a torpedo bomber, and G.24/35 for a general reconnaissance aeroplane. Detail design work began in March 1937. The prototype (L 4441) first flew on 15 October 1938, powered by two 1,065 hp Bristol Taurus II radials in place of the Perseus originally planned. Specification 10/36 was framed to cover production aircraft, seventy-eight of which had been ordered in September 1936, and the Beaufort I entered production in 1939. Initially this was armed with one 0·303 in machine-gun in the port wing and two in the dorsal turret; later, a rear-firing gun was added in an off-set blister beneath the nose, and some aircraft also had twin K guns in the nose and two others in beam positions. Bristol built nine hundred and sixty-five Beaufort I's, first deliveries being made to No 22 Squadron, Coastal Command. In January 1940 a Beaufort from this unit came close to sinking the battle cruiser *Gneisenau* in Brest harbour on 6 April 1941, and Beauforts of No 86 Squadron played an important part in trying to prevent the 'Channel dash' by the *Gneisenau*, *Scharnhorst* and *Prinz Eugen* early in 1942. Other RAF Beaufort squadrons in the United Kingdom and Mediterranean included Nos 39, 42, 47, 203, 217, 415 and 489. They remained in service until replaced by torpedo-carrying Beaufighters in 1943, their duties including mine-laying. At the outset the Beaufort had also been chosen for production in Australia. In November 1940 one aircraft was flown with 1,200 hp

Pratt & Whitney R-1830-S1C3G Twin Wasp engines, becoming the prototype for four hundred and fifteen similarly powered Beaufort II's for the RAF. Many of these were completed, and others later converted, as operational trainers, with a dorsal turret faired over. Another Twin-Wasp engined prototype was flown in Australia in May 1941, and up to August 1944 seven hundred Beauforts were built there. These comprised fifty Mk V, thirty Mk VA, forty Mk VI, sixty Mk VII and five hundred and twenty Mk VIII. These differed chiefly in the engine variant or equipment fitted, though the enlarged fin introduced on the Mk VII later became standard on all Australian Beauforts. They served with the RAAF in the Solomons, Timor, New Guinea and several other Pacific battle areas. In November 1944 forty-six aircraft were converted into Mk IX troop transports. A Mk III was proposed, but not built, with Merlin XX engines and Beaufighter 'long-range' outer wing sections; one Mk IV was completed, with 1,750 hp Taurus engines.

30 De Havilland Mosquito
One of the outstandingly versatile aeroplanes of any era, the D.H.98 Mosquito was first conceived, in 1938, as a day bomber fast enough to outrun enemy fighters and thus carry no armament. Not until March 1940 was firm official interest shown in the design, fifty then being ordered. Three prototypes were built, the first and second of these

(W4050 and W4051) being completed in bomber and photo-reconnaissance configuration respectively. They flew on 25 November 1940 and 10 June 1941. The initial fifty aircraft included ten PR Mk I and ten B Mk IV, and the first operational Mosquito sortie was flown by an aircraft of the former batch on 20 September 1941. The B IV's entered service with No 105 Squadron in May 1942, and two hundred and seventy-three Mk IV's were eventually built. In addition to three de Havilland factories in the United Kingdom, contributions to overall Mosquito production were also made by Airspeed (one hundred and twenty-two), Percival (two hundred and forty-five) and Standard Motors (one hundred and sixty-five). De Havilland built altogether five thousand and seven Mosquitos, four thousand four hundred and forty-four of them during the war period. In addition, two hundred and eight (Mks 40–43) were built by de Havilland Australia, and one thousand one hundred and thirty-four (Mks VII, 20–22 and 24–27) by de Havilland Canada. Wartime Mosquito production totalled six thousand seven hundred and ten, with a further one thousand and seventy-one completed after VJ-day. Mosquitos quickly established a reputation for their excellent flying qualities, their unequalled talent for destroying pin-point targets, and for having easily the lowest loss rate of any aircraft in service with Bomber Command. Mosquito IV's originally equipped the Pathfinder Force, which later employed also the high-altitude Mk IX and the second most numerous variant, the Mk XVI; and photo-reconnaissance counterparts of these three Marks constituted the principal wartime PR variants of the Mosquito. From early in 1944 the most popular Mosquito weapon was the 4,000 lb (1,814 kg) 'block-buster' bomb, carried in a specially bulged bomb bay retrospectively fitted to all Mks IX and XVI and several Mk IV's. About one thousand two hundred Mosquito XVI's were built, and were later flown with auxiliary pinion fuel tanks to increase their range. The NF Mk II, FB Mk VI and other fighter and fighter-bomber variants are described in the *Fighters, Attack and Training Aircraft 1939–45* section.

31 Junkers Ju 88

The most adaptable German warplane of World War 2, and among the most widely used, the Ju 88 was evolved to a 1937 requirement issued by the RLM for a fast, well-armed multi-purpose aeroplane. The first prototype (D-AQEN) was flown on 21 December 1936, powered by two 1,000 hp DB 600A in-line engines. The second prototype was essentially similar, but in the third the powerplant was a pair of Jumo 211A engines, and the Jumo was to power the majority of Ju 88's subsequently built. The characteristic multi-panelled glazed nose section first appeared on the fourth prototype. A pre-series batch of Ju 88A-0's were completed during the summer of 1939, and delivery of the first Ju 88A-1 production models began in September. The A series continued, with very few gaps, through to the A-17, and included variants for such specialised roles as dive bombing, anti-shipping strike, long range reconnaissance and conversion training. Probably the most common model was the A-4, which served both in Europe and North Africa. This was the first version to incorporate modifications resulting from operational experience gained during the Battle of Britain; it had extended-span wings, Jumo 211J engines, increased bomb load and defensive armament. Twenty Ju 88A-4's were supplied to Finland, and others to the *Regia Aeronautica*. The Ju 88B, evolved before the outbreak of war, followed a separate line of development to become the Ju 188, and the next major production model, chronologically, was the Ju 88C fighter series. The Ju 88D (over one thousand eight hundred built as D-1, D-2 and D-3) was a developed version of the A-4 for the strategic reconnaissance role. Next bomber series was the Ju 88S, powered by 1,700 hp BMW 801G radials (in the S-1), 1,810 hp BMW 801TJ's (S-2) or 1,750 hp Jumo 213E-1's (S-3). Apart from powerplant, the S sub-types were basically similar to one another, and differed from the earlier bombers in having a smaller, fully rounded glazed nose. They were less heavily armed, and carried a smaller bomb load, but performance compared with the A and D series was considerably better. The Ju 88T-1 and T-3 were photo-reconnaissance counterparts of the S-1 and S-3. Production of bomber and reconnaissance variants of the Ju 88 totalled ten thousand seven hundred and seventy-four, just over 60 per cent of the overall total. Other major versions are dealt with in the *Fighters, Attack and Training Aircraft 1939–45* section. Towards the end of the war many Ju 88 airframes ended their days rather ignominiously as the explosive-laden lower portion of *Mistel* composite attack weapons, carrying a Bf 109 or Fw 190 pick-a-back fashion to guide them on to their targets.

32 Douglas DB-7 series

Douglas submitted its Model 7A design in a 1938 U.S. Army competition for a twin-engined attack bomber, and was authorised to build prototypes for evaluation. The first appeared as the improved Model 7B, with 1,100 hp Twin Wasp engines and a tricycle undercarriage, first flying on 26 October 1939. First customer was France, which ordered one hundred in February 1939; the first U.S. orders, for one hundred and eighty-six A-20's and A-20A's, followed three months later. These, with the manufacturer's designation DB-7, had a narrower but deeper fuselage. The first DB-7 was flown on 17 August 1939, with 1,050 hp Twin Wasps. On 14 October French DB-7 orders were increased to two hundred and seventy, the second batch to have uprated engines; six days later a further hundred were ordered, designated DB-7A and having 1,600 hp

Wright Cyclones. Little more than a hundred DB-7's had been delivered before the fall of France in 1940, and the remainder were diverted to Britain. The DB-7's were initially named Boston I and II by the RAF, but later converted into Havoc I fighters; the DB-7A's became Havoc II. In February 1940 Britain ordered one hundred and fifty DB-7B's (not to be confused with the original Model 7B). These were similar to the DB-7A, but with seven 0·303 in guns instead of the latter version's six 7·5 mm guns. The RAF ultimately received seven hundred and eighty-one, named Boston III. Nine hundred and ninety-nine A-20B's were built for the U.S. Army. Features of the RAF's Boston III were incorporated into eight hundred and eight A-20C's for the USAAF. Of these, two hundred and two went to the RAF designated Boston IIIA. Next major U.S. variant was the A-20G, two thousand eight hundred and fifty being built with the 'solid' nose of the fighter variants and bomb-carrying capacity later increased to 4,000 lb (1,814 kg). Production batches of the A-20G varied in armament, and some carried a ventral fuel tank. The four hundred and twelve A-20H's were similar apart from their 1,700 hp Twin Wasp engines. A one-piece moulded transparent nose characterised the A-20J (four hundred and fifty built) and A-20K (four hundred and thirteen built), known in the RAF as the Boston IV and V. Overall production of the DB-7 'family', including the Havoc fighter models,

totalled seven thousand three hundred and eighty-five, and came to an end in September 1944. Almost half of this output went to the U.S.S.R., but USAAF and RAF variants served in all theatres of the war, undertaking a wide range of operational duties beyond those for which they were designed. Small quantities were employed by the U.S. Navy, and by the air forces of Brazil and Canada.

33 Douglas A-26 Invader

Although nowadays best known for its operational service in Korea, the Congo and Vietnam, the Douglas Invader's design was actually begun in January 1941, well before the U.S. entered World War 2. It was initiated as a successor to the Douglas A-20 Havoc, and in June 1941 the USAAF ordered three prototypes. The first of these was flown on 10 January 1942, but each was completed to a different configuration. The original XA-26 was an attack bomber, with a 3,000 lb (1,361 kg) internal bomb load, twin guns in its transparent nose section and two others in each of the dorsal and ventral turrets; the XA-26A, a night fighter, had a solid radar-carrying nose, four cannon in a ventral tray and four 0·50 in guns in the upper turret; while the XA-26B had a shorter nose mounting a single 75 mm cannon. In the initial production model, the A-26B, the armament was changed yet again (see caption on page 49), and the bomb load increased. Later production batches introduced R-2800-79 engines with water injection, boosting the power and performance at altitude, the number of nose guns was increased to eight, and additional gun-packs, rocket projectiles or 2,000 lb (907 kg) of bombs could be carried beneath the wings. To concentrate the fire-power even more, the dorsal guns could be locked forward and fired by the pilot. Five hundred and thirty-five water-injection A-26B's were built, following the initial eight hundred and twenty by Douglas's Long Beach and Tulsa factories. The Invader made its European operational debut in the autumn of 1944, and its first Pacific appearance early in 1945. The A-26C, which appeared in 1945, also saw limited service before the war ended. This had the twin-gun transparent 'bombardier' nose, but was otherwise similar to the B model. With the arrival of VJ-day, large numbers of Invader orders were cancelled, but even so, one thousand and ninety-one A-26C's were completed. In Europe alone, A-26 series aircraft flew over eleven thousand sorties and dropped more than eighteen thousand tons of bombs for the loss of sixty-seven aircraft in combat; curiously, despite their formidable firepower, they destroyed only seven enemy aircraft during this period. After the war, redesignated in the B-26 series after the Martin Marauder was withdrawn in 1958, they became a standard post-war USAF type, and the latest models continue to serve in Vietnam some twenty-five years after their first operational mission.

34 Martin Baltimore

The Baltimore was designed specifically to British requirements, to provide an improved successor to the Martin 167 operated by the RAF as the Maryland. It appeared as the Martin 187, the first production aircraft (there was no separate prototype) flying on 14 June 1941, some thirteen months after the RAF had placed an order for four hundred. These were built as Baltimore Mks I (fifty), II (one hundred) and III (two hundred and fifty), all being similarly powered and having four wing guns and one rearward-firing and four-downward-firing ventral guns. Only the dorsal armament distinguished them, the Mks I and II having single and twin Vickers K guns respectively, while the Mk III had a Boulton Paul four-gun turret. The Baltimore was given the USAAF designation A-30, although none served with the American forces. Lend-Lease supplies included two hundred and eighty-one Baltimore IIIA's (identical to the Mk III), two hundred and ninety-four Mk IV's and six hundred Mk V's, bringing overall manufacture to one thousand five hundred and seventy-five before production ended in May 1944. The Baltimore IV (illustrated) replaced the Boulton Paul turret by a twin-gun Martin turret, and the Baltimore V was similar except for the up-rated 1,700 hp R-2600-29 engines. The Baltimore, like the Maryland, served exclusively in the Middle East theatre, where it equipped several squadrons of the RAF from the spring of 1942 onward. Two squadrons of the South African Air Force were also equipped with them, and several were operational in the Balkans area, especially over Yugoslavia, with the *Stormo Baltimore* of the Italian Co-Belligerent Air Force in 1944-45. A few others were handed over to the Royal Navy for non-operational duties.

35 Martin B-26 Marauder

Finishing the war with a combat loss rate of less than 1 per cent, the Marauder more than vindicated its early reputation as a 'widow maker', which arose chiefly from the high accident rate created by inexperienced pilots handling an unfamiliar and unusually heavy aeroplane. As the Martin 179, its design was entered for a 1939 U.S. Army design competition and was rewarded by an immediate order for two hundred and one aircraft without the usual prototype preliminaries. The first B-26, flown on 25 November 1940, exhibited a modest armament, compared with later models, of only five defensive guns. Delivery to USAAC units began in 1941, in which year there also appeared the B-26A, with heavier calibre nose and tail guns, provision for extra fuel tanks in the bomb bay and for carrying a torpedo beneath the fuselage. One hundred and thirty-nine B-26A's were completed, making their operational debut from Australian bases in the spring of 1942. The B-26 also appeared in action from Alaskan and North African bases. Then followed the B-26B, with uprated engines and increased armament. Of the one thousand eight hundred and eighty-three built, all but the first six hundred and forty-one B-26B's also introduced a new, extended-span wing and taller tail. The B-26B made its operational debut in Europe in May 1943, subsequently becoming one of the hardest-worked Allied medium bombers in this theatre. One thousand two hundred and ten B-26C's were built, essentially similar to the later B models. These were succeeded by the B-26F (three hundred built), in which the wing incidence was increased with the purpose of improving take-off performance and reducing the accident rate. The final model was the B-26G, which differed only slightly from the F; nine hundred and fifty G models were completed, the last being delivered in March 1945. Of the overall U.S. production supplies to the RAF under Lend-Lease included fifty-two B-26A's (as Marauder I's), two hundred B-26F's (Marauder II) and one hundred and fifty B-26G's (Marauder III). Many other Marauders were completed for the USAAF as AT-23 or TB-26 trainers, and some for the U.S. Navy as JM-1's.

36 PZL P.37 Łoś (Elk)

This elegant Polish medium bomber was among the best of its type to appear in the 1930s, but lack of appreciation of its qualities by the Army authorities controlling aircraft procurement for the Polish Air Force denied it the commercial and operational successes that it deserved. The original design, by Jerzy Dabrowski, received approval from the Department of Aeronautics in October 1934, and was developed under the designation P.37. In August 1935 work began on two flying prototypes and a static test airframe, and the P.37/I flew late in June 1936 with two 873 hp Polish-built Bristol Pegasus XIIB engines. This prototype, and nine of the first ten similarly powered Łoś A production aircraft, had a single fin and rudder. The P.37/II prototype, and all other production Łoś bombers, had a twin-tail assembly. The P.37/II, which flew in April 1937, was prototype for the Łoś B, differing principally in its more powerful Pegasus XX engines and an ingenious cantilever main landing gear. Orders were placed for twenty more Łoś A's and one hundred and fifty Łoś B's, the majority to be delivered by 1 April 1939. Delivery of the Łoś B began in autumn 1938, when the existing Łoś A's were fitted with dual· controls and transferred to operational conversion training with No 213 Squadron. The Army used devious means to denigrate the P.37's operational worth, cutting back military orders for the Łoś B in April 1939 when only a hundred had been completed. The P.37/II was refitted with several alternative engines, including the Gnome-Rhône 14N.1 of 970 hp and the 14N.20/21 of 1,050 hp, which were intended for use in the proposed Łoś C and Łoś D export models. Before the outbreak of war PZL had received encouraging orders from Bulgaria, Rumania, Turkey and Yugoslavia; and had good prospects of further sales or licences in Belgium, Denmark, Estonia and Greece. However, none of these aircraft were delivered, and the Polish Air Force itself had only some ninety Łoś bombers on charge when the war began. Of these, thirty-six were with Nos 211, 212, 216 and 217 Squadrons of the Tactical Air Force's Bomber Brigade which had been formed in the previous summer. In the second week of fighting nine more were acquired, but twenty-six of the forty-five operational machines were lost during the sixteen days before the U.S.S.R. invaded Poland from the east. The surviving aircraft, with twenty-seven others from Brzesc airfield, were withdrawn to Rumania, in whose colours they subsequently fought against Soviet forces. Variants included an abortive heavy fighter project with an eight-gun 'solid' nose, and the P.49/I Miś (Teddy Bear). The latter, incomplete when the war started, was the prototype for a more powerful and more heavily armed bomber version.

37 Mitsubishi Ki-21

The Ki-21 won an exacting design competition initiated by the Japanese Army Air Force early in 1936, and the first of five prototypes was completed in November of that year. With improved fields of fire for the defensive guns, and 850 hp Nakajima Ha-5-*Kai* engines replacing the Mitsubishi Kinsei Ha-6's of the first prototype, it was accepted for initial production as the Ki-21-Ia, or Type 97 heavy bomber. It entered JAAF service in 1937, and in 1938 Nakajima began to contribute to the production programme, delivering its first Ki-21 in August. The Model 1A was quickly succeeded by the Model 1B (Ki-21-Ib), into which were built modifications resulting from combat experience during the fighting with China. Increases were made in protective armour for the crew, defensive armament and the sizes of the flaps and bomb bay. The Model 1C (Ki-21-Ic) had increased fuel and an extra lateral gun. A wider-span tailplane was introduced on the Model 2A (Ki-21-IIa). Mitsubishi began the development of this late in 1939, replacing the former power-plant by 1,490 hp Ha-101 engines. The Ki-21 was a standard Army bomber at the time of Pearl Harbor, and was subsequently encountered in Burma, Hong Kong, India, Malaya, the Netherlands East Indies and the Philippines. Under the Allied code-naming system, the Ki-21 was known as 'Sally', although the name 'Gwen' was briefly allocated to the Model 2B (Ki-21-IIb) before it was recognised as a Ki-21 variant. The Model 2B was the final production variant of this now-obsolescent bomber, recog-nisable by the turret replacing the dorsal 'greenhouse' of the earlier models. With its appearance, many earlier Ki-21's were withdrawn either for training or for conversion to MC-21 transports. Shortly before the war ended, nine Ki-21's were made ready as assault transports at Kyushu, to transfer demolition troops to Okinawa, but only one reached its target. Production came to an end in September 1944 after one thousand seven hundred and thirteen had been built by Mit-subishi, plus three hundred and fifty-one by Nakajima (up to February 1941). Just over five hundred transport counterparts of the Ki-21 were built by Mitsubishi, designated MC-20 in their civil form and Ki-57 (code-name 'Topsy') in military guise. Proposals for a Ki-21-III version were shelved in favour of the Ki-67.

38 Mitsubishi G4M

The G4M was evolved to a 'range-at-all-costs' specification, issued by the Japanese Navy in 1937 for a twin-engined medium bomber. Kiro Honjo, who led the design team, could only accomplish this by packing so much fuel into the wings that no armour protection could be provided for the fuel tanks or the crew. Then, after the prototype G4M1 had flown in October 1939, Mitsubishi were instructed to adapt the design for bomber escort duties, with increased armament and a crew of ten. Thirty G6M1's, as this version was known, had been built and service tested before the JNAF admitted their performance was inadequate and abandoned the pro-ject. The aircraft subsequently served as G6M1-K trainers and later still as G6M1-L2 troop transports. By the end of March 1941, however, fourteen more G4M1 bombers had been flown, and in April this version was accepted for service with the JNAF as the Model 11 land-based attack bomber. The G4M1 had a single 20 mm tail gun, with 7·7 mm guns in each of the nose, ventral and dorsal positions; powerplant was two 1,530 hp Mitsubishi Kasei 11 radials. The G4M1 was used by Japan in pre-war operations in south-east China, and by the time of her entry into World War 2 there were some one hundred and eighty G4M1's in service with the JNAF. They scored a number of early successes, but the 1,100 gallons (5,000 litres) of unprotected fuel in their tanks made them extremely vulnerable and the bomber soon became known to U.S. gunners as the 'one-shot lighter'. Three months after particularly heavy losses in the Solomons campaign of August 1942, Mitsubishi began work on the G4M2 Model 22. This had an improved armament, and 1,850 hp Kasei 21 engines with methanol injection; the fuel capacity was increased, but still the tanks remained unprotected. Nevertheless, the G4M2 became the major production model, appearing in five other versions: the G4M2a Model 24 (bulged bomb doors, Kasei 25 engines); G4M2b Model 25 (Kasei 27's); G4M2c Model 26 (total of two 20 mm and four 7·7 mm guns); G4M2d (for flight-testing the Ne-20 turbojet engine); and the G4M2e Model 24-J (four 20 mm guns and one 7·7 mm). Model 24-J's were later adapted as carriers for the Ohka suicide aircraft. Late in 1943, in the face of continuing heavy losses, Mitsubishi built sixty examples of the G4M3a Model 34 and G4M3b Model 36. These carried a reduced fuel load of 968

gallons (4,400 litres), in fully protected tanks, in a much-re-designed wing. Total production of G4M's (Allied code name 'Betty') amounted to two thousand four hundred and seventy-nine aircraft, many of which were converted to 20-seat troop transports towards the end of the war. Flight trials of a G4M3c Model 37, with exhaust-driven superchargers were partially completed before VJ-day; another project, the G4M4, was abandoned.

39 Mitsubishi Ki-67 Hiryu (Flying Dragon)

Design of the Ki-67, led by Dr Hisanojo Ozawa, began late in 1941 to a JAAF specification issued early that year. The first prototype was flown at the beginning of 1943, and by the end of that year fifteen Ki-67's had been completed. The Hiryu showed a considerable advancement over earlier Army bombers, not only in performance but in the degree of armour protection afforded to the crew members and the fuel installation. It was ordered into production in Model 1A form (Ki-67-Ia) early in 1944, and began to enter service during the summer. First combat appearance of the Ki-67 (code-named 'Peggy' by the Allies) was during the Battle of the Philippine Sea, where it was flown by Army crews but operated as a torpedo bomber under the direction of the Japanese Navy. The Model 1A was soon supplanted in production by the Model 1B (Ki-67-Ib), in which the former's flush-mounted beam guns were replaced by transparent blisters. By the end of the war

Mitsubishi had built six hundred and six Hiryus, while others had been completed by Kawasaki (ninety-one), Nippon Hikoki (twenty-nine) and the Army Air Arsenal (one). The majority of Ki-67's operated from Kyushu, and were encountered during the final year of the war in the Iwo Jima, Marianas and Okinawa battle areas, among others. Some became test-beds for the proposed Ki-67-II (two 2,500 hp Ha-214 engines), but this was still incomplete when the war ended. One development that did materialise was the Ki-109 'heavy' fighter. This replaced the originally proposed Ki-69 escort fighter version of the Hiryu, and the later Ki-112 project of 1943. Two Model 1B bombers were assigned early in 1944 to the Tachikawa Army Air Arsenal, where they were converted to mount a 75 mm Type 88 cannon in the nose, the only other armament being a 12·7 mm tail gun. Twenty of these 4-seat fighters were built, but Mitsubishi's inability to deliver any of the Ha-104ru turbo-supercharged engines intended for them caused them to be fitted with the same non-supercharged units as the bomber versions. With these they were unable to reach the combat altitude necessary to carry out the task for which they had been built – interception of the B-29 Superfortress bombers attacking Japan.

40 Nakajima Ki-49 Donryu

The first prototype Ki-49 was flown in August 1939, having been designed to a JAAF specification issued at the end of the preceding year. It was followed by a second prototype, each being powered by Nakajima Ha-5B engines. The Ki-49 had been evolved as a replacement for the Mitsubishi Ki-21, with the object of overcoming the slow speed and poor defensive armament of the latter; but the prototypes proved less than 20 mph (32 kmh) faster than the Ki-21, had a poor operational ceiling and were armed only with a single 20 mm cannon and two 7·92 mm machine-guns. Some improvement was made in subsequent prototypes, and in the Ki-49-I Model 1 which entered production in the late spring of 1940, by installing 1,250 hp Ha-41 engines. One hundred and twenty-nine Ki-49-I's were built at Ota, and the name Donryu was bestowed by the manufacturer, after the well-known Shinto shrine there. (A colloquial translation of Donryu is 'Dragon Swallower'.) In the Allied coding system the Ki-49 was known as 'Helen'. The Ki-49-IIa, the next production version, had three additional 7·92 mm guns; in the Ki-49-IIb all five machine-guns were of 12·7 mm calibre. Six hundred and forty-nine Ki-49-II's were built by Nakajima, fifty by Tachikawa and a small number by Mansyu. The parent company also completed six examples of a Ki-49-III, with 2,500 hp Ha-117 engines, but this version was not developed, and production of the Donryu ceased in December 1944. First operational appearance of the Ki-49-I was on 19 February 1942, when a force of them attacked Port Darwin in Australia from New

Guinea. The Ki-49-II, which entered service in the following September, was encountered in the China-Burma-India theatre, the Netherlands East Indies, Formosa and the Philippines. After the Leyte Island campaign, in which many were lost, they were extensively used for suicide attacks, though some were employed for mine detection and coastal patrol. A Ki-49, carrying Emperor Hirohito's envoy to Okinawa to sign the surrender agreement on 19-20 August 1945, made the last flight of the war by a JAAF aircraft. Such was the insistence on engine power and defensive armament that the Ki-49 inevitably suffered from having a small bomb load and inadequate range. Three Ki-58 fighter proto-types, based on the Ki-49-IIa, were built with five 20 mm and three 12·7 mm guns; and two Ki-49-III's were converted as formation leaders with the designation Ki-80.

41 Mitsubishi Ki-46

The Ki-46, in terms of aerodynamics and performance one of the best Japanese aircraft to serve during World War 2, was designed by Tomio Kubo to a JAAF require-ment issued in December 1937. The specification was a rigorous one, for a fast, high altitude, long range, twin-engined reconnaissance aero-plane capable of speeds more than 50 mph (80 km/hr) faster than the latest western single-engined fighters. These demands were met by ingenious weight-saving and excellent streamlining, and the first prototype, powered by 875 hp

Mitsubishi Ha-26-I engines, was flown in November 1939. The aircraft entered immediate pro-duction as the Ki-46-I, or Army Type 100 Model 1 Command Reconnaissance monoplane. The initial thirty-four aircraft were similarly powered, and were armed with a single 7·7 mm Type 89 machine-gun on a movable mount-ing in the rear cabin. They were used mostly for service trials and crew training, the main production version being the Ki-46-II Model 2, which first flew in March 1941. One thousand and ninety-three Model 2's were built, with 1,080 hp Ha-102 engines providing enhanced per-formance. Delivery of these began in July 1941, initially to JAAF units in Manchuria and China. The Ki-46 (code named 'Dinah' by the Allies) subsequently appeared in virtually every theatre of the Pacific war. A few Ki-46-II's were also used by the Japanese Navy, and others were converted in 1943 to Ki-46-II-Kai operational trainers, with a second, raised cockpit behind the pilot's cabin. In December 1942 two prototypes were flown of the Ki-46-III, and six hundred and nine Model 3's were completed. The Ki-46-IIIa featured a modified nose canopy, eliminating the former step in front of the pilot's cabin, carried additional fuel and dispensed with the dorsal gun. Four prototypes were also built in 1945 of the Ki-46-IVa, basically similar but with turbo-supercharged Ha-112-IIru engines, but no production was undertaken. The entire one thousand seven hundred and forty-two Ki-46's were built by Mitsubishi at Nagoya and, later, at Toyama. In 1944, however, a substantial quantity of Model 3's began to be converted to Ki-46-III-Kai fighters by the Army Aeronautical Research Institute at Tachikawa for Japanese home defence. Conversion involved a 'stepped' nose, broadly similar to the original one, housing two 20 mm Ho-5 cannon and, between the front and rear crew cabins, a 37 mm Ho-203 cannon fixed to fire forward and upward. The Ki-46-IIIb, of which a few were built for ground attack, was similar, but omitted the dorsal cannon. Projected fighter variants included the Ki-46-IIIc (twin Ho-5's) and Ki-46-IVb (two nose-mounted Ho-5's).

42 Yokosuka P1Y1 Ginga (Milky Way)

The Ginga, code-named 'Frances' by the Allies, was evolved to a Japanese Navy 15-Shi (1940) requirement for a land-based bomber and dive bomber, though the first of several prototypes was not flown until early 1943. Designated Y-20, it was a handsome, well-built aeroplane with retractable under-wing air brakes. With its construction simplified and additional armour protection for the crew, the bomber was accepted for the JNAF as the P1Y1 Model 11. Production was undertaken by the Nakajima factories at Koizumi and Fukushima, which had built nine hundred and six Ginga bombers by the end of the war; delivery to combat units began in spring 1944. The Ginga was employed chiefly from land bases in Japan, especially from the island of Kyushu. In place of the usual single dorsal gun, some aircraft had a turret mounting twin 12·7 mm or 20 mm guns. Despite excellent flying qualities, the Ginga's operational career was restricted by the lack of skilled production staff, efficient pilots and fuel. Difficulties were also encountered with the Homare engines, which had been installed at the direction of the Navy. At Okinawa, many Gingas were employed as suicide aircraft. Kawanishi, invited to develop a night-fighter version of the Ginga, decided to replace the troublesome Homare with the more reliable Mitsubishi Kasei 25 radial of 1,850 hp. Kawanishi proposed two new variants – the P1Y2 bomber and the P1Y2-S night fighter – but preference was given to the latter type. A prototype was flown in June 1944, and ninety-six production aircraft, designated P1Y2-S Model 26 Kyokko (Aurora), were built. They carried elementary AI radar, and were armed with three 20 mm cannon, one on a movable mounting in the rear cabin and the other pair fixed to fire forward and upward from amidships. Despite Japan's urgent need of a strong home defence, the P1Y2-S had still only reached trials units when the war ended. The only operational night fighters were a few P1Y1-S conversions of Nakajima-built bombers. Some of these had a hand-operated dorsal turret with two 20 mm cannon, but none carried radar. One Ginga was used in 1945 to flight-test the Ne-20 turbojet engine. A further night fighter, P1Y3-S with 1,990 hp Homare engines, was projected but not built; and another proposed variant, the Ginga-Kai, was to have acted as parent aircraft for the Model 22 version of the Ohka suicide aircraft.

43 Heinkel He 177 Greif (Griffin)

The fact that the He 177 was the only German long-range strategic bomber to go into series production during World War 2 was doubtless due chiefly to the official indecision and political interference with its development that gave little chance of its initial design faults being satisfactorily overcome before it was pressed into service. Had it been permitted a natural and uninterrupted development, its story might have been very different, for it was basically a conventional design in all but one respect. This was the radical decision to employ pairs of coupled engines, each pair in a single nacelle, driving a single propeller. It was designed to a 1938 specification for a dual-purpose heavy bomber and anti-shipping aircraft, and was, unbelievably, required to be stressed for dive bombing. The first prototype, flown on 19 November 1939, just managed to keep within the overall weight limits of the specification, but service variants of the He 177 became progressively heavier. More ominous, however, was the curtailment of the first flight due to engine overheating, which was to plague the He 177 throughout its career. Eight prototypes were completed,

followed by thirty-five pre-production He 177A-0's built by Arado and Heinkel and one hundred and thirty Arado-built He 177A-1's. The early aircraft in this batch were used for further trials, and after a brief and unhappy operational debut the remainder were also withdrawn from service. From late 1942 they were replaced by one hundred and seventy Heinkel-built A-3's and eight hundred and twenty-six A-5's which had longer fuselages and repositioned engine nacelles. Main combat area of these models was the Eastern Front, where the bomber's use also for ground-attack produced some interesting variations in armament. Other He 177A's were employed as transports, and certain variants were equipped to carry Hs 293 or FX 1400 missiles externally. A few A-6's were built, but by now attention was being diverted to developing the *Greif* with four separately mounted engines. When the German forces evacuated Paris the prototype He 274A (formerly the He 177A-4) was still awaiting its first flight at the Farman factory at Suresnes. One He 177A-3 airframe became the four-engined He 277, to which Heinkel gave the false designation He 177B to overcome official disapproval of the re-engined design. This flew late in 1943 with four 1,730 hp DB 603A engines, followed by two more prototypes and a small production batch, but these did not enter squadron service.

44 Curtiss C-46 Commando

Designed by Curtiss-Wright in 1936 as a 36-seat commercial airliner designated CW-20, the prototype of this capacious transport (NX 19436) first flew on 26 March 1940. It was evaluated by the U.S. Army, under the designation C-55, but was then restored to civil standard and purchased by BOAC, who named it *St Louis* and operated it as a 24-seater between Gibraltar and Malta and on longer routes. The USAAF ordered an initial twenty-five, further modified and having 2,000 hp Pratt & Whitney R-2800-43 Twin Wasp engines, for service as C-46 troop and freight transports. Originally named Condor III, the C-46 was later renamed Commando, and was produced in substantial numbers for the USAAF and U.S. Navy. The two major production models were the C-46A (one thousand four hundred and ninety-one built) and C-46D (one thousand four hundred and ten), the former having a single, large loading door while the latter had double freight doors and a remodelled nose section. The B, C, G, H, K and L variants were experimental models that did not go into production, the other Army models being the single-door C-46E (seventeen built) and double-door C-46F (two hundred and thirty-four built). These were counterparts to the A and D models, with R-2800-75 instead of -51 engines. One hundred and sixty R5C-1's (corresponding to the C-46A) were also built for the U.S. Marine Corps, with whom they performed invaluable supply and casualty evacuation duties. The Army aircraft, employed predominantly in the Far East, became

famous for their round-the-clock flights across the Himalayas to keep open the supply routes between Burma and China. They first appeared in Europe in March 1945, when they were used to drop paratroops during the Rhine crossing. Compared with the civil prototype, the military Commando could airlift up to 40 troops, 33 stretcher cases or a 10,000 lb (4,536 kg) payload of freight or military equipment.

45 Douglas C-47 Skytrain series

First Douglas Commercial transports to be acquired by the U.S. services were a number of DC-2's (Army C-32A and C-34, Navy R2D-1), followed by thirty-five C-39's with DC-2 fuselages and the DC-3's tail surfaces and outer wing panels. The principal wartime versions of the DC-3 were the Twin Wasp-engined C-47 Skytrain, C-53 Skytrooper and the Navy R4D series, differing in minor detail only, except for their function. The first nine hundred and fifty-three C-47's were troop or cargo transports; they were followed in 1942 by four thousand nine hundred and ninety-one C-47A's, and from 1943 by three thousand one hundred and eight C-47B's, all by Douglas. One hundred and thirty-three TC-47B's were also built, for training duties. The Skytrooper, as its name implied, was specifically a troop transport, of which Douglas produced one hundred and ninety-three C-53's, eight C-53B's, seventeen C-53C's and one hundred and fifty-nine

C-53D's from 1941 to 1943. Seventeen C-117A VIP transports were delivered in 1945. Commercial airline DST's (Douglas Sleeper Transports) or DC-3's impressed for war service included thirty-six with designations C-48 to C-48C, one hundred and thirty-eight C-49 to C-49K, fourteen C-50 to C-50D, one C-51, five C-52 to C-52C, two C-68 and four C-84. The Skytrooper preceded the C-47 into service (October 1941), despite its higher designation number; the first Skytrains were delivered in January 1942. More than one thousand two hundred were supplied under Lend-Lease to the RAF, by whom they were known as Dakota Mks I to IV. They first entered service with No 31 Squadron in Burma in June 1942. Additional roles included casualty evacuation and glider towing. Total wartime production of military DC-3's, which ended in August 1945, amounted to ten thousand one hundred and twenty-three, mostly built by Douglas. Nor was this all: in addition to about seven hundred supplied to the U.S.S.R. under Lend-Lease, the Soviet engineer Boris Lisunov spent some time at Douglas prior to initiating production of a Soviet-built version known as the Li-2 (formerly PS-84). Some two thousand were built in the U.S.S.R., including some with a gun turret just above and behind the crew cabin. Licence production was also undertaken in Japan, where Showa built three hundred and eighty L2D2's and L2D3's for the JNAF (code-named 'Tabby' by the Allies) and Nakajima completed a further seventy.

46 Consolidated PBY Catalina

First flown as the XP3Y-1 on 21 March 1935, the Consolidated Model 28 was the first U.S. military flying boat with cantilever wings. Sixty were ordered as PBY-1's in 1935, deliveries (to Squadron VP-11F) beginning in October 1936. Fifty PBY-2's followed in 1937-38, and in the latter year three PBY-3's and a manufacturing licence were sold to the U.S.S.R. The Soviet version, designated GST, was powered by M-62 engines. Orders for the U.S. Navy continued with sixty-six PBY-3's and thirty-three PBY-4's, the latter introducing the prominent lateral observation blisters that characterised most subsequent versions. The RAF received one Model 28-5 for evaluation in July 1939, resulting in an order for fifty aircraft similar to the U.S. Navy's PBY-5. The RAF name Catalina was subsequently adopted for the PBY's in USN service. During 1940 the RAF doubled its original order, and others were ordered by Australia (eighteen), Canada (fifty), France (thirty) and the Netherlands East Indies (thirty-six). Of the U.S. Navy's original order for two hundred PBY-5's, the final thirty-three were completed as PBY-5A amphibians, and an additional one hundred and thirty-four were ordered to -5A standard. Twelve later became RAF Catalina III's, and twelve more were included in the NEI contract. Seven hundred and fifty-three PBY-5's were built, and seven hundred and ninety-four PBY-5A's, fifty-six of the latter for the USAF as OA-10's. Lend-Lease supplies to Britain included two hundred and twenty-five PBY-5B's (Catalina IA) and ninety-seven Catalina IVA's with ASV radar. Production continued with the tall-finned Naval Aircraft Factory PBN-1 Nomad (one hundred and fifty-six, most of which went to the U.S.S.R.) and the similar PBY-6A amphibian (two hundred and thirty-five, including seventy-five Army OA-10B's and forty-eight for the U.S.S.R.). Canadian Vickers-built amphibians went to the USAAF (two hundred and thirty OA-10A's) and RCAF (one hundred and forty-nine Cansos). Boeing (Canada) production included two hundred and forty PB2B-1's (mostly as RAF Catalina IVB's), seventeen RCAF Catalinas, fifty tall-finned PB2B-2's (RAF Catalina VI) and fifty-five RCAF Cansos. Total U.S./Canadian production of PBY models was three thousand two hundred and ninety, to which were added several hundred GST's built in the U.S.S.R.

47 Saab-18

The Saab-18 originated, under the project designation L 11, as a twin-engined recconaissance aircraft, two prototypes being ordered in November 1939 and February 1940. By the time the first of these flew on 19 June 1942 changing tactical requirements had caused it to be developed primarily as a light day bomber and dive bomber. In general configuration it closely resembled the Dornier Do 215 bomber, except that the crew cabin was offset to port to improve the pilot's downward vision. With 1,065 hp Twin Wasp engines, the prototype had been somewhat underpowered; nevertheless, in July 1942 production was started of an initial batch of sixty aircraft with these engines, and these began to enter *Flygvapnet* service in June 1944 in B 18A bomber and S 18A reconnaissance forms. On 10 June 1944 the prototype was flown of the B 18B, powered by two of the 1,475 hp Daimler Benz DB 605B in-line engines which by then were being licence-built in Sweden for the Saab-21 fighter. The production B 18B's, one hundred and twenty of which were completed, did not enter service until after the war (1946). They had a maximum internal bomb load of 3,307 lb (1,500 kg), a fixed armament of one 7·9 mm and two 13·2 mm guns, ejection seats for the pilot and navigator, and provision for carrying rocket projectiles beneath the wings. The final production version was the T 18B, whose prototype was flown on 7 July 1945; sixty-two were built. Originally intended as a torpedo-bomber, the T 18B served finally in the attack role, carrying a two-man crew and armed with one 57 mm Bofors gun and two 20 mm cannon. This version remained in service until 1956.

48 Dornier Do 217

A substantial number of Do 217 prototypes were built, the first of them flying in August 1938 and generally resembling a scaled-up Do 215B. All of the first six incorporated a novel four-leaf air brake, opening umbrella-style in operation and forming an extension of the rear fuselage when retracted. This feature proved troublesome to operate and was discarded on later models. First major series was the Do 217E, which entered production in 1941 following service trials with a small pre-series batch of Do 217A-0's in the preceding year. Numerous E sub-types appeared, powered by various models of the BMW 801 radial engine and differing in armament and other equipment. The Do 217E-5 carried additional radio gear for launching and guiding two underwing Hs 293 missiles. Many E-2's later became Do 217J night fighters. The next bomber series, with a redesigned and even more bulbous nose than its predecessors, was the Do 217K (1,700 hp BMW 801D). The K-2 and K-3 sub-types could carry special anti-shipping weapons beneath extended wings of 81 ft 4⅜ in (24·80 m) span. In-line engines – 1,750 hp DB 603A's – appeared in the Do 217M series, many of which were also converted later for night fighting as the Do 217N. Final production model, a reconnaissance version, was the Do 217P (also with DB 603A's), but only six of these were built. The Do 217W (or Do 216) twin-float torpedo bomber project remained uncompleted, and only prototypes were completed of the much-developed Do 317. Total output of Do 217 variants reached one thousand seven hundred and

thirty, all except three hundred and sixty-four of these being bomber models. The Do 217 night fighters are described in Book I *Fighters, Attack and Training Aircraft 1939–45.*

49 **Dornier Do 17 and Do 215**
The Do 17 was evolved originally as a 6-passenger, high-speed mailplane for Deutsche Luft hansa, the Do 17V1 first prototype making its maiden flight in the autumn of 1934. Three single-finned prototypes were built for DLH, but the extreme slimness of the aeroplane was its commercial undoing, the narrow fuselage demanding extraordinary agility by passengers in order to reach their seats. However, the RLM decided to evaluate the design in its efforts to procure a new medium bomber for the *Luftwaffe*. Further prototypes were ordered, the first of them (Do 17V4) setting the future design pattern by having twin fins and rudders. The specially stripped Do 17V8, with boosted engines, created a considerable stir at the Zürich International Military Aircraft Competition in July 1937, when its performance clearly outshone even the best of the single-seat fighters being displayed. By this time two production versions of the aircraft were already in *Luftwaffe* squadron service, and in 1938 joined the Condor Legion in the Spanish Civil War. These were the Do 17E-1 bomber, with 750 hp BMW VI engines and a 1,764 lb (800 kg) bomb load, and its reconnaissance-bomber counterpart, the Do 17F-1. Impressed by the V8's performance at Zürich, the Yugoslav Govern-

ment ordered twenty of an export version, designated Do 17K and powered by 986 hp Gnome-Rhône 14N radials, which improved both speed and range. This model was later licence-built in Yugoslavia, and when Germany invaded the country in April 1941 seventy were in service; the few that survived the fighting were allocated to the Croatian Air Force after the Nazi occupation. To maintain the Do 17's performance in relation to contemporary fighters, two new production models appeared with supercharged engines. These were the Do 17M (900 hp Bramo 323A) and Do 17P series (865 hp BMW 132N), otherwise generally corresponding to the E and F models. Two experimental series, the Do 17R and Do 17S, between them gave rise to the Do 17U, a pathfinder bomber with DB 600A engines, and then to the Do 17Z. The latter, with Bramo 323A or 1,000 hp Bramo 323P's, featured a more angular, bulbous front fuselage, and over five hundred Z models were built for bombing, reconnaissance and training. Two of the pre-production Do 17Z-0's, redesignated Do 215V1 and V2, became foreign demonstrators with Bramo and Gnome-Rhône engines respectively. The only foreign order received was from Sweden, for eighteen Do 215A-1's with DB 601A engines, but these were taken over by the *Luftwaffe* before delivery. They were followed by one hundred and one Do 215B's, most of which were similar except for the B-5, a night fighter/intruder version with a six-gun 'solid' nose. Development

subsequently continued as the Do 217, described separately.

50 Armstrong Whitworth Whitley

Oldest of the three standard RAF twin-engined bombers at the outbreak of World War 2, the Whitley was designed to Specification B.3/34, and the first prototype (K 4586) was flown on 17 March 1936. Thirty-four Mk I Whitleys were built, powered by 795 hp Armstrong Siddeley Tiger IX radial engines, and the first deliveries were made to No 10 Squadron in March 1937. Late-production Mk I's introduced dihedral on the wings, which became standard for all subsequent machines. The forty-six Mk II's were followed by eighty Mk III's with 920 hp Tiger VIII engines and a retractable ventral turret aft of the wing trailing-edge. A change was made to in-line engines in the Mks IV and IVA, thirty-three and seven of which were completed with 1,030 hp Merlin IV and 1,145 hp Merlin X engines respectively. Merlin X's were also adopted for the main wartime version, the Mk V, of which one thousand four hundred and sixty-six were produced. This was redesigned with a longer fuselage and tail fins of a modified shape. One hundred and forty-six Whitley VII's were produced for general reconnaissance work with Coastal Command, having increased range and carrying ASV radar for anti-shipping patrols. A number of Mk V's were later converted to Mk VII standard. Strictly speaking, the Whitley was obsolete as a bomber by the outbreak of war, when the RAF had two hundred and seven (mostly Mks I to IV) on charge; and its first operational missions were leaflet-dropping and security patrols. However, in company with Hampdens, Whitleys made the first bombing raid of the war on German soil on 19-20 March 1940, and in June 1940 became the first British bombers to attack a target in Italy. Their front-line career ended late in 1942, when even the reconnaissance versions were withdrawn, but they continued to serve for the remainder of the war in the valuable, if less glamorous, roles of troop and freight transport and glider tug. Fifteen Whitley V's were converted for freighter duties with BOAC in the spring of 1942, but (except for one casualty) were returned to the RAF by 1943.

51 Handley Page Hampden

Following the Whitley and Wellington, the Hampden was the third of Britain's trio of twin-engined medium bombers to enter service, two hundred and twenty-six being on RAF strength on 3 September 1939, serving with ten squadrons. Designed to the same Specification (B.9/32) as the Wellington, the first of the two Hampden prototypes (K 4240) flew for the first time on 21 June 1936. An initial order, for one hundred and eighty Hampden Mk I's to Specification 30/36, followed two months later, and these began to be delivered from September 1938, the first recipient being No 49 Squadron. In production Hampdens the rather ugly square-cut nose section was replaced by a curved Perspex moulding, the rear gun installations were modified and Pegasus XVIII's replaced the original Pegasus P.E.5S(a) engines. Even with these improvements, the Hampden was a disappointment operationally, the field of fire being very limited and the extremely narrow fuselage produced excessive fatigue for the 4-man crew. Later attempts to mitigate the bomber's defensive shortcomings by fitting twin guns in each of the rearward-firing positions improved the situation only marginally. Nevertheless, Hampdens continued in operational service with Bomber Command, principally on night bombing raids or minelaying, until September 1942, and many of them continued in service as torpedo bombers or reconnaissance aircraft with Coastal Command for a year or more after this. During their service Hampdens took part in the first bombing raids on Berlin and in the first of the 1,000-bomber raids on Cologne. One thousand two hundred and seventy Hampdens were built in the United Kingdom by Handley Page (five hundred) and English Electric (seven hundred and seventy). In Canada, Canadian Associated Aircraft Ltd also completed one hundred and sixty in 1940-41. Two Hampdens were re-engined with 1,000 hp Wright GR-1820-G105A Cyclones as prototypes for a Mk II version, but this did not go into production. Concurrently with the first RAF order, however, a contract had also been placed for one hundred of a variant with 1,000 hp Napier Dagger in-line engines, named Hereford; this order was later increased to one hundred and fifty. These were built by Short Bros & Harland, but due to powerplant problems, many of these were later re-engined to become Hampdens. Those that remained as Herefords served with operational training units only.

52 Fiat B.R.20 Cicogna (Stork)

The B.R.20 (indicating *Bombarda-mento Rosatelli*, after its designer) was evolved in 1935 to provide the *Regia Aeronautica* with a fast, well-armed light bomber. The prototype's first flight, on 10 February 1936, was soon followed by the initial production B.R.20, with 1,000 hp Fiat A.80 RC 41 engines and various detail modifications. The first of these entered service with the 13° *Stormo Bombardamento Terrestre* in September 1936. Before the outbreak of World War 2 Fiat also built two B.R.20L, these being demilitarised models for international com-petitions and record flights. From the summer of 1937, B.R.20 bombers became engaged in the Spanish Civil War, and in June 1940 this type equipped four bomber *Stormi*, some two hundred and fifty having been built up to that time. Mean-while, late in 1939 the prototype had been flown of the B.R.20M (for *Modificato*), an improved version characterised chiefly by its somewhat longer fuselage, better-contoured nose section and strengthened wings. About sixty of these were in service in June 1940, and series production continued until summer 1942, at

which time five hundred and eighty had been completed. The majority of these were built as B.R.20M's; at least a hundred were B.R.20's, but many of these aircraft were later brought up to B.R.20M standard. They were used regularly during the early part of the war for bombing duties in the Mediterranean area, the Eastern Front, and, briefly, with the *Corpo Aereo Italiano* based in Belgium for attacks on the United Kingdom. By the end of 1942, when they began to be replaced by later types, their main duties were coastal reconnaissance and convoy patrol, and many others were employed as operational trainers. Late in 1940 Fiat flight-tested the first prototype of a much redesigned model designated B.R.20*bis*, and a second was flown in 1942. This version had increased armament and bomb load, installed in a considerably refined fuselage with a nose section reminis-cent of the Heinkel He 111 and He 115. The use of 1,250 hp Fiat A.82 RC 32 engines gave a marked increase in performance, but only a dozen or so of this model appear to have reached squadron service. In 1938 eighty-five B.R.20's were supplied to Japan, where they were used by the JAAF as an interim type in China pending quantity deliveries of the Mitsubishi Ki-21.

53 North American B-25 Mitchell

North American Aviation was awarded an immediate production contract for its NA-62 design, without the usual preliminary prototypes, and the first B-25 was flown on 19 August 1940. By the end of the year twenty-four had been delivered, all except the first nine having the gull-winged appearance that was a characteristic of the bomber. They were followed in 1941 by forty B-25A's, then by one hundred and nineteen B-25's with dorsal and ventral gun turrets. First operational unit was the 17th Bombardment Group, which began to receive its B-25's in 1941. Production continued with one thousand six hundred and nineteen B-25C's and two thousand two hundred and ninety B-25D's from early 1942, and in April that year B-25B's flying off the USS *Hornet* made their epic raid on Tokyo. The B-25E and F were experimental models, production continuing with the B-25G, which carried two 0·50 in guns alongside a 75 mm cannon in a new 'solid' nose. Four hundred and five B-25G's were built, and a hundred and seventy-five earlier Mitchells were modified to carry a total of ten 0·50 in guns. An even more heavily armed 'gunship' was the B-25H, one thousand of which were produced with the 75 mm nose cannon and fourteen 0·50 in guns; this entered operational service in February 1944, joining the earlier multi-gunned Mitchells on anti-shipping strikes in the Pacific battle areas. Final production model, the B-25J (four thousand three hundred and eighteen built), reverted to the standard bomber nose, but retained the forward placing of the dorsal turret introduced on the H model. Mitchells in U.S. service operated predominantly in the Pacific war

zone, but large numbers were supplied elsewhere during the war. Two hundred and forty-eight B-25H's and four hundred and fifty-eight B-25J's were transferred to the U.S. Navy from 1943 as PBJ-1H's and -1J's, most being operated by Marine Corps squadrons. Eight hundred and seventy Mitchells of various models were supplied to the U.S.S.R. under Lend-Lease; twenty-three Mitchell I's (B-26B) and five hundred and thirty-eight Mitchell II's (B-25C and D) were received by the RAF; and others were supplied to Brazil (twenty-nine), China (one hundred and thirty-one) and the Netherlands (two hundred and forty-nine).

54 Lockheed Hudson

The Hudson was evolved at short notice, in 1938, to meet a British requirement for a coastal reconnaissance aircraft to supplement the Anson. Essentially, it was a militarised version of the Model 14 commercial airliner that had flown in July 1937, and an initial RAF order was placed for two hundred. The first of these was flown on 10 December 1938; deliveries of Hudson I's to Britain began in February 1939, the first recipient being No 224 Squadron. On arrival, many were fitted with twin-gun Boulton Paul turrets. On the outbreak of war the RAF had seventy-eight Hudsons on strength, and on 8 October 1939 one of them destroyed the first German aircraft to fall to RAF guns in the war. Lockheed supplied three hundred and fifty Hudson I's and twenty similar Hudson II's before introducing the Mk III, with more powerful Cyclone engines and ventral and beam guns. Four hundred and twenty-eight of this version were ordered. The only other direct purchases were three hundred and nine Hudson V's with 1,200 hp Twin Wasp engines. Many other Hudson's reached the RAF under Lend-Lease, however. These included three hundred and eighty-two Cyclone-engined Mk IIIA's, and thirty Mk IV's and four hundred and fifty Mk VI's with Twin Wasp engines. In 1941 the Hudson was given USAAF designations: A-28 for the Twin Wasp version and A-29 for the models with Cyclone engines. Eighty-two A-28's and four hundred and eighteen A-29's went to the USAAF, except for twenty A-28's that were transferred to the U.S. Navy with the designation PBO-1. In service with Squadron VP-82, one of these became the first U.S. aircraft of the war to destroy a German submarine. The Hudson continued in front-line service with Coastal Command until 1943-44, but undertook a variety of wartime duties that included agent-dropping, transport and operational training.

55 Lockheed Ventura

As the Hudson was evolved from the commercial Lockheed Model 14, so was the Ventura a militarised form of the larger Model 18, also instigated at the request of the British Purchasing Commission in 1940. The initial RAF contracts were for six hundred and seventy-five aircraft, of which the first one hundred and eighty-eight were delivered from summer 1942 as Ventura Mk I's, following the first flight on 31 July 1941. They entered service with No 21 Squadron of Bomber Command in October 1942 and made their first operational sorties early in the following month. The Ventura II and Lend-Lease IIA which followed had a different variant of Double Wasp engines, an increased bomb load of 3,000 lb (1,361 kg) and two additional guns in the fuselage. However, the Ventura was less successful in daylight operations than had been hoped, and deliveries were halted after about three hundred had been delivered. The remaining IIA's were acquired by the USAAF as B-34's, and more than three hundred others from previous RAF contracts became B-34A Lexington bombers or B-34B navigation trainers with the USAAF. The proposed Ventura III (B-37) with Wright Cyclone engines was cancelled after delivery of only eighteen of the U.S. Army's order for five hundred and fifty, and subsequent production concentrated upon the PV-1 model for the U.S. Navy, ordered in September 1942. This model had R-2800-31 Double Wasps, a 'solid' nose, six defensive guns, provision for external drop tanks and the ability to carry depth charges or a torpedo as an alternative to bombs. One thousand six hundred PV-1's were built, three hundred and fifty-eight of which went to RAF Coastal Command and several Commonwealth air forces as Ventura GR Mk V's. Twenty-seven of the Ventura II's originally intended for Britain were acquired by the U.S. Navy and designated PV-3 (PV-2 being the designation already allotted to a Ventura development known as the Harpoon).

56 Lockheed Lodestar

The pre-war Model 18 Lodestar commercial transport was selected by the U.S. Army for wartime production, three hundred and twenty-five being built as standard Army and Navy paratroop transports with the designation C-60A. A proposed freighter version with large cargo-loading doors was to have been built in even larger numbers, but this contract was cancelled. However, a variety of assorted civil Model 18's were acquired for war service under several separate designations. Those in USAAF service included thirty-six C-56 to C-56E; thirteen C-57 and seven C-57A; ten C-59; thirty-six C-60; and one C-66. The U.S. Navy designations R50-1, -2, -5 and -6 correspond to the USAAF's C-56, C-59, C-60 and C-60A, while the R5O-3 and -4 were 4-seat and 7-seat executive transports respectively. Many of the impressed commercial Model 18's were returned to their former owners during 1943-44, very few remaining in service beyond this date. Although not in service in great numbers, the Lodestar performed a wide range of duties that included troop and cargo transport, casualty evacuation and glider training. More than two dozen civil Lodestars were also impressed into service with the RAF, to whom

Lend-Lease deliveries included ten Mk IA and seventeen Mk II. Twenty aircraft corresponding to the American C-56B version were supplied to the Royal Netherlands Indies Army Air Corps.

57 Armstrong Whitworth Albemarle

The A.W.41 Albemarle was designed by Armstrong Whitworth to Air Ministry Specification B.18/38, for a twin-engined medium bomber of mixed wood and metal construction that could be contracted extensively to firms outside the aircraft industry. Two prototypes were completed by Armstrong Whitworth, and the first flight was made by the second of these (P 1361) on 20 March 1930. Completion of the entire production run of six hundred aircraft was entrusted to A. W. Hawkesley Ltd at Gloucester, but only the first thirty-two (designated Mk I Series 1) were completed as bombers. For this role they were to have had a 6-man crew, including two gunners to man the four-gun dorsal turret and the retractable 'dustbin'-type, two-gun ventral turret; the dorsal turret was offset slightly to port to simplify access to the rear fuselage. The Albemarle, although it also had a fixed, shock-absorbing tailwheel, was the first British military aircraft with a retractable nosewheel undercarriage to enter service. The first production aircraft was completed in December 1941, but the Albemarle never served in its intended role, and these thirty-two aircraft were instead converted for transport duties. Deliveries began to No 295 Squadron at Harwell in January 1943. Subsequent Albemarles were designated ST (Special Transport) or GT (General Transport), and were completed as follows: ninety-nine ST Mk I, sixty-nine GT Mk I, ninety-nine ST Mk II, forty-nine ST Mk V, one hundred and thirty-three ST Mk VI and one hundred and seventeen GT Mk VI. These were further subdivided into Series according to variations of equipment or role. The eight ST Mk I Series 1's had only twin dorsal guns, with a sliding hood over them; the fourteen ST Mk I Series 2's had Malcolm glider-towing gear; the ST Mk VI's were Series 1's with a starboard side rear freight door; and the GT Mk VI's were Series 2's with additional radio equipment and no dorsal armament. The Mk II could operate as a 10-man paratroop transport, and the Mk V (otherwise similar to the Mk II) was fitted with fuel jettison equipment. All were powered by Bristol Hercules XI engines, though there was a project for a Merlin-engined Mk III, and one Mk IV was completed with 1,600 hp Wright R-2600-A5B Double Cyclones. Other RAF squadrons to operate the Albemarle included Nos 296 and 297 (in the United Kingdom and in North Africa), and No 570; small numbers also served with Nos 161 and 511, and some (ten?) Albemarles were supplied to the Soviet Air Force. Large numbers took part in the Allied landings in Sicily (July 1943), Normandy (June 1944) and at Arnhem (September 1944).

58 Beech UC-45 Expediter

This was the military version of the pre-war Beech Model 18, one of the most adaptable twin-engined aeroplanes ever built: developed versions are still in production, and operate in all parts of the world. First military orders were placed before Pearl Harbor, the U.S. Army ordering eleven 6-seat C-45's (Model B18S) and twenty 8-seat C-45A's in 1940-41. Also in 1941 came the first orders for a 5-seat navigation trainer version, the AT-7 Navigator, five hundred and seventy-seven of which were ultimately delivered. The first mass-produced military transport version was the C-45B, basically the same as the A but with interior layout modified to Army requirements. Two hundred and twenty-three C-45B's were produced for the USAAF, one hundred and twenty-one similar aircraft were supplied to Britain under Lend-Lease as Expediter Mk I's. Five went to the Royal Navy, the remainder to the RAF. The 'Utility Cargo' designation first appeared on the two UC-45C's adopted by the USAAF; the two UC-45D's and six UC-45E's were 5-seaters similar to the AT-7 and -7B trainers. Major production transport was the 7-seat UC-45F, one thousand one hundred and thirty-seven of which were delivered to the U.S. Army from 1944. An additional two hundred and thirty-six were supplied to the RAF, and sixty-seven to the Fleet Air Arm, by whom they were known as the Expediter II. Subsequent trainers included seven AT-7A's, with convertible twin float or ski landing gear, and nine AT-7B's, which were basically 'winterised' AT-7's. Five of this model were supplied to the RAF. Final USAAF variant was the AT-7C, with R-985-AN-3 engines; five hundred and forty-nine were completed. A development of the AT-7 for bombing training was the AT-11 Kansas, one thousand five hundred and eighty-two of which were completed; thirty-six were later converted to AT-11A's for navigation training. Many Expediters were used by the U.S. Navy, with JR (Utility Transport) series designations: the Navy's JRB-1, -2, -3 and -4 corresponded to the Army C-45, C-45A, C-45B and UC-45F respectively. Navy counterpart to the AT-7 was the SNB-2. Several other aircraft served as USAAF photographic aircraft, with the name Discoverer. These included fourteen F-2's, thirteen F-2A's (converted from transport models) and forty-two F-2B's.

59 Focke-Wulf Fw 189 Uhu (Owl)

The Fw 189 was designed originally to a 1937 specification for a tactical reconnaissance aircraft. The Fw 189V1 prototype (D-OPVN), first flown in July 1938, was an unorthodox aeroplane, with two 430 hp Argus As 410 engines mounted in slender booms that also carried the tail assembly. The crew members were accommodated in an extensively glazed central nacelle. A second and third prototype were completed to generally similar configuration, the Fw 189V2 carrying guns and external bomb racks. The first series

version to go into production was the Fw 189B dual-control trainer, three B-0's and ten B-1's being completed in 1939-40. Production of the first reconnaissance series began in the spring of 1940, ten Fw 189A-0 pre-series aircraft being followed by the A-1, the better-armed A-2 and a smaller quantity of A-3 trainers. First deliveries to the *Luftwaffe* were made in the autumn of 1940, but it was not until the end of the following year that the Fw 189 began to appear in front-line units in any numbers. Thereafter the *Uhu*, as it was known to its crews, became employed in increasing numbers, especially on the Eastern Front. It was popular with those who flew it, and its delicate appearance belied what was in fact an adaptable, manoeuvrable and sturdily built aeroplane. Production of the Fw 189A series was undertaken by the parent company, which built one hundred and ninety-seven, excluding prototypes; at the Aero factory in Czechoslovakia, which built three hundred and thirty-seven; and at Bordeaux-Mérignac in France, where two hundred and ninety-three were completed. Small numbers were supplied to the air forces of Hungary and Slovakia. Meanwhile, in 1939 the Fw 189V1 had been reflown after being modified to have a very small but heavily armoured central nacelle seating two crew members. This and the generally similar Fw 189V6 were prototypes for a proposed attack version, the Fw 189C, but the latter did not go into production. The float-fitted Fw 189D, the Fw 189E with Gnome-

Rhône engines, and the more powerful Fw 189G were all projects that did not come to fruition, but a small number of Fw 189F-1's, with 580 hp As 411 engines, did become operational.

60 Blohm und Voss Bv 138

A product of Hamburger Flugzeugbau, the aircraft division of the Blohm und Voss shipbuilding company, the prototype of this three-engined flying boat was designated Ha 138V1 when it made its first flight on 15 July 1937. A second prototype, with a modified hull and tail surfaces, was flown on 6 November 1937, both being powered by 600 hp Junkers Jumo 205C engines. In 1938 the 'Ha' designations were discarded, the third machine to be completed being designated Bv 138A-01. This was the first of six pre-production aircraft, embodying a much-enlarged hull, redesigned booms and tail, and a horizontal wing centre section. Production began late in 1939 of twenty-five similar Bv 138A-1's, intended for well-equipped, long-range maritime patrol duties, but this initial version was not a conspicuous success, and the first pair were actually employed as 10-passenger transports in Norway. It made its combat debut in October 1940, at about which time the A-1 was beginning to be replaced by the Bv 138B-1, twenty-one of which were built with a turret-mounted nose cannon, a similar gun in the rear of the hull and 880 hp Jumo 205D engines. The major version in service was the Bv 138C-1, two hundred and twenty-seven of which were produced between 1941 and 1943. The C-1, with more efficient propellers and a 13 mm upper gun, offered slightly better performance and defence than its predecessor. Despite an indifferent start to its career, the Bv 138 eventually proved to be both robust and versatile, and was employed with increasing effect both on convoy patrol in Arctic waters and, in association with the U-boat patrols, on anti-shipping missions over the North Atlantic and the Mediterranean. A few were also converted for sweeping or 'degaussing' minefields (these were designated Bv 138MS), and many more were adapted for launching from catapults.

61 C.R.D.A. Cant. Z.506B Airone (Heron)

The Z.506 first appeared as a 12-passenger commercial transport, the prototype (I-CANT) making its first flight in 1936 with Pratt & Whitney Hornet engines. Small batches of Z.506A's (760 hp Cyclones) and Z.506C's (750 or 800 hp Alfa Romeos) were delivered, from 1936 to 1938, to the Italian airline Ala Littoria, during which time successively improved world records for speed, distance and payload-to-height were established by various machines. Meanwhile, in July 1936 the prototype was handed over to the Italian Air Ministry, leading to the evolution of a bomber/torpedo bomber version, the Z.506B. This carried a crew of five and had a redesigned fuselage whose chief features were a raised cockpit, seating the two pilots in tandem; a ventral gondola, incorporating a forward bomb aimer's position, the bomb bay and a rear defensive gun position; and a strut-braced tail-plane. The bomb bay could accommodate two 1,102 lb (500 kg) bombs, various combinations of smaller bombs up to a total of 1,984 lb (900 kg) or a single 1,764 lb (800 kg) torpedo. A pair of Breda-SAFAT 12·7 mm machine-guns were installed in a retractable Breda M.1 dorsal turret. The Z.506B Serie I entered production at Monfalcone in 1937, thirty-two being completed and delivered to the *Regia Aeronautica* during 1938. Some of these joined Italy's *Aviazione Legionaria* in Spain at the end of that year, where they were employed primarily for rescue or reconnaissance missions. By June 1940 production at Monfalcone had reached ninety-five Serie I and later models, others had been completed by Piaggio at Finalmarina, and Z.506B's in Italian service included twenty-nine of an order for thirty placed by the Polish Government in 1938. Principal Airone formations in 1940 were the 31° *Stormo da Bombardamento Marittimo* at Elmas (Sardinia) and the 35° *Stormo B.M.* at Brindisi. The Airone was active in its primary role during the early part of the war, but after the Greek islands campaign of 1941 all aircraft of this type were diverted to maritime patrol duties of various kinds, serving, *inter alia*, with the 139°, 147°, 170° and 199° *Squadriglie da Ricognizione Marittimo*. After the Italian capitulation, twenty-three Z.506B's became part of the *Raggruppamento Idro* (seaplane group) of the Co-Belligerent Air Force based at Taranto. By this time the principal service variant was the Serie XII, the gross weight of which had been raised by improvements in bomb-carrying capacity (to 2,645 lb = 1,200 kg) and defensive armament. It has not been possible to establish individual details of intermediate Serie numbers, nor of overall Airone production. The only other wartime variant identified was the Z.506S (for Soccorso = help), a conversion of the Z.506B for air/sea rescue. Some of these served in *Luftwaffe* colours, five were among the Co-Belligerent Air Force's acquisitions in 1943, and a further twenty conversions were made by Siai-Marchetti after the war for the reconstituted *Aeronautica Militare Italiano*, with which they served until 1959.

62 Junkers Ju 52/3m

Although it first entered military service as a bomber, it is as a transport aeroplane that the Ju 52/3m began and ended its career. Developed from the single-engined Ju 52 flown in October 1930, the first of the Ju 52/3m trimotors made its maiden flight in 1932, and for several pre-war years they were used widely by Deutsche Lufthansa and other airlines, notably in South America. Several hundred were delivered to the *Luftwaffe* in 1934-35 in bomber configuration, but they were regarded only as interim equipment, pending the arrival of such types as the He 111 and Do 17. Thus, in their first operational role, in the Spanish Civil War of 1936-39, they were employed principally as troop transports. The early production models were powered by 600 hp BMW 132A engines; the first version to introduce the higher-powered BMW 132T was the Ju 53/3mg5e. Principal production model was the Ju 52/3mg7e, with enlarged cabin doors, autopilot and other detail improvements; this could be fitted out either as an 18-seat troop transport or as an ambulance with provision for 12 stretchers. In these two roles the Ju 52/3m served for many years with the *Luftwaffe*, by whom it was popularly known as 'Iron Annie'. Their best-known action came with the invasion of Norway in April 1940, in which nearly six hundred of these transports were engaged. Almost as many were in action during the invasion of France and the Low Countries, and in both campaigns well over a quarter of the Junkers transports involved were lost. Nevertheless, they continued to figure prominently in such subsequent Nazi campaigns as those in Greece, Libya and Crete. Other duties undertaken by the Ju 52/3m during its *Luftwaffe* career included those of supply transport and glider tug, and some aircraft were fitted with electromagnetic 'de-gaussing' rings for clearing minefields. Most models had provision for interchangeable wheel, ski or float landing gear. Overall production of the Ju 52/3m between 1934 and 1944, including civil models, amounted to four thousand eight hundred and forty-five aircraft. Of these, two thousand eight hundred and four were built in Germany between 1939 and 1945. Many pre-war com-

mercial Ju 52/3m's were impressed for military service, and when the war was over several hundred were allocated to many foreign airlines, assisting them to re-establish their pre-war services until more modern types became available. A few remain in airline service today.

63 C.R.D.A. Cant. Z.1007 Alcione (Kingfisher)

The most important wartime contemporary of the S.M.79 Sparviero was another trimotor bomber, the Z.1007 designed by Ing Filippo Zappata. The first prototype flew towards the end of 1937, others following during the ensuing year and a half, and the Z.1007 entered production in 1939. The early aircraft for the *Regia Aeronautica* carried a light defensive armament of four 7·7 mm guns, and were powered by 840 hp Isotta-Fraschini Asso IX RC 35 Vee-type engines, installed in annular cowlings that gave them the appearance of being radials. This initial version was soon followed by the principal model, the Z.1007*bis*, in which a change was made to 1,000 hp Piaggio radials, resulting in a considerably improved performance. This version had increases in wing span and overall length, and a strengthened undercarriage, all permitting it to operate at higher gross weights; and defensive armament was improved. Eighty-seven Alcioni were in service when Italy entered the war. Of all-wood construction, the Alcione was unusual in being built in both single- and twin-finned forms; production was undertaken by IMAM

(Meridionali) and Piaggio, as well as by CRDA. As an alternative to its internal load, the Z.1007*bis* could carry a pair of 450 mm (17·7 in) torpedos under the fuselage, and the type was also employed for reconnaissance. The Alcione saw most of its wartime service in the Mediterranean area and North Africa, but also served on the Eastern Front, standing up well to extremes of climate despite its wooden construction. A later version, the Z.1007*ter*, appeared in *Regia Aeronautica* service towards the end of 1942. It had 1,175 hp Piaggio P.XIX engines and a reduced bomb load, but was not built in substantial numbers. The parallel Z.1015, with 1,500 hp Piaggio P.XII RC 35 engines, was likewise surpassed by the promise of an even better design, the Z.1018, which had flown in 1940.

64   Savoia-Marchetti S.M.79 Sparviero (Hawk)

The S.M.79, designed by Alessandro Marchetti, originated as the prototype (I-MAGO) of an 8-seat commercial transport, making its first flight in October 1934. Several record flights, with various powerplants, were made in 1935-36, leading to the completion of the second prototype as a military bomber, powered by three 780 hp Alfa Romeo 126 RC 34 engines. This entered production as the S.M.79-I Sparviero, characterised by the dorsal hump which caused it to be nicknamed *il Gobbo* (the hunchback) when it entered service. The 8° and 111° *Stormi Bombardamento Veloce* (High Speed Bomber Groups)

achieved some considerable success with their Sparvieri during the Spanish Civil War, and forty-five S.M.79-I's were ordered in 1938 by Yugoslavia. In 1937 service trials were begun of the S.M.79-I equipped to carry one 450 mm (17·7 in) torpedo, and later two, beneath the fuselage. These trials indicated that, with more powerful engines, the Sparviero could easily carry two of these weapons externally, and in October 1939 production began of the S.M.79-II, to equip the *Squadriglie Aerosiluranti* (Torpedo Bomber Squadrons) of the *Regia Aeronautica*. Apart from one batch with 1,030 hp Fiat A.80 RC 41 engines, all S.M.79-II's were powered by the Piaggio P.XI radial. Production was sub-contracted to Macchi and Reggiane factories, and in June 1940 there were nearly six hundred Sparvieri, of both models, in Italian service. The S.M.79 was active during World War 2 throughout the Mediterranean area, in North Africa and the Balkan states, its duties including torpedo attack, conventional bombing, reconnaissance, close-support and, eventually, transport and training. After the Italian surrender in 1943 about three dozen continued to fly with the Co-Belligerent Air Force, while the pro-German *Aviazione della RSI* employed several S.M.79-III's. This was a cleaned-up version, without the ventral gondola, and had a forward-firing 20 mm cannon. The S.M.79B was a twin-engined export model, with an extensively glazed nose, and was first flown in 1936. It was built for Brazil (three), Iraq (four) and Rumania (forty-eight), each version with a different power-plant. The Rumanian I.A.R. factories also built the S.M.79B under licence with Junkers Jumo 211D in-line engines. Overall Italian production of S.M.79 variants, including export models, reached one thousand three hundred and thirty before output ceased in 1944.

65 Petlyakov Pe-8

The Pe-8 was evolved to meet a 1934 Soviet Air Force specification for a long range heavy bomber, and originally bore the designation ANT-42, indicating that it was a product of the A.N. Tupolev design bureau. Its military designation was TB-7. When the Soviet designation system was changed at the end of 1940 credit was given to Vladimir Petlyakov, who had led the team responsible for its design. The proto-type bomber first flew on 27 December 1936, with 1,100 hp Mikulin M-105 engines, and later trials were conducted with an M-100 engine mounted in the fuselage to drive a supercharger for the four propulsion engines. Late in 1939, when the TB-7 entered production at Kuznets, it was powered by AM-35A engines, which did not require this clumsy arrangement in order to maintain the bomber's excellent speed-at-altitude performance. The aircraft entered service during 1940, and in the summer of 1941 carried out their first major attack of the war when a formation of Pe-8's raided Berlin. They continued to make similar deep-penetration raids behind the German lines. Mean-while, attempts to improve the design had begun early in 1941 with the installation of M-30B diesel engines, whose greater fuel economy offered an even longer range. Unfortunately, this powerplant proved unsatisfactory in other ways, and trials with M-82 radials revealed an unacceptable loss of performance; eventually, the withdrawal from production of the AM-35A led to the installation, from 1943, of M-82FN fuel-injection radial engines in production Pe-8's. This version introduced various aero-dynamic improvements, evolved by I. F. Nyezval after Petlyakov's death in 1942, and the nacelle gun instal-lations were omitted. Design changes and powerplant difficulties were chiefly responsible for Pe-8 pro-duction coming to an end in 1944, the total number built being com-paratively small by Soviet wartime standards. In 1942 one Pe-8 made a flight of more than 11,000 miles (17,700 km) from Moscow to Washington and back via Scotland, Iceland and Canada.

66 Short Stirling

The Stirling was a victim of its own Specification (B.12/36), because of which its wings were of such low aspect ratio that its operational ceiling was limited and its bomb bay could take no single weapon larger than 2,000 lb (907 kg) in size. The prototype (L 7600), preceded in 1938 by flight trials of the P.31 half-scale wooden prototype, made its first flight on 14 May 1939. It crashed on landing, but a second machine (L 7605) was flown on

3 December 1939. In May 1940 the first production Stirling Mk I made its maiden flight, and deliveries of this version began in August 1940 to No 7 Squadron. The initial order for one hundred Stirlings was soon increased, and after the 1939 Munich crisis stood at one thousand five hundred. Hercules XI engines of 1,595 hp in the Mk I replaced the 1,375 hp Hercules II's of the two prototypes. Two conversions were made as Mk II prototypes, with 1,600 hp Wright R-2600-A5B Cyclone engines, but this model never went into production. The major service version was the Mk III, which in addition to Hercules XVI engines introduced a new-style dorsal gun turret. Two Mk III's were converted in 1943 as Mk IV prototypes, the latter version being produced for both paratroop transport and glider towing duties. The Mk IV was basically similar to the Mk III, except for the removal of some or all gun turrets and having, in the paratrooper version, an exit hatch aft of the bomb bay. The final version, the Mk V, was an unarmed passenger or cargo transport with a fuselage rear-loading door and an extended nose section which hinged sideways to provide an additional loading facility. Short Bros built five hundred and thirty-two Mk I, six hundred and eighteen Mk III, four hundred and fifty Mk IV and one hundred and sixty Mk V; in addition, one hundred and ninety-one Mk I and four hundred and twenty-nine Mk II were completed by Austin Motors. The Stirling I first went into action on 10 February

1941, with an attack on an oil storage depot at Rotterdam, and throughout 1942 began mounting the heavy bombing of enemy targets later continued by the Halifax and Lancaster by night and the U.S. Fortress and Liberator by day. It figured in the first and many subsequent thousand-bomber raids, and was the first Bomber Command type fitted with the 'Oboe' blind-bombing device. Before their transfer to less belligerent duties in the later war years many Stirlings also carried out minelaying duties.

67 Focke-Wulf Fw 200 Condor

The Fw 200V1 prototype (D-AERE *Saarland*), which first flew on 27 July 1937, was designed by Dr Kurt Tank as a 26-passenger commercial transport for Deutsche Lufthansa, and prior to World War 2 the Fw 200A and Fw 200B also served with Danish and Brazilian operators. Two other prototypes were acquired by the RLM, later becoming personal transports for Hitler and his staff, but the first suggestion to employ the Condor for maritime patrol came from Japan. None of the aircraft ordered by Japan were in fact delivered, but the Condor was adapted, as the Fw 200C, for ocean patrol and bombing duties with the *Luftwaffe*. In spite of this it was as a military transport that the Fw 200C was first employed operationally, during the invasion of Norway in the spring of 1940. Early production Fw 200C's were powered by 830 hp BMW 132H engines and carried a crew of 5, but with successive variations in armament the crew later increased to 7 men, and from the Fw 200C-3 onward Bramo 323R engines became the standard power-plant. The Fw 200C-1 first entered service in the maritime role towards the end of 1940, with *Kampfgeschwader* 40, followed by the C-2 and C-3 models during 1941. The principal sub-type was the C-4, with more advanced radar and radio equipment, which entered production early in 1942. Subsequent variants included the C-6 and C-8, adapted to carry two Hs 293 guided missiles. The latter was the final military variant, a total of two hundred and seventy-six Condors (including prototypes) having been built when production ended early in 1944. Considering the small quantity built, the Condor established a considerable reputation as a commerce raider during the early war years, operating independently or in conjunction with U-boat patrols against the Allied convoys. It was not ideally suited to the rigours of maritime warfare, however, and many were lost through structural failure when indulging in strenuous manoeuvres. When its initial successes began to diminish after the appearance of the CAM ships and such Allied types as the Beaufighter and Liberator, it was progressively transferred to the transport role for which it had first been designed.

68 & 69 Boeing B-17 Flying Fortress

In service from beginning to end of the U.S. participation in World War 2, the B-17 was evolved in 1934 for a USAAC design competition for an offshore anti-shipping bomber. In 1935 the prototype was completed, as the Boeing 299, and flew for the first time on 28 July 1935, powered by four 750 hp Pratt & Whitney Hornet engines. A change of power-plant, to 1,000 hp Wright Cyclones, was specified for the thirteen Y1B-17's and one Y1B-17A that were then ordered for evaluation; after trials, these were placed in service as the B-17 and B-17A respectively. The initial production batch comprised thirty-nine B-17B's, with modified nose, larger rudder and internal improvements. They were followed by thirty-eight B-17C's (higher-powered Cyclones and revised armament), twenty of which were supplied to the Royal Air Force in 1941 as the Fortress Mk I. The B-17D, forty-two of which were ordered for the USAAF, was generally similar, and most American C's were later converted to D standard. It was the B-17E which first introduced the huge, sail-like fin and rudder that characterised all subsequent Fortresses, and the much-improved defensive armament on this model included, for the first time, a tail gun turret to cover the blind spot to the rear of the bomber. Five hundred and twelve B-17E's were built by Boeing, including forty-five which became the Fortress IIA of the RAF. American B-17E's, serving in the United Kingdom, made the first raids on European targets by the U.S. Eighth Air Force in August 1942, and this version also served extensively in the Pacific theatre. The next model, the B-17F, was sub-contracted to Douglas and Lockheed-Vega factories which, with Boeing, built three thousand four hundred and five. Nineteen of these were supplied to the RAF as the Fortress II, and forty-one others were converted to F-9 series photographic reconnaissance aircraft. The same three companies combined to build eight thousand six hundred and eighty examples of the last production model, the B-17G; eighty-five of these became Fortress III's with RAF Coastal Command and ten others were converted to F-9C's. The B-17G was characterised chiefly by its 'chin' turret with two additional 0·50 in machine-guns, a feature later added to many B-17F's in service. Forty-eight B-17G's were allocated to the U.S. Navy and Coast Guard, with whom they performed ASR or early warning patrol duties; these aircraft were designated PB-1G or PB-1W respectively, the latter having large ventral radomes. About fifty other Flying Fortresses, adapted to carry a lifeboat under the fuselage, were redesignated B-17H and employed on air/sea rescue work. The Flying Fortress's principal sphere of activity during World War 2 was in Europe, where the E, F and G models were the mainstay of the U.S. heavy day bomber attacks on enemy targets.

70 **Boeing B-29 Superfortress**
Design of the Superfortress began well before America's entry into World War 2, when the Boeing Model 345 was evolved to a USAAC requirement of February 1940 for a 'hemisphere defense weapon'. In August 1940 two prototypes, designated XB-29, were ordered by the USAAF, and the first one was flown on 21 September 1942. It was a much larger aeroplane than Boeing's earlier B-17 Fortress, and was characterised by its circular-section, pressurised fuselage and remote-controlled gun turrets. Powerplant was four 2,200 hp Wright R-3350-13 Cyclone radial engines. By the time of the first flight, nearly seventeen hundred B-29's had been ordered. The first pre-production YB-29 Superfortress flew on 26 June 1943, and squadron deliveries began in the following month to the 58th Bombardment Wing. The first operational B-29 mission was carried out on 5 June 1944, and the first attack upon a target in Japan on 15 June 1944. It was during this month that the Superfortresses moved to the bases in the Marianas Islands, from whence they subsequently mounted a steadily increasing bombing campaign against the Japanese homeland. Apart from the direct damage caused by this campaign, it was responsible for many Japanese aircraft from other Pacific battle fronts being withdrawn for home defence duties, although comparatively few types were capable of indulging in effective combat at the altitudes flown by the American bombers. Superfortresses also carried out extensive minelaying in Japanese waters; a hundred and eighteen others became F-13/F-13A photo-reconnaissance aircraft. Finally, two B-29's brought the war to its dramatic close with the dropping of atomic bombs on Hiroshima and Nagasaki on 6 and 9

August 1945. Shortly after VJ-day over five thousand Superfortresses were cancelled, but when B-29 production ended early in 1946 the three Boeing factories had completed two thousand seven hundred and fifty-six B-29's and B-29A's; in addition, six hundred and sixty-eight B-29's were manufactured by Bell, and five hundred and thirty-six B-29's by Martin. Three hundred and eleven of the Bell machines were converted to B-29B's with reduced armament.

71 Avro Lancaster

The Lancaster was a direct development of Avro's unsuccessful Manchester twin-engined bomber, its prototype (BT 308) being originally the Manchester III, complete with triple tail unit, modified by the installation of four 1,130 hp Merlin X engines in place of the two Vulture engines of the Manchester. This prototype flew on 9 January 1941, being followed just over nine months later by the first production Mk I, of which delivery began (to No 44 Squadron) shortly after Christmas 1941. The first Lancaster combat mission came on 2 March 1942, and the first bombing raid, on Essen, followed eight days later. The Lancaster I, fitted successively with Merlin XX, 22 or 24 engines, remained the only version in service throughout 1942 and early 1943, and an eventual total of three thousand four hundred and forty Mk I's were completed by Avro, Armstrong Whitworth, Austin Motors, Metropolitan-Vickers and Vickers-Armstrongs. Avro completed two prototypes for the Lancaster II, powered

by 1,725 hp Bristol Hercules radial engines as a safeguard against possible supply shortage of Merlins. In the event no such shortage arose, but three hundred production Lancaster II's were built by Armstrong Whitworth. The other principal version, the Lancaster III, was powered by Packard-built Merlin 28, 38 or 224 engines; apart from a modified bomb-aimer's window, this exhibited few other differences from the Mk I. Most of the three thousand and twenty Mk III's completed were built by Avro, but one hundred and ten were manufactured by Armstrong Whitworth and one hundred and thirty-six by Metropolitan-Vickers. The Mark numbers IV and V applied to extensively redesigned models that eventually became the Lincoln, while the small batch of Mk VI's were Mk III's converted to Merlin 85 or 87 engines in redesigned cowlings. The final British variant was the Mk VII, one hundred and eighty being built by Austin with Martin dorsal turrets mounting twin 0·50 in guns. In Canada, Victory Aircraft Ltd manufactured four hundred and thirty Lancaster X's, which had Packard-Merlin 28's and were essentially similar to the Mk III. The Lancaster's bomb-carrying feats were legion. It was designed originally to carry bombs of 4,000 lb (1,814 kg) in size, but successive modifications to the bomb bay produced the Mk I (Special) capable of carrying first 8,000 lb (3,629 kg) and then 12,000 lb (5,443 kg) weapons, and culminating in the 22,000 lb (9,979 kg) 'Grand Slam' armour-piercing weapon designed by Barnes Wallis. This remarkable engineer also designed the skipping bomb carried by the Lancasters of No 617 Squadron in their epic raid on the Moehne and Eder dams on 17 May 1943.

72 & 73 **Handley Page Halifax** The H.P.57 came into being as a redesign of the twin-Vulture-engined H.P.56 evolved to meet Air Ministry Specification P.13/36, after it had become apparent that the Vulture would be unsatisfactory. The H.P.57 was a much-enlarged design, drawn up around four Rolls-Royce Merlin engines, and the first of two prototypes (L 7244) was flown on 24 September 1939, by which time an initial contract had already been placed. Deliveries of the Halifax Mk I, to No 35 Squadron, began in November 1940, and the bomber made its operational debut in a raid on Le Havre on the night of 11-12 March 1941. The early machines became known as Mk I Series I, being followed by the Mk I Series II with a higher gross weight and Series III with increased fuel tankage. The first major modification appeared in the Mk II Series I, with its two-gun dorsal turret and uprated Merlin XX engines. The Mk II Series I (Special) had a fairing in place of the nose turret, and the engine exhaust muffs omitted; the Series IA first introduced the drag-reducing moulded Perspex nose that became a standard Halifax feature, had a four-gun dorsal turret, and Merlin 22 engines. Variants of the Mk II Series I (Special) and Series IA, with Dowty landing gear instead of the

standard Messier gear, were designated Mk V Series I (Special) and Series IA. One thousand nine hundred and sixty-six Mk II's and nine hundred and fifteen Mk V's were built. One other important modification appearing in the Mk II Series IA was the introduction of larger, rectangular vertical tail surfaces, designed to overcome serious control difficulties experienced with earlier models. The Perspex nose and rectangular fins characterised all subsequent Halifaxes, whose only serious drawback now was a lack of adequate power. Thus, in the Mk III, which appeared in 1943, the Merlin powerplant was abandoned in favour of Bristol Hercules radial engines. The Mk III became the most numerous Halifax variant, two thousand and ninety-one being built. The Mk IV was a project that remained uncompleted, the next operational models being the Mks VI and VII, the former powered by 1,675 hp Hercules 100, while the latter reverted to the Hercules XVI as used in the Mk III. These were the final bomber versions, and compared with earlier models were built in relatively small numbers. Halifax production ended with the Mk VIII supply transport and Mk IX paratroop transport, the final aircraft being delivered in November 1946. Six thousand one hundred and seventy-six Halifaxes had then been built, by a widely sub-contracted wartime programme that included English Electric, Fairey, Rootes Motors and the London Aircraft Production Group as well as the parent company. The Halifax remained in service with Bomber Command throughout the war, making its last operational sortie on 25 April 1945. Its work included many special-duty missions, including agent-dropping and radar countermeasures, and it also served in the Middle East. After the war Halifaxes remained in service for a time with Coastal and Transport Commands, the last flight being made by a Coastal Command GR Mk VI in March 1952.

74 & 75 Consolidated B-24 Liberator

To the Liberator go the distinctions of being built in greater numbers and more variants than any other U.S. aircraft of World War 2, and of serving in more combat theatres, over a longer period, than any heavy bomber on either side. It originated as the Consolidated Model 32, a major feature of which was the exceptionally high aspect ratio Davis wing that gave the Liberator its prodigious range. Allied to this was the deep, capacious fuselage that enabled the aircraft to carry a large bomb load and also made it eminently suitable as a transport. The sole XB-24 prototype flew on 29 December 1941, followed by seven YB-24 service trials aircraft and thirty-six production B-24A's. One hundred and twenty were also ordered by the French Government, but these were diverted to Britain, the first few being designated LB-30 or -30A and used by BOAC for transatlantic ferry flying. Twenty others went to RAF Coastal Command as Liberator I's, equipped with an early form of ASV

radar. The first B-24A deliveries to the USAAF were made in June 1941, followed by nine B-24C's with turbo-supercharged engines and revised armament. The first U.S. version actually to serve in the bomber role was the B-24D, which was essentially similar to the B-24C except for its R-1830-43 engines and increased gross weight. Production of the B-24D, including ten by Douglas, totalled two thousand seven hundred and thirty-eight. Two hundred and sixty were supplied to the RAF as the Liberator III and IIIA (the former having Boulton Paul gun turrets), plus a further one hundred and twenty-two, fitted with 'chin' and ventral radar fairings and Leigh airborne searchlights, which served with Coastal Command as the Liberator Mk V. In mid-1943 those USAAF B-24D's engaged on anti-submarine patrol were transferred to the U.S. Navy, by whom they were redesignated PB4Y-1. Seven hundred and ninety-one B-24E's were built by Convair (as Consolidated was now known), Douglas and the Ford Motor Co, distinguishable from the D model chiefly by their modified propellers; while North American contributed four hundred and thirty B-24G's, some of them with a powered gun turret installed in the nose. An Emerson nose turret and R-1830-65 engines characterised the B-24H, three thousand one hundred of which were completed by Convair, Douglas and Ford. These three companies, plus North American, then manufactured six thousand six hundred and seventy-eight B-24J's, with a Motor Products nose turret and a ventral Briggs ball turret. One thousand two hundred and seventy-eight B-24J's became the RAF's Liberator Mk VI bomber and Mk VII for general reconnaissance. Nine hundred and seventy-seven were delivered to the U.S. Navy, also receiving the designation PB4Y-1 and having, in most cases, radar in place of the ventral turret. Other armament variations characterised the B-24L (one thousand six hundred and sixty-seven by Convair and Ford) and B-24M (two thousand five hundred and ninety-three, from the same factories). Ford had completed seven examples of the single-finned YB-24N, and forty-six similar RY-3's which were delivered to the U.S. Navy, when further contracts (for over five thousand B-24N's) were cancelled in May 1945. The Liberator, although sharing a substantial part of the bombing of Europe with its contemporary, the Boeing Fortress, was even more prominent in the Pacific theatre, where its excellent range was particularly valuable. It also gave considerable service as a transport aircraft, two hundred and seventy-six B-24D-type aircraft being completed as C-87's for this role; close on one hundred Liberators of various types were adapted as F-7 series photo-reconnaissance aircraft; and others were utilised as cargo transports, tanker aircraft and flying classrooms. In addition to those serving with the U.S. forces and the RAF, considerable numbers also operated with the Canadian and other Commonwealth air forces.

When Liberator production ended on 31 May 1945 the total output of all variants had reached eighteen thousand one hundred and eighty-eight aircraft.

76 Short Sunderland

The Sunderland, eventually to become the RAF's longest-serving operational aircraft, was first delivered to No 230 Squadron in Singapore early in June 1938. Its design, based upon the successful C Class 'Empire' flying boats of Imperial Airways, was evolved to Specification R.2/33, and the prototype (K 4774) was flown on 16 October 1937 with 950 hp Pegasus X engines. With Pegasus XXII's and revised nose and tail armament, the Sunderland Mk I entered production in 1938, and by 3 September 1939 forty were in service with four RAF squadrons. Ninety Mk I's were eventually completed, including fifteen by Blackburn. This company also built five of the forty-three Sunderland II's which, from the end of 1941, began to replace the Mk I's in service. The Mk II introduced Pegasus XVIII engines, with two-stage superchargers, a twin-gun Botha-type dorsal turret in place of the 'midships gun ports, an improved tail turret and ASV radar. Rising operating weights now necessitated redesign of the hull planing bottom, and the Mk II on which this was tested thus became the prototype for the chief production model, the Sunderland III. The first Short-built Mk III flew on 15 December 1941; the parent company eventually produced two hundred and eighty-six Mk III's, while a further one hundred and seventy were built by Blackburn. It was No 10 Squadron of the Royal Australian Air Force which first experimented with a group of four machine-guns in the nose of the Sunderland III. This proved so successful, both against enemy submarines and aircraft, that many Sunderlands were subsequently operated with this total armoury of ten guns, their bristling defence earning them the respectful nickname *Stachelschwein* (porcupine) from their German adversaries. The designation Sunderland IV was given originally to a larger, heavier development with 1,700 hp Bristol Hercules engines, eight 0·50 in machine-guns and two 20 mm cannon. In the event, only two prototypes and eight production aircraft were built; they were given the new type name Seaford, but after a brief service appearance were later converted into Solent commercial transports for BOAC. Final military variant was the Mk V (one hundred built by Shorts and fifty by Blackburn), with 1,200 hp Pratt & Whitney R-1830-90 Twin Wasps as powerplant and improved ASV equipment. The Sunderland V entered service in February 1945, and was the last version to serve with the RAF, finally retiring in 1958. Sunderlands exported post-war to the French *Aéronavale* (nineteen) and the RNZAF (sixteen) served until 1960 and 1966 respectively.

77 Kawanishi H8K

The 13-Shi (1938) specification to which Dr Kikuhara designed the first prototype H8K1 was an exacting one, and in its initial trials early in 1941 the flying boat gave little indication of its future promise, having a lack of stability on the water and a marked tendency to 'porpoise'. Various modifications were made to this and the three pre-production H8K1's of 1941, all of which were powered by 1,530 hp Mitsubishi Kasei 11 engines. As finally accepted for production in February 1942, the H8K1 Model 11 had a deeper hull, with a more efficient planing bottom, and enlarged vertical tail surfaces. Thirteen production H8K1's were built at Kohnan. They carried a crew of 10 and were armed, like the pre-series machines, with a single 20 mm tail gun, one 20 mm and two 7·7 mm guns in the nose turret and a 7·7 mm gun in each of the beam blisters. Operational debut of 'Emily', as the H8K was later dubbed by the Allies, was made by the three pre-series H8K1's. These made an abortive attack on Pearl Harbor early in March 1942, flying from the Marshall Islands and refuelling from submarine tankers *en route*. The production H8K1 was an excellent hydrodynamic design, with a performance equal or superior to any other flying boat in service during the war. In 1943 it was superseded by the H8K2 Model 12, with more powerful Kasei 22 engines and increased armament. This was employed throughout the Pacific theatre, its maximum endurance of nearly 27 hours enabling it to carry out extremely long range maritime patrol, bombing and reconnaissance duties. Late production H8K2's carried ASV radar in the bow, the beam observation blisters being omitted. One hundred and twelve H8K2's were completed during 1943-45, plus thirty-six examples of a transport version, the H8K2-L Model 32 Sei-Ku (Clear Sky). This could carry up to sixty-four passengers, or a mixed load of passengers and cargo. It was recognisable by double rows of fuselage windows and a reduced armament of a single 13 mm and 20 mm gun respectively in the nose and tail. The first prototype H8K1, re-engined in 1943 with Kasei 22's and converted to a passenger layout, served as the trials aircraft for this version. Two H8K3 Model 22's were essentially late production H8K2's fitted experimentally with retractable wing-tip floats (originally planned for the first prototype) and a retractable dorsal turret. Later they were re-engined with Kasei 25b's and were redesignated H8K4 Model 23. Neither went into production, and the projected H8K4-L Model 33 transport was never completed.

78 Kawanishi H6K

One of the most efficient Japanese aircraft of the late 1930's, the Kawanishi H6K flying boat was designed to a JNAF specification of 1934, and three of the five prototypes had flown by the end of 1936. Two of these, and one other machine, had their original 840 hp Nakajima Hikari 2 engines replaced later by 1,000 hp Mitsubishi Kinsei 43's, in which form they were delivered to the JNAF for squadron service in January 1938 under the designation H6K1. The fifth machine served as prototype for the initial production version, the H6K2 Model 11, nine more of which were built. The designation H6K3 was allocated to the next two aircraft, which were completed as transports. They were later restyled H6K2-L, and a total of eighteen was eventually delivered to Japan Air Lines as 16-seat commercial and military transports. The early military models flew operationally with the JNAF during the Sino-Japanese conflict, but by the outbreak of World War 2 the principal version in service was the H6K4 Model 22. Initially, this had been built with Kinsei 43 engines, but from August 1941 the standard powerplant became the more powerful Kinsei 46, permitting higher operating weights. Sixty-six Model 22's, later code-named 'Mavis' by the Allies, were in JNAF service at the time of Pearl Harbor, and eventually between two and three times this number were completed, several of them as H6K4-L transports. An attempt to prolong the flying boat's career resulted in the H6K5 Model 23, with 1,300 hp Kinsei 53 engines, but the satisfactory evolution of the later H8K from the same stable rendered such a course unnecessary, and only a comparatively small number of H6K5's were built. Most 'Mavis' flying boats ended their careers in the transport role, but by the end of 1943 they had virtually disappeared from service. A total of two hundred and seventeen H6K's, of all versions, were built.

79 Messerschmitt Me 323

Messerschmitt's huge transport glider, the Me 321 *Gigant*, had been produced only in small numbers before it was realised that the need to use rocket assistance and three twin-engined Bf 110's to get it into the air was uneconomical. Ing Degel of Messerschmitt was therefore given, early in 1941, the task of evolving from it an aeroplane that could take off under its own power. His solution, calculated also to avoid making demands upon German engine production, was to install Gnome-Rhône 14N engines, already in production in Occupied France. At first it was supposed that four of these engines would suffice, and ten prototypes were completed to this configuration. The first, designated Me 323V1, was flown in April 1941, but it soon became apparent that four engines were inadequate, and in August 1941 the first of five six-engined prototypes was flown. When manufacture of the Me 321 glider ended in January 1942, the six-engined Me 323 entered production. The initial model was the Me 323D-1, of which just over two dozen were built. One example was also completed of the Me 323D-2, to compare the merits of two-blade wooden propellers with the three-blade metal ones of the D-1. The D-1's five MG 131 machine-guns remained the minimum basic armament of the main production model, the Me 323D-6. However, additional weapons were often carried, and there were reports of some Me 323's with as many as eighteen machine-guns on board. In 1943 one hundred and forty Me 323D-6's were built, and Messerschmitt delivered nineteen examples of the Me 323E-1, whose basic armament included a power-operated turret, mounting a 20 mm MG 151 cannon, installed above the centre engine nacelle on each wing. In 1944, before having to devote its resources to the Me 262 jet fighter, Messerschmitt had begun production of the Me 323F-1, powered by Gnome-Rhône 14R engines. Production was then transferred to the Zeppelin plant at Friedrichshafen, where a few F-1's were re-engined in mid-1944 with 1,340 hp Jumo 211F engines, but little further output was undertaken. The Me 323 was an invaluable supply transport on the Eastern Front, where it first appeared, but in North Africa and elsewhere its slow speed and difficult handling made it an easy prey for Allied fighters. After heavy losses during the evacuation of Tunisia little more was heard of this huge aeroplane, and further projected versions remained uncompleted.

80 Yokosuka MXY-7 Ohka (Cherry Blossom)

Most Japanese *Kamikaze* (Divine Wind) suicide air attacks were made by existing service aircraft adapted for the purpose, but one aircraft developed specifically for this role was also met operationally. This was the Ohka piloted flying bomb, developed to a project initiated by the Japanese Naval Air Research and Development Centre and evolved by the Yokosuka Naval Air Arsenal. Design work began in August 1944, priority production by several factories starting in September. The only version to reach combat status was the Model 11, seven hundred and fifty-five of which were built up to March 1945. Powered by a three-barrelled rocket motor and carrying a 2,645 lb (1,200 kg) warhead in the nose, the Ohka was attached beneath the belly of a G4M2e parent aircraft, the bomb doors of which were removed in order to accommodate it. The Ohka was carried to about 50 miles (80 km) from its target, when it was launched from a height usually around 27,000 ft (8,200 km) at an airspeed of some 200 mph (320 km/hr) to complete its journey alone. The pilot maintained it in a glide towards the target, using the rocket motor only for the last few miles and the ultimate steep dive. Fifty Ohka Model 11's were aboard the carrier *Shinano* when it was sunk by U.S. forces *en route* to the Philippines in November 1944. The aircraft was first encountered operationally on 21 March 1945, when sixteen Ohkas, with their parent aircraft and an escort of thirty Zero fighters, were intercepted while making for a U.S. task force about 300 miles (480 km) from Kyushu. All of the Ohka-carrying bombers, and half of the escorting fighters, were destroyed without a single weapon being launched. Sub-sequently, about three hundred Ohkas were allocated to the Okinawa area; probably no more than a quarter of these were launched at Allied targets, but these were enough to persuade their victims, at least, that perhaps the code name *Baka* (Japanese for 'fool') bestowed by the U.S. Navy was after all something of a misnomer. The only other version built in quantity was the Model 22, about fifty of which were completed. This had a 13 ft 6¼ in (4·12 m) wing span, was 22 ft 6⅞ in (6·88m) long, and had a gross weight of 3,197 lb (1,450 kg) including a 1,323 lb (600 kg) warhead. Powerplant was a TSU-11 jet engine, the compressor of which was driven by a 110 hp Hatsukaze piston-engine to provide 441 lb (200 kg) of thrust. The intended parent aircraft was the P1Y1 Ginga, but the Ohka 22 had a disappointing performance and did not go into service. The Model 33, proposed in April 1945, was incomplete when the war ended. Intended for air-launching from the G8N1 Renzan four-engined bomber, it would have had a 1,047 lb (475 kg) st Ne-20 turbojet and a warhead comparable to the Model 11. Project studies were also made for Models 43A (with folding wings) and 43B, to be launched from sub-marine-based and land-based cata-pults respectively.

INDEX